LIBERTY, JUSTICE AND THE STATE

LIBERTY, JUSTICE AND THE STATE

Paul O'Hara

To order additional copies of this book, contact:
Xlibris
1-800-455-039
www.Xlibris.com.au
Orders@Xlibris.com.au
793196

Contents

Introduction

Politics could be described as a kind of bartering that enables us to overcome the discontinuities in our lives by resolving conflicts in a peaceful rather than unruly manner, and seeking a sphere in which there is some common or general accord. It is thus the art of compromise, conciliation, and negotiation rather than brute or naked force where it concerns meaningful and effective decision-making. It is also an attempt to establish some legitimate authority in response to the different needs that arise in society, and create a system of benefits and burdens that are binding on all. To this extent it is about the means and not the end, or at least the sufficiency of any means as opposed to the morality or immorality of any end. How to achieve what is good is thus to achieve what is useful, or at least the best strategy or plan that suits those circumstance at hand. In this case we do not say that if the end is right or wrong then the means are value-free, but that since the means are value-laden then the end is value-free. Given that wielding a blunt instrument is neither ethical nor unethical, the best we can hope for is a more ethical approach to the fashioning of any singular or conjugate set of means. So it is with our diplomats in their consular dealings and our policy makers in the world of home affairs.

There is another view however that suggests that the difference between the political and the non-political hinges on the distinction between a 'public' and a 'private' good, with the assumption that what is true of the one must also be true of the other. That is, that politics is an ethical activity that replaces right behaviour with just behaviour; that it is the pursuit of human betterment through ostensibly public means just as ethics is the pursuit of human betterment through ostensibly private means. In answer to the question where this line should be drawn the most common reply is between civil society and that entity we call 'the state'. State institutions such as the government, the judiciary and the armed forces could be regarded as public because they touch all aspects of communal life. On the other hand, institutions such as the family, business conglomerates, trade unions and divers clubs could be regarded as private because they support only limited aims and are voluntary to join just as well as voluntary to quit. (Although of course, not voluntary to join in the case of the family.) This may also generate a particular perception of public life as being good in one sense but bad in another. Participation in the activities of the state may be deemed worthwhile if this is seen to involve interaction amongst individuals who are both free and equal in their regard for one another. On the other hand, state participation may be seen in a negative light if this restricts our range of choices, and especially in the case of the family if it interferes with our commitments and our everyday pursuits.

But if politics is concerned principally with questions about 'the state' a related question concerns its origin, whether it has evolved naturally or whether it is a purely human artifice borne of certain indispensable needs. This controversy has a long history dating back to the Greeks, and Aristotle's is typical of the kind of approach that supports the former. Political associations are regarded as 'natural' progressions starting with those that are simple and then working towards those that are more complex. The pairing of a male and a female is essential for the sake of procreation, and that introduces the basic unit of the family. The pairing of a master and a slave is essential for the sake of legitimate rulership, and that introduces the primacy of mental dexterity over physical strength. What we mean by the head of any household is then extended to include the head of any village, although in this case the lord or master acquires a certain status which demands the loyalty of all his subjects. A convening of several villages is then the basis for that association which has ultimately come to know as the state.

In respect to an an artifice or convention there are various ways in which this may be viewed, but let us suppose it concerns the actual condition that men might be in at any given time. In the account that Hume provides, justice is not something 'natural' in the sense of something inveterate but something that may be rendered entirely useless when certain conditions or circumstances conspire to this end. Under circumstances where nature is bountiful, then this will engender a greater spirit of generosity in the way that men deal with one another. On the other hand, if nature is niggardly in the supply of its goods, then this will engender a more selfish approach in the way that men deal with one another. However, in the more usual circumstance where there is a degree of sufficiency rather than insufficiency, men will judge it in their 'best interest' to control their desires, to allocate their goods, and to enjoy the benefits of what they have fairly struggled and worked for. In other words, justice is somewhere between generosity and selfishness where it concerns a certain sentiment, and abundance and scarcity where it concerns a certain endowment.

To treat of an artifice or convention in these terms however is not exactly what we mean by the striking of any contract, since that assumes some original condition or a 'state of nature' from which men might wish to free themselves. In his classic work *Leviathan* Hobbes postulates such a state, or some impoverished condition in which the lives of men are 'solitary, poor, nasty, brutish and short'. However, there are several points that need to be made about this alleged 'state of nature' or a primitive condition prior to the advent of civilised society. Firstly, it was not Hobbes' intention to give an accurate description of any condition in the way that an anthropologist might, this was merely a working hypothesis that suited his particular needs. In contrast to what Aristotle takes to be a natural development, what Hobbes is arguing is that men must gain control of their baser instincts if they are to achieve a more 'harmonious' state of coexistence.

In fact, if one were to speculate on a possible 'state of nature' then this would probably be more in keeping with the way that Locke regards the matter. At a time when men lived solely by hunting and gathering, there was no general scarcity and hence no need either for men to regulate or reign in their desires. Such a situation would not have made them selfish, rather the reverse, it would simply have made them less mindful of any competing claims. In others words it would have made them neither selfish nor unselfish, since where there are no grounds for a division neither is there for those sentiments of liberality and greed. (Compare this to the biblical account in the book of Genesis). Claims would only become necessary when resources dwindled and needs increased to the point where no man could be certain to retain those things he had acquired through his industry and good luck. Thus, from an historical point of view it appears that Locke may have been a good deal closer to the mark.

Another point that needs to be made is that a contract theory of government is rather an idealized account of the way that power might be wielded in everyday life, and certainly not a true reflection of the way that different states are actually related to one another. In *The Prince* Machiavelli takes an entirely different approach, since to seize and retain a principality requires not trust but guile, clever machinations, and a degree of brute strength. However, we also need to be clear about the difference between a contract or a promise when this is *binding* on a person and a contract or a promise when this is *freely afforded* and yet also *revoked* by a person. When Machiavelli suggests that a ruler neither 'can nor ought to keep his word when this is hurtful to him' then this is not prudent or practical but rather immoral and unconscionable no matter what the time or circumstance.

What is really important about the contract theory is not that it gives an accurate account of the origin of the state but rather that it raises the average man to the status of a self-sufficient agent. Power is not the exclusive domain of any deity or potentate, rather something worked out by men as a compromise, and which stakes their equal rights against their unequal needs. The other thing that it does is place the relation between force and freedom in stark relief. In the case of

Hobbes and Locke the conflict that exists between different wills can only be overcome if we recognize the need to prioritize our objectives, if we place order above disorder (Hobbes) and the majority above the minority (Locke). In Rousseau's case however this assumes a rather different guise, since here the will of the individual must be completely subordinate to the good of the community. Adding to this, Hegel posits an ideal state in which there is no conflict between what the individual aspires to and what the state in fact delivers. Rather, it is the state that shapes men's behaviour in keeping with their more primitive and ineluctable desires.

Let us express these different viewpoints in the following way: (a) If physical force is self-negating then spiritual freedom is self-expanding (where the former is the means to the latter). (b) If physical force is self-expanding then spiritual freedom is self-negating (where the latter is the means to the former). The implication in this second is that power may be wielded arbitrarily or capriciously, and hence, that we should place a check on those who have been entrusted with the running of the state. The implication in the case of the first is that physical force is purely nugatory, and hence, that a criminal may redeem himself if he willingly embraces any penalty imposed by others or those acting on behalf of the state. The problem in this case is that although we may admit that punishment and evil can be compared in their effects, we would not necessarily say that they can be *annulled* in their effects. Or at least, no matter how much remorse the evil-doer might feel this cannot undo the deed once it is done. The rights of the victim, thus, must always have a different basis to the rights of the criminal.

When we say that rights and duties are correlated what we mean is that they are conditioned by what a person may sensibly regard as the basis for his freedom, and that includes the ability to both *think* and to *act* freely. The ability that a person has to act in such and such a way will always be conditioned by the force that may be applied to prevent him from so doing, and that is true not only of man but of every sentient being. Hence it is a right that is contingent upon a duty and not a duty that is contingent upon a right, because a right is what is simply *permitted* whereas a duty is what is strictly *required*. Neither would we distinguish between the internal and external side of a right. Rights may be guaranteed by the state but they cannot be produced by the state. And if the state is not the originator of rights then neither do they originate in man's spiritual or moral nature (understood in some ineluctable way). Rather do they arise in conjunction with a set of needs and a range of interests that are necessarily quite diverse.

Taking our duties to be substantive therefore the question that might well be asked is this—what is the difference between a duty that is relative and a duty that is absolute? It is sometimes held that this concerns the difference between those that do and those that do not assume some correlative right. The problem with this is that it only begs the question what the *relevance* is of any such right to being with. For instance, in the way that one says there is an 'absolute duty' to act benevolently even though there is no correlative right, would one also say there is an 'absolute duty' to refrain from homosexuality even though this is not the breach of any seeming or correlative right? In the one case, what we appear to be dealing with is something *more* than what duty requires, in the other, of something *less* than what justice requires. There are those who would argue that homosexuality is strictly forbidden because it is a moral imperative and that is all we require; there are those on the other hand who would argue that to the degree it does not infringe on another's right then neither is there ground for its simple prohibition.

We might thus prefer to approach this from the viewpoint of what is meant by an absolute right, that is, the wherewithal rather than the inability to enjoin a particular end. A good example would be something like the right to marry or the right to make a will. (And thus, as something that corresponds to the 'sanction of nullity') This then leads on to a distinction between an absolute duty and a relative right, but only on the assumption that it is the right that is preeminent. An 'absolute' duty is thus defined as something that is perfect (i.e. legal) but neither private, positive, nor strictly proprietary. Again however, we are treating of this in a purely derivative way, that is, what we are really saying is that it is the right that is perfect (or imperfect), public, private, and strictly proprietary. Hence a person who is acting in his public capacity has the 'absolute duty' to do what is good for the community and not simply for himself. A parent has the 'absolute duty' not to abuse or neglect a child, but that is not the same as the 'positive' duty to be kind when he has to.

Where it concerns the question of positive and negative duties, we might treat of this in terms of a more or less civilized condition of man, or at least the necessary prerequisite for a condition that is orderly rather than disorderly in its ends. In the case of a negative duty, this concerns the claim to certain goods that each deems to be exclusively his own. In the case of a positive right, this concerns the right that each has to the use of those possessions, but also quite specifically, with the support and assistance of his fellows. That is, it concerns the fact that if there is joint agreement about the existence of proprietary rights then there must also be an agreement about the protection of just such a set of rights. And of course, that means that a person will come to the assistance of his neighbour if and when he is required.

In the case of positive duties and negative rights this is what we would expect of a state of society when it has become more enterprising and advanced. Rather than there being a division or rights and duties, both are active, only in the one case, active in respect to one's fellows, and in the other active in respect to oneself. In one respect (what we mean by a positive duty) this means to act from a spirit of mutual or brotherly love, that is, to be sympathetic and supportive when is necessary. From another viewpoint (what we mean by a negative right) this means permission to do what one might otherwise deem inapposite, that is, to perform an act of generosity outside the range of one's normal and everyday tasks.

Chapter 1

On the Different Affections of Men

It is common to divide the active powers of nature into two categories —those that proceed from nature as a set of efficient causes, and those that proceed from nature as a set of immanent causes. So far as it concerns the first, then we need to consider this against the backdrop of forces such as gravity, electricity, corpuscular attraction etc which do not presuppose any superintendent cause, or what we mean by a rational agency pursuing some rational end. On the other hand, so far as we suppose there to be a cause that links *every* train of events, so far as we suppose the universe to be ordered rather than desultory, then what this implies is a necessary cause on which depend those divers effects that proceed in a purely adventitious way. Thus, we have the existence of an active force in conjunction with both active and inactive things, and an active force peculiar to active things, but which applies to inactive things as well. Gravitation for instance, is an active force that applies to both active and inactive things. A man on the other hand, is an active thing, and which may command another thing (a horse) to pull a wagon or a plough. The motions that we observe in different living beings thus leads us to the belief in a Supreme Being whose essence lies not outside but rather within the compass of its own capacity and strength. Of the various powers that reside in living organisms on the other hand, we might divide these into (a) appetites, (b) instincts, and in the case of man (c) aesthetic tastes as well.

An appetite could be defined as a drive that arises within the individual and that craves to be satisfied, principally those of hunger, thirst, and sex. An instinct on the other hand is somewhat more complex, it is a natural response to certain stimuli which protects us from the rigours of our environment and those dangers that lie in wait. An instinct however is not necessarily what we mean by a reflex. Thus, by the alternate contractions and relaxations of the throat a man swallows, by the movements of the jaw he bites and chews, through inhaling and exhaling he breathes. By the exertion of certain autonomic nerves, he salivates and sweats, and yet in a way he knows nothing of this, only that there is a meal to be eaten or a task to be done. In the animal kingdom certain body parts have been sculpted to perform a variety of tasks, as for instance the baleen in the case of a whale, the tusks in the case of a boar, or the claws in the case of cat. But again, no consideration is given as to how these may be used, either for attack, defence or the capturing of food. There are many circumstances where an action must be done so swiftly there is no time to decide on how it should be done. When we feel we are falling there is a natural tendency to recover our balance and remain upright, but we do not logically connect this with any activity in the inner ear. In the same way, when there is a sudden movement in our direction there is a natural tendency to blink our eyes, to raise our hands, to turn our backs or lift our legs. These responses are the legacy of our ancestral history, in no way are they the simple products of our rationality, our volition or our will.

Habit is different from instinct in that it is not something we are born with but something we acquire, and could be defined as the disposition to do something as the result of having done it many times before. It may also raise questions about the kinds of patterns that not only are but *should* be acquired, that is, the kind of habits that are adjudged to be expedient rather than unhelpful. Hence there is such a thing as a good or bad dress sense, a good or bad accent, a good or bad hair style. Whilst animals certainly possess an ability to mimic one another this is rarely outside the boundaries of play, whereas in the case of man not only does he have the capacity to copy what he finds worthy but parody what he finds quirky, thus inspiring mirth through a comparison at both extremes. As self-conscious beings, not only do we seek to emulate our heroes, but also deride our enemies by focusing on those habits that bespeak a sense of self- neglect.

When appetite becomes more settled and includes an end to be attained, then this constitutes the nature of a desire. By desire and aversion what we mean are the agreeable or disagreeable sensations which arise in connection with something we apprehend to be good in the case of the former and bad in the case of the latter. But we may also need to distinguish between desire and aversion when this assumes objects that are or are not antithetical in their kind, or at least that is, when there is a lack of desire but not a will to be displeasing. In the way we often refer to the objects of love and hate, it is natural to regard these as exhibiting characteristics that are either repugnant or agreeable in themselves. On the other hand, and as concerns our more rudimentary needs, whilst with eating or drinking it is difficult to construe its pursuit as anything *less* than a wish to survive, in the case of sex it is difficult to construe its avoidance as anything *more* than a lack of libido. Hence, although we may have a willingness to be tender that does not necessarily imply a willingness to make love, but if we have a wish to be healthy then this most certainly must include a willingness to be fed.

For the most part, a desire is something we tend to associate with what we hope to surmount rather than what we hope to obtain, and that is relief from what causes us injury rather than procurement of what causes us joy. Even where it concerns the question of a cool or calm desire then this is rarely the pursuit of anything universal; more often than not it is simply an attempt to shift the balance from a surplus of ill to a surplus of good. And that is why, when treating of the object of desire, we need to be careful not to confound it with desire as it is in itself, or desire in the sense of a *willing* as what is real or objective in itself. If the source of joy were nothing more than the sense of joy that accompanies any fleeting desire, then a man who conquers Mt Everest would have no more reason to feel satisfied than a child who consumes an ice cream but in one almighty gulp. This is also why when there is an equal mixture of good and evil, or when we are equally repelled and attracted by the same object, we tend to regard this as a cause of inaction and not the reverse, that is, as something that settles our urges rather than taking us back and forth.

We also need to attend to a distinction between the desire that arises in conjunction with the apprehension of what is antecedently painful, and the kind of desire that is nurtured through an *opinion* of what is good and evil. Of the former, that is the appetites, then any number could be enumerated, but in the case of sex this may also involve a certain dispositional aspect, since as we have already stated, abstention could well be construed as the absence of desire, not what was displeasing in and of itself. In the case of our aesthetic pleasures on the other hand e.g. reading a poem, listening to a recital, contemplating a work of art, then it is clear that what this hinges on is a judgement about the object and what is in the object, not any uneasy sensation we are hoping to quell or allay. In the same way, we may also form judgements about the behaviour of men such that those actions we account generous we also deem praiseworthy, and those we account miserly we also deem blameworthy.

This also highlights the difference between the way we might treat the subject with respect to our external senses, and how we might treat of it with respect to our intellective powers. From the latter viewpoint, what we mean by good and evil are not conflicting but rather quite compatible states, or at least compatible from the viewpoint of what is mutually supportive or destructive at its very most core. To say that two things are qualitatively different does not mean they cannot be quantitatively the same, it simply requires a more synoptic approach to what it means to be 'quantitatively the same'. And this provides an introduction to what we mean by the metaphysic of desire. To begin with, it should be clear that what we mean by being repulsive is not the same as what we mean by being repelled nor being attractive what we mean by being attracted. Being fair or being ugly may well be regarded as objective characteristics, but in any given circumstance it may not be immediately clear whether one person will be attracted or repelled by another. In the same way, although chemical elements in combination may well produce discernible effects, this cannot always be gleaned from their constituents or any class that they belong to. Fundamentally it is 'being attractive' which contrasts with 'being repelled', and 'being repulsive' which contrasts with 'being attracted'—there is a difference when we separate the object from any agent and the essence from any accident. So far as the object of desire may be an agent for change then what was originally neither attractive nor repulsive may become so, only more directly where it concerns the former. Consider the way a comb is able to impart a charge to a scrap of paper when it is rubbed against a woollen jersey. The paper is attracted to the object that has *become* attractive, which in turn derives from the object that *is* attractive. Where however it concerns the question of 'being repulsive', although this is clearly not consistent with 'being attracted' it may nonetheless involve the capacity to both attract and repel, or at least attract and *absorb* or *expel*. In this case what we mean by attraction is essentially the activity of absorption and what we mean by repulsion is essentially the activity of expulsion.

So far as it concerns our aesthetic tastes then what is needed for this is a degree of intellection, those pleasures and pains that arise from the contemplation of both orderly and irregular objects. To this we might subjoin the idea of an object that is either present, absent, or expected. Present good raises joy, absent good raises desire, expectant good raises hope. Present evil raise sorrow, absent evil raises aversion, expectant evil raises fear. The apprehension of a good that is readily available arouses within us the desire for its procurement. The like apprehension of impending ill arouses within us the desire for its avoidance. The apprehension of a good not present but which is guaranteed in the future arouses within us a sensation of joy, as with honour, when our actions are a fit object for the praise and esteem of our fellows. The apprehension of an evil not present but which is guaranteed in the future arouses within us a sensation of sorrow, as with shame, when our actions are a fit object for the contempt and disdain of our fellows. Joy arising from the flattery of others is what we call conceitedness. Sorrow arising from the cajolery of others is what we call dejectedness. The apprehension of a good not present but which is likely in the future arouses within us a sensation of hope. The apprehension of an evil not present but likely in the future arouses within us a sensation of fear. The apprehension that the delivery of any future good may be thwarted arouses within us a sense of frustration. The apprehension that the delivery of any future evil may be thwarted arouses within us a sense of relief. Hope without the apprehension of a why or what, is cheeriness. Fear without the apprehension of a why or what, is terror. But whereas hope and fear are sustained by an element of doubt (what we expect but do not know) if we remove that doubt then what we have in the first instance is self—complacency and in the second only lamentation or despair.

In respect to the question of a proper object, then we need to treat of this in terms of a distinction between (a) the absent, (b) the accessory and (c) the distinct. What we mean by the first of these, an object *in abstentia,* is the kind of condition that gives rise to those confused and uneasy sensations that are known as the passions. Pity when not attended with any genuine concern may very easily descend into ridicule or voyeuristic delight, as when someone falling clumsily draws ridicule or indifference to their plight. Disapprobation when not attended with any concern for the magnitude of the wrong may well descend into peevishness or irascibility, as when a person reacts quite heatedly because someone has stood on his toe. However, we may also need to distinguish between this kind of situation and one in which there is a discernible object but not connected with any particular end. That is, when something that was originally a means, by association with what it is the means to, becomes desirable in and of itself. To be fond of someone it could be said is not only to be desirous of that person's company but to be protective of him (or her) as well, just as, to hate someone may not only be to shun that person's company but to be indifferent towards any suffering they may feel. Of course, in saying this we are not suggesting that what is an object of love must always be an object of praise, since we may also disconnect the object from the end as in the case of sex outside of marriage (lust), fame outside of attribution (ambition), or money outside of giving (greed). There is also the instance when a passion may be deflected or dispersed, as when the shame that is felt by the agent redounds on his family or his friends.

Where it concerns an object that is distinct, then we need to distinguish between something that is apprehended to be the source of certain qualities and something that is principally the cause of good or evil. Thus, love and hate are emotions that arise in conjunction with the apprehension of certain qualities that we deem good or bad, worthy or base. On the other hand, so far as one person is the cause of another's misery, as with teasing or fault-finding, then so also is he its object as well. And the same applies in the case of congratulation, only here where one person is the cause of another's weal and not his woe. Where it concerns an object that is indirect, then this concerns the manner in which we respond rather than the manner in which we act, given the apprehension of a person as having some status or value relative to our own. Being envious is a way of responding to someone we perceive to be the embodiment of what we wish we could be. Being compassionate is a way of responding to someone we perceive to be the embodiment of what we wish we could avoid. And how we respond will depend entirely on how we are disposed relative to those means or that condition we find at work in ourselves.

To be distinct in the way we have just suggested means there can be no ambivalence in respect to either an origin or an end. In the case of something such as teasing then that means the cause and the object will be the same. (That is, a bully will always be a bully no matter the circumstance). In the case of something such as jealousy, that means joining the object with the cause in a way that invites a response. In the case of emotions such as love and hate on the other hand there may be a degree of uncertainty about the way such a relation should be viewed. If the object is real and not imaginary then it will always proceed from without, but that may not be the same for the cause, especially in the case of a person who experiences rancour and self-loathing. Under these circumstances the cause of what is hateful may express itself in various ways, since such a person may vent his anger on anything within his immediate surrounds. Neither would we say that someone who hates something necessarily seeks to destroy it, just as someone who loves something necessarily seeks to preserve it. There can only be destruction or preservation if there are two things equivalent in their strength, and so from this standpoint there is no more reason why love should conquer hate than hate should conquer love. Perhaps it would be more accurate if we said that he who imagines that what he loves will be destroyed *hopes* it will not be, and he who imagines that what he hates will be destroyed *fears* it will not be.

In our treatment of the *will* we also need to be careful that we do not confound the meaning of what may be true at one level with the meaning of what may be true at another. As we have already stated, there is a kind of desire that arises in conjunction with what is antecedently painful, and in that case what we are dealing with is something *necessitated* as a means. We do not have a choice if we wish to stay the pangs of hunger; rather, we are driven to seek the means for getting it under control. (Of course, we do not mean driven in any exaggerated sense, only what it is natural or normal for a person to do). At the next level it may sometimes be necessary to connect the will with either the presence or the absence of desire. For instance, where it concerns sexual gratification then rarely is there complete neutrality, occasionally only pleasures of the imagination, but for the most part sensual gratification as well.

However, at the level of the affections there is something more we need to consider, and that is the kind of spontaneity that arises in conjunction with a range or diversity of means. At this level the idea of 'not willing' must be given a more positive signification, that is, not just the willing of different objects but the willing of different means. There are various ways we might approach this, sometimes when it does and sometimes when it does not suppose the existence of antithetical means. For instance, it could be said that the 'calm' or 'reasonable' desire to become wealthy may sometimes necessitate a means which will temporarily leave a person short of funds. On the other hand, the vehement desire we call avarice may recommend a completely different set of means. This however is not necessarily the way we might view the relation between 'seeming' self-interest on the one hand and 'true' benevolence on the other. There are those who would argue that to be selfish means not to will to be generous, just as to be generous means not to will to be selfish. But what this rests on is the supposition that 'not willing' is simply the absence of anything willed, or at least the absence of anything willed as a separable means. In the broad scheme of things no one can say how much of a person's 'interest' is mixed with the interests of others, or how far a person may be able to distance himself from any ill effects that may occur down the track. And the same could be said for sentiments such as honour and shame. Whether a person is accorded honour or made to feel ashamed may be just a matter of the circumstances he finds himself in, not a necessary sequel to two things antithetical in themselves. Or at least, that if they are antithetical in themselves, they may not necessarily be fair in their apportionment, a sense of shame not always being preceded by an event for which there is the least discernment of blame. And that is why, although we tend to use the word *selfish* in a variety of contexts that does not mean there is any such thing as a 'selfish' as opposed to more 'benevolent' affection.

So far as it concerns the relation between prudence and benevolence then in practice we would not seek to distinguish between the happiness of any individual and the happiness of any other, or at least not where it concerns the question of any fair allocation of what is good. On the other hand, neither would we allow that generosity may be the means to being quite prudent or that prudence may be the means to being quite generous. Leaving aside the question of any cumulative gain, what is self-directed is not the same as what is other-directed, even if this difference may not always be so easy to discern. In acting benevolently or even sympathetically, what a person does is make the welfare of another principally but not exclusively the object of his concern. In the same way, when a person acts with a view to his own good there may well be unexpected consequences that are favourable or unfavourable to the agent. To act impartially means to act in a way that neither augments nor diminishes the weal of others; to act selfishly is to act in a way that is prejudicial to either the rights or the needs of others. For example, a disabled yachtsman circumnavigating the globe can hardly be doing so for the sake of the common good, but that is not to say he may not be an inspiration to others with similar difficulties in their lives. Hence what is self-regarding in one sense is not necessarily what is selfish in another. What we mean by prudence and imprudence however are not what we mean by benevolence and malevolence, since what the latter assume is that pleasure and pain may be pursued independently, whereas with the former they do not. To act imprudently is not what it means to act with evil intent; rather, it only implies that a person is lacking in wisdom and foresight, not that he has a surfeit of cunning and guile.

Such notwithstanding, to say that being heedless is not to act with evil intent does not mean there should not be a reasonable regard for the self, only we would tend to approach this in terms of what is more rather than less than its proper degree. When a person has too great a regard for himself then this tends to issue in the sentiments called pride, vanity and self-conceit. The difference between pride and vanity stems from the fact that in the case of the former there is at least some degree of objectivity whereas in the latter there is not. Whilst the proud man seeks recognition for his deeds, he is perfectly able to remove himself when the situation demands that he should. Although he may well have the desire that his actions be pleasing to others, this impulse is not so great he would ever grovel at their feet. The vain man on the other hand is so convinced of his own self-worth he will welcome any morsels that are left sitting on the plate—his well-being depends on others, on their flattery and their gifts.

But to be vain in this sense is not necessarily what it means to be haughty and aloof. The haughty man is neither beholden to others nor respectful of their wishes. He has a sharp wit, a quick temper, and a constant need to assail his opponents with sharp and stinging words. But if pride, vanity, and aloofness could be said to constitute an overestimate of self then at the other extreme do we have despondency, humility, and self-abuse. If pride is a kind of vice then so also is its opposite, since if it is not natural for a person to overestimate his worth then neither should he underrate it. Taken in one way, humility may be something that exhibits itself in a touching smile, a respectful bow, a conciliatory speech. Taken in another way (servility), humility may be something that exhibits itself in a demeaning glance, a bended knee, or as a subterfuge for jealousy and ambitious intent.

So far as it concerns the difference between benevolence and beneficence, then we need to distinguish between a motive, an act, and an effect. In the case of beneficence, the act is contained in the effect, while in the case of benevolence the motive is contained in the act. Hence for benevolence we may have both a motive that engages with an end and a motive that is indifferent towards an end. What we mean by pure benevolence is a motive that is indifferent towards an end. What we mean by mixed benevolence is a motive that is connected with an end. And the same could be said in the case of malevolence. In the case of the former what we have is the appearance and the reality of affording someone good; in the case of the latter the appearance and the reality of affording someone harm. Mixed benevolence occurs when there are conflicting means in conjunction with the production of something good. Mixed malevolence occurs when there are conflicting means in conjunction with the production of something bad.

When we say that benevolence and malevolence are equally pure or equally mixed it should be clear that what we mean by the former is that if there is a bifurcation in the end then there must also be a bifurcation in the means. And hence, that so far as prudence and benevolence are concerned it is not a matter of which may be the means or which may be the end. Of course, it is true that beneficence might be characterized in a way that is either positive or negative, in the former case where we mean the fruitful distribution of what is good and, in the latter, the prodigal distribution of what is good. Likewise, for maleficence we might characterize this as either positive when it is cool and calculated, or negative when it is hasty and ill thought out. But in respect to any likely sanction then on no account does this apply to what is exclusively one or the other. In acting benevolently what the agent does is make the welfare of others his primary concern, and without the prospect of receiving anything significant in return. A philanthropist who provides an endowment for disabled children may well be buoyed by any publicity this receives, but in no way could this be seen to supply a motive for how he has behaved (or at least for any sanction other than which could be called 'natural', that is, a good conscience) Likewise, a suicide bomber hell-bent on causing widespread panic will hardly be dissuaded by any reprisals that might ensue, either to his family, his friends, or the country of his origin..

Chapter 2

Free will vs Determinism

To begin our account of the will, let us consider the basic difference between (a) determinism, (b) compatibilism, and (c) libertarianism. What we mean by a *determinist* is someone who believes that every event that occurs, be that organic or inorganic, must do so in accordance with a system of natural laws, and that if we knew all the antecedent causes and conditions then we could predict with complete certainty any event that can or might be likely to occur. This is not to say we *do* know all the circumstances that surround any given event, but there is no doubt that physics and psychology point us towards a set of laws that are operative in both our physical and mental lives. Even a person's conscious state or his conscious intentions can be traced back to activities in the brain, and since all events are the result of other events in accordance with strict laws, this applies no less to our mental activities as well.

What we mean by a *compatibilist* is someone who believes that freedom and necessity can be reconciled, but only in terms of the stirrings and activities of the whole, not anything that may done in isolation from everything else. The laws of physics should not be confounded with the laws of psychology; the latter may indeed determine how a person will act in accordance with his instincts or his drives, but this is very different when it is his *motivation* that is at stake. That is, it is not a question of what we may or may not do as what we can or cannot *avoid*. For the most part there is not the least discrepancy between freedom and compulsion in the actual choices we make, whether in respect to the lesser of two evils or that which is supplied on more affirmative grounds. If a stranger accosts you and demands you hand over your wallet then even in the absence of any physical threat you may well accede to it, and the *reason* you do so is because you value your life more than you do the loss of your possessions. When the government has to decide whether it should outlaw a street protest then this will depend upon a counting of the costs, that is, whether the benefits to public safety will outweigh the basic right to free speech (Or least this is certainly true in most democracies). A person's choices are a product of all those different things that make him what he is, be that his habits, his beliefs, or simply the genes he has inherited from his parents. So far however as it concerns a question of events that are completely random and the causes that bind us to just such events, here there is no evidence for anything at work in the shaping of the self.

What we mean by a *libertarian* is someone who believes in a rational and not appetitive will, that is, that there is both a power to discriminate between right and wrong (by the indifferent apprehension of an end) and the power to affirm what is right or wrong (by the indifferent application of a means). The intellect therefore presents an object to the will, and the will either accepts or rejects it according to that judgement it forms. This of course is not to say that there is no such thing as an *appetitive* will, only, we must distinguish between deliberation in the sense of (a) doing or omitting a deed according to whether it is desired or abhorred, and (b) deciding or resolving on a course when what this involves is some intelligent or predetermined plan. As we will see later, the difference between proposing and inducing a belief centres on the fact that although we may have a genuine intent, circumstances may at times conspire to prevent us from achieving exactly what we had hoped for. Hence, it is not freedom that should be made conditional upon what is not necessary, but rather necessity that should be made conditional upon what is not free.

Another claim is that a person's general disposition does not of itself dictate his actions but only establishes the limits for *how* in the main he might act. For instance, given a degree of risk for some one behind the wheel of a car, it is difficult to say how he might react to a dangerous situation otherwise than in terms of (a) his age and experience (b) his present state of mind, (c) other relevant factors such as intoxication or being sleep deprived. Thus, it is not so much a change in circumstance that will necessitate a change in the way we behave, rather, those different responses that *might* arise in conjunction with any significant change of events. Under certain circumstances being inclined or loathe to do something may solely reside in a state of mind, under other circumstances or to achieve success, it may be critical if one is fit and well, and at other times there may be significant forces which simply cannot be controlled.

Now let us consider some of the traditional arguments in favour of determinism, by comparing it with any kind of indeterminism. As we have already seen, a compatibilist is someone who believes that freedom and necessity can be reconciled, but only if we define the former as the absence of any impediment and the latter as the power to impede or constrain a person in any decisions that he makes. So far as it concerns the activities of the intellect, or the will, then this is nothing more than the capacity to countenance certain effects, or the alternate urgings to do and forbear concerning any matter currently at hand. A man therefore may be viewed in either of two ways; his character or what he has become by virtue of his accomplishments, and what he *will* become by virtue of those urges on which his acts are based. However, one of the issues with this is that it does not pay due regard to the difference between those motives that are in keeping with our *sentiments* and those motives that imply the existence of certain *restraints*. That is, a certain bifurcation may occur if we do not give equal status to what we do as the result of desire and what we do in connection with any particular lack of it. To wish to do something could be construed as having a sufficient impetus, whereas to ignore something could be viewed as having an insufficient impetus, and thus that all that matters is some threshold for how we act, not the question of any specific or differentiated response. For instance, if someone offers you a piece of chocolate you may either accept or reject it, but you would hardly say that someone with a sweet tooth was motivated to resist chocolate in the same way he was to partake of it. That is, his reason for rejecting it may have more do with his waist line or the preservation of his teeth. Thus, to avoid or ignore something may not be same as to openly reject it, just as, not to close the window because you are tired is not the same as not to close the window because it is humid and muggy.

Compare this however with the kind of motivation that is based on our hopes and our fears, when there is not just some internal spring but some external sanction as well. A person may behave in a certain way because he hopes to be rewarded, or he may behave in a certain way because he fears he will be punished, but in neither case is there the kind of division that we witnessed before. Rewards and punishments may be equally efficacious in shaping the way we behave; hence, a person may be just as likely to omit something because he hopes to be rewarded as embark on something because this is what his duty tells him. There is a world of difference between (a) avoiding a piece of chocolate because it is fattening (b) paying your taxes because you fear the department of revenue (c) cheating on your wife because you know you can get away with it and (d) donating to a charity because it engenders a sense of self-complacency. In terms of what could be called a moral resolve, then on no account should this be viewed as a choice between doing good and avoiding evil but rather between doing and avoiding both good and evil. The argument that one should pursue good directly and avoid evil indirectly seems to stem from the basic misconception that the one is not formally but only *materially* excluded from the other, so that to pursue evil does not include the avoidance of good, but that to pursue good *must* involve the avoidance of evil. If the use of a person's will amounted to nothing more than doing what was good for him, then you would no more be entitled to say that a person was acting in the sure knowledge of doing evil than you would that its distribution could be anything but what was perfectly just. Furthermore, and as should be readily apparent, even the law admits that a different standard applies to an act done in the heat of the moment and something done after due deliberation. A person who kills another behind the wheel of a car may be charged with culpable driving but not necessarily with manslaughter; a person who kills another while protecting his property may be charged with manslaughter but not necessarily with murder—and this is different yet again for someone who commits treason or is caught spying for a foreign country. It is nonsense to suggest that a person should be punished for his rashness no less than for his forethought, any more than that our actions are predetermined, or in the case of an abusive upbringing, something adding to and not detracting from the guilt. If we cannot seek absolution by embracing any influences from the past, neither can we, by denying there may be any planning in the future.

There is another theory that asserts that the difference between freedom and necessity concerns only the difference between incumbent ends and the suprasensible realm to which they belong, and hypothetical ends and the physical realm to which they belong. Not only that, but that the problem of accountability can only be solved if we regard the individual as outside the determinants of space and time - if not discontinuous with the future then at least discontinuous with the past (Kant). And yet the question still remains; how can we be *free* to behave as we do if our lives are already settled from the start, or is it just the case that action must always be viewed in connection with certain prior influences and events? Consider, in respect to the relation between the consequent and its ground, the sense in which it might be said that the present is conditional upon the past but not the future upon the present. If we speculate that some event will occur in the distant future but are not sure it will actually take place, then neither can we be sure of that condition on which it is based, and so, tracing all this back to the present neither can we be sure that anything in our immediate future will be conditional upon anything in our immediate past. And yet to profess this kind of reasoning is also to ignore the question whether we can be sure of all the intermediate links stretching from one event to the next, or how far in reviewing any particular sequence we can be sure we have arrived at the very first one.

The upshot of arguing that there is an absolute ground for every assemblage of events is that the past and the future become a dividing point for the absolute certainty about an origin and the absolute equivocation about any end. If we adopt the view that nothing in the future can be gleaned from anything in the present, but that something in the present may be gleaned from something in the past, then what this suggests could be only one of two things. Either the *whole* of the future will be conditional upon the *whole* of the past so that one is simply an iteration of the other, or, there will be no connection between the two, and nothing can be learnt about the one through any examination of the other. However, by regarding causality as pertaining solely to the realm of what is sensible, it is clear (a) that the past may be used to make reliable predictions about the future (by the method we call induction), and (b) that the future may be used to lend a certain colouration to the past (through what we call historiography). In this way we can avoid the judgement that what we mean by the future is really just ambivalence about any ending, and that what we mean by the past is really only certainty about any origin.

The fact too that what we are dealing with is something *sui generis* is not to say it will be perceived any differently from anything altogether lacking in just this respect. If the difference between a free and a predetermined act cannot be discerned in the nature of their effects, then how, or by what means can we convince ourselves that there has been any true willing at all? That is, how can the reality of a free cause be evident if it does not stand out from the mainstream of everyday events? And that is why freedom and causality should never be connected in any fundamental way—the one is just as much progressive as the other is regressive, the one (causality) is just as much in keeping with a stable conception of space as the other (freedom) is with a plastic conception of time. What we mean by a cause is something that mediates between two events and which fixes this relationship, but what we mean by the will is something entirely inventive, both with respect to the future and with respect to the past. And if this fact be granted, that causality pertains to the realm of phenomenal and not noumenal things, then it presents no problem in positing some starting point if one considers that such is accidentally, and not essentially, dormant or in a state of rest. That is, from the determination of an object's essence it should be clear it will not always be in motion or at rest, but could be either at any given time. On the other hand, to argue that something may be both the origin and end of itself is to commit to the idea that doing will always be prior to being, since if something is moving then it must always be moving no matter what the time or place. As we have elsewhere argued (*The Limits of Knowledge*) in order for something to be and to change this must not only be from potentially what-is but potentially what-is-not, otherwise what-is could only be construed as what-must-be but is not yet and what may-be as what-was but is no more.

There is also a way of addressing the issue by suggesting that a person's conduct proceeds from a certain fixed and innate character— that we can tell precisely what he will do from knowledge of any original state and then by weaving all these different strands together. It seems there are two ways we may regard the relation between a sum of particular acts and the ground or the reason for their being. Either, a person's character is something that comprises the sum of his multifarious acts, and all these together afford an abstract of what he is, or, the whole is necessarily mirrored in each part; the whole can be *read* in each part, or constructed from a single part, as we find in an essay by Schopenhauer:

> As a botanist knows a plant in its entirety from a single leaf, as Cuvier from a single bone constructed the whole animal, so an accurate knowledge of a man's whole character may be attained from a single characteristic act . . (Free will vs Determinism).

A bad deed or a bad will therefore, is no less reflective of our true self than is the opposite, a good deed or a good will. The only problem with this is that it does not permit any possible garnering of an end independently of a means, or indeed, allow any ends that may be genuinely antithetical in themselves. For if honour and infamy are the sorts of things that are etched or engraved on a person's soul then a bad will has no more the chance of producing good works than a good will has the chance of producing wicked ones. And yet is it not also the case that we sometimes say of a person that he is acting out of character just as much as we do that he is acting 'true to form'? What we mean by repentance therefore cannot be a simple change in knowledge or a form of corrected knowledge, rather, a genuine change of heart, an admission that one's past misdeeds were not just inadvertent but thoroughly mistaken as well. Only in this way can the future and the present be joined through a total transformation of the past.

Perhaps we can better appreciate this if we consider how motives may sometimes be connected with or abstracted from, their particular ends, or when the goodness or badness of an act is subservient to the suitability or inappropriateness of such and such a means. Let us say that the reason for a person not paying his debts or keeping his promises is the prospect of short-sighted gain; that there are times and circumstances where it is simply convenient or opportune to renege on one's commitments. But let us say there are also times when it might be advisable to pay one's debts, perhaps because there is no other way to keep the wolf from the door. What we have here then is not so much a conflict of motives as a conflict of means, what it is that serves the end of self-interest rather than any question of a *rightful intent*. That is, it is only our knowledge of a certain set of circumstances that causes us to behave as we do, not the realization that certain forms of behaviour are inherently right and others inherently wrong. It may be inherently right to meet our obligations or our duties but that is not to say this is *all* we can do; rather, it is having such and such a state of mind which will predispose us to achieving such and such an outcome.

So far as it concerns the kind of approach we call libertarian, what is characteristic of this is the belief that (a) the present agent is the sole cause of action and not his historically determined character, and (b) the agent always has the last say even though he may also be influenced by a range of factors not entirely within his control. One of the objections to this is that if there is freedom from any original stimulus, or if in fact our choices are not compatible with our interests, then to act morally simply means to act arbitrarily or without any reason at all. That being said, it may still be necessary to distinguish between any inner stimulus that can be expressed through some outer act, and those outer influences that may be at work only because there is a simple lack of desire. As we have already argued, because there is no inner stimulus does not mean there may not be some directionless act as commonly occurs when we are lazy or bored.

A much more serious objection however is that the way this doctrine is expressed may not be altogether clear or coherent. As a starting point let us approach this through a discussion about freedom and justice, and what it is that we mean by a just or a fitting desert. Where it concerns the question of a legal right or a legal duty then there is both the sense in which a person's actions may terminate upon the weal or woe of others, and the sense in which they may be shaped through a set of pre-determined ends. This end is not simply the agent's interest but what is moral and upright as well. To say that justice is based on a sentiment, as perhaps resentment for injuries incurred, may not be to give a sufficient explanation for just exactly how this applies, or at least, how it differs from a principle discerned through purely rational means. A system of legal sanctions must serve a twofold purpose—it calls the agent to account for his past acts and directs him towards something better. It is just as certain that a person should be punished for his misdemeanours as it is that certain factors may militate against his guilt. It is just as certain that a person should be rewarded for his benefactions as it is, under certain circumstances, that he should be forgiven for his mistakes. A just or fitting desert in this context means making a person accountable to his peers, and this can only be discerned through the actions of the the judiciary and the courts.

On the other hand, if you are going to argue that it is justice that presupposes freedom and not freedom justice, then a question could be raised about the propriety of prohibiting certain acts or of raising certain rules. That is, given a conception of freedom that is *apriori*, then a sanction can only be that upon which certain actions *must* terminate in the case of what is free and *ought not* terminate in the case of what is necessary, or at least what is unavoidable. The problem with this is that although it appears to place a check on obdurate or wilful behaviour, the true meaning of justice simply vanishes, since the grounds for punishing wrong-doing may not be so clear at all. All we have is a simple *petitio principii*—the rule of justice does not follow upon the will of God, rather, the will of God must reflect what is 'fitting and just'. And yet apart from the observation that to act justly is not to act arbitrarily this gives no indication as to the real *efficacy* of just such a will. No doubt the Almighty will reassure Himself about that blueprint he has laid down, but it is not altogether clear how this might apply in the realm of quite fallible men. Or, if there is not this claim about divine goodness, there is the attempt to derive a right from some unshakeable law, as when it is said that the right to punish an adulterer necessarily stems from the law that prohibits such an act. When pressed further on the question of such a punishment, the answer may vary widely, from a fine, to a whipping, to a stoning, or even to death. There is no legal code that perfectly represents "the will of God", only the different customs that cause different societies or social institutions to behave in the way that they do.

Let us pursue the subject of freedom by relating it to those sanctions we would call (a) moral (b) legal, (c) natural, and (d) religious. So far as it concerns the meaning of both moral and legal sanctions, then in the case of the former this concerns what is agreeable to one's community or one's peers, in the case of the latter, what is positively commanded or proscribed. And since a person's character may be formed with either of these ends in view, the law gives greater weight to penalties than it does to fostering what may be for a person's own good. That is, it is more interested in dissuading a person from acting wrongly than it is in persuading him to adopt a standard he may never have been capable of at the outset. There are two ways we might approach the question of punishment, and they are (a) that to act wrongly is to invite punishment as its normal and necessary accompaniment (that is, where the evil is intrinsic) or (b) that punishment is no less an evil than what it is intended to offset, and so, must be weighed against the greater evil of allowing the deed to go unchecked (that is, where the evil is extrinsic). The first of these is the kind of argument that would be favoured by a retributivist, or the advocate for a just and a fitting desert, the second by a utilitarian, or an advocate for what is simply permissible or allowed. Notwithstanding what we have just said about the dual character of punishment, we would probably incline towards the latter; it is better that we improve men than simply allow them to wallow in the mire. Certainly, there is a problem with free will in the sense of what is either given or returned, if punishment is really nothing more than an after-effect, much as a hangover is something that follows a heavy bout of drinking. To argue that a person is not only due but also has the right to his own punishment (Hegel) is to subvert the only true meaning of a *right*, that is, as something which may be enforced but only in connection with some *common* store of good.

Not only that, but since the citizens of any state may seek to benefit through both its privileges and its rules, to act in accordance with the latter is surely the only thing that can be justified in and of itself. To enact a law is also to require that it be obeyed but only if it can be shown to be in keeping with the common good. Of course, a retributivist might argue that in putting a person to death we are not only making him accountable to his peers but to his Maker as well. In addition, critics of utilitarianism argue that a severe penalty may be appended to a trivial offence simply because it achieves the desired result, and hence, that in the overall picture it may be working against justice just as much as it is in support of it. On the other hand, this only begs the question how right and power are connected, that is, whether the power that the state has to end a person's life also gives it the right to do so, even if the enormity of the crime suggests that it really ought to. Allowing the state to exercise its powers in extreme ways may be to open the flood gates, or at least, invite the prospect of critical and irrevocable mistakes. Not only is it wrong to terminate a life when a person has been wrongly convicted but also if he has stolen a loaf of bread—and on what grounds can we be sure the judiciary will never overstep this mark?

Now let us consider the proposition that freedom and constraint are as one in their origin, that the former is merely an implicit agreement between acting dutifully and acting *from* a sense of duty, or making duty the very object and end of our acts. There is a difference between obedience to the law which permits of any exemption from the law, and that feeling which follows necessarily from the doing of what is worthy and just in itself. In the case of the latter it is our conscience that is at work, in the case of the former only cunning that directs us or what is simply expedient we should do. The feeling of reverence or a certain moral rectitude is what we call the promptings of our conscience—they attend upon the doing of the deed and mirror the sense of our having done well or ill. The reason we comply with the law is because we deem that it is just, but it is not 'just' if we choose to obey the law simply out of self-interest or because it is prudent we should do so.

And yet to what extent this is a credible account of duty really hinges on the question of our basic motivation, and whether to be seemly necessarily means to be disinterested as well. To experience guilt and remorse may well be a fitting response on any given occasion, but that does not of itself indicate what is evil or tarnish a person for the rest of his life. It merely indicates that a person *is* feeling badly, not necessarily *why* he is feeling badly. A parent may feel guilty at the loss of a child even if through a simple misadventure; a crash survivor may feel guilty because many lives have been lost—in neither case however does this follow upon a bad act, merely an unreasonable expectation one could have done more than one did. Of course it could be argued that how a person feels in the aftermath of any action is the necessary consequence of such an action, but it is quite another thing to suggest that the basis for acting rightly is the same as the basis for acting wrongly, if what they elicit is entirely the same response. It may be true that a person who acts rightly has virtue or duty as his end, but it does not follow that a person who acts wrongly has also depravity and indifference as his end. That is, so far as the end in question is something manifest or concrete, we need to consider self-interest, not duty, in both a form that is permissible and a form that is pernicious. It may well be a sin if you fail to report a colleague even though you know he has been stealing, but it is not a sin if you obey the law and yet do not do so from a sense of what is upright in itself.

In respect to the question of divine sanctions, the issue that presents itself is how a certain prescience or omniscience can be reconciled to the capacity that all men have to be sinful, just as they do to be virtuous. The idea that God can foresee the entire course of a person's life raises the question of how a person can in any sense be said to be free, since either the will of God antecedes the will of man or the will of man antecedes the will of God, but it cannot be both. And so, assuming the Almighty could never be inferior to his creations, the notion of free will has been introduced as a kind of escape clause (the book of Genesis), that is, to ensure that men in some sense can always be made accountable for their deeds. What is meant by sin therefore implies a distinction between what is simply permitted as distinct from what is objectively willed. A system of divine sanctions would therefore be effective in allowing a person to freely pursue a course of behaviour whilst ultimately issuing in either punishment or reward. What is problematic about this however is that although it seems to have broken the cycle in one respect it has also joined it in another. Looked at from the viewpoint of the wicked, it is certainly true that this may prevent him from seeking their own demise, if not even his own reform. On the other hand, looked at from the viewpoint of the virtuous, it seems that even they may be no better motivated than to seek out greater and more everlasting gains. (Or at least in the case of supererogation, if something is permitted then it is not necessarily rewarded)

Perhaps we can better appreciate this if we consider the question of moral accountability from the viewpoint of the way we might regard our future and the way we might regard our past. If we survey the totality of our acts or our intelligible character as a whole, then we can have both a sense of our commitment to the future and our deliverance *from* the past, and a sense of our deliverance from the future and accountability *for* what is past. Let us consider in the first place what it means to have an obligation to the future. So far as there is a set of positive sanctions that influence and shape our behaviour then it should be clear that what we mean by being generous or noble does not consist in acting prudently, in seeking greater and more everlasting gains. If this were so then acting rightly would simply amount to acting selfishly, and acting wrongly short-sightedly, given that there is just this standard to which everyone must comply. Where it concerns the question of punishment, we would likewise tend to regard this as something in the order of external compulsion. That is, we would want to address the reasons a person has for acting as he does if it is clear he could not have been free to consult his best interest, or was simply distracted from his aims. To commit evil therefore does not hinge on any settled state of mind, rather, on the uncertainty about any end or the uncertainty about any means. What we are dealing with therefore could be described as the problem of *good and better effects*—how we can overcome the necessity of pursuing greater and more everlasting gains at the same time as removing any basis for their opposite.

Where on the other hand it concerns our obligation to the past and what we might or could have done, then this is the capacity we have to do or desist from any action, and not make choices which are little more than wishful thinking. This power, the power of *not*-willing, is something we should steadfastly keep safe; otherwise who and what we are would be no more than how we were programmed, and from the moment of our birth. It would be like believing that evil was a congenital condition and that we should not just pity a person because he has Huntington's disease but censure him for this as well. But to return to what we have earlier said about repentance, the fact that we have an awareness we could have acted otherwise creates in us a sense of guilt, together with whatever misery we may have visited upon our fellows. It then becomes a difficult matter to separate this from the effects of true contrition, or due recompense to our victims and others we have injured along the way. This however, rather than pertaining to our future aspirations might best be described as the problem of *bad and worse effects*. The future has been darkened for us because of those sins and transgressions that are constantly re-emerging in our dreams.

Chapter 3

On the Meaning of a Moral Resolve

Broadly speaking, there are two ways we might regard a particular doctrine, as either (a) instrumental, where it concerns a comparison of means in respect to the same end, or a comparison of ends in respect to the same means, or (b) unconditional, where it concerns a comparison between something which is singular and something which is manifold, or the relativity of such and such a means and the absoluteness of such and such an end. Consider for instance how the relationship between public and private good may be viewed in either absolute or instrumentalist terms. In the case of the former what this supposes is a purely qualitative difference, adherence to the rule that the one should never be appended to the other but either completely included in or excluded from its being. Pursuit of private good should never be a rule for the seeking of what is publicly useful, since so long as we admit the broader ends of humanity this will necessarily have an impact on our purely private state of being. On the other hand, it may also be possible to treat of this relationship in a much more facile and less intractable way. The means to private happiness could well be said to reside in those things that surround us—and to this extent do they afford us delight in the way they are utilized; not necessarily disappointment in the way they are misused. In the same way, the means to public happiness could well be said to reside in those things that challenge and inspire us; and to that extent will we be both favourably and adversely disposed to the designs of our fellow men.

Now let us address the meaning of a motive in connection with a rational or appetitive will. There are two broad issues that arise in connection with a moral choice, and they are (a) whether reason or desire can be accounted as the motive for moral action, and thus, whether it is an unconditional end which informs a conditional means or a conditional means which informs an unconditional end, and (b) whether pursuit and avoidance are contrary but also independent in their nature, or whether pursuit and avoidance are contrary but also connected in their nature. Let us consider the first of these. In terms of the relation between reason and desire it is easy enough to see how the former may be subordinated to the latter, but not how the latter may be subordinated to the former. And that is because if we make reason the very object of an act, then it is unclear how anything sensible or affective could be construed as the means to just such an end. As sensuous beings it seems perfectly clear we are under the strict necessity to pursue pleasure and avoid pain, that we have certain indispensable needs, and that these needs must always be met. On the other hand, what could also be argued is that this could never constitute the basis for a moral resolve, otherwise, what was desirable could only be what we desire, and what was contemptible could only be what we despise. An authentic choice must therefore rest on two things that are not just *materially* but *formally* excluded from one other, that is, where both may be the possible objects of pursuit and avoidance. But even in these terms, it should never be our aim to posit reason as the ultimate end of our acts—only the notion of rational ends as reflective of the notion of a practical or politic means.

Neither by a moral choice do we mean anything which might rest on a spirit of indifference per se—be that the indifferent apprehension of a means (by the use of the will), or the indifferent apprehension of an end (by the light of our reason). In the first instance what is meant by the will concerns only a seeming disparity between good and evil, so that to seek an increase in the one is to seek an increase in the other, and likewise, to seek a decrease in the one a similar decrease in the other. In no way however would we describe this as a regulated will. On the other hand, neither should it be thought to proceed from a difference between full and inadequate knowledge where this concerns the simple *recognition* of an end, since moral truths are not like logical truths that unreservedly command our assent. The indifferent apprehension of an end, something so to speak which is known by the light of reason, is very far from establishing the means or the motives which give rise to our acts. And since there will always be a bifurcation in the motives so must there always be a bifurcation in the ends. What we might understand by a good or a bad will is not something that can be approached in any purely elemental way as neither can its products, malicious desire on the one hand or benevolent intent on the other. A great and well-intentioned mind (Einstein) could unearth the principles behind nuclear fission and wish that this not be misused, but a great and well-intentioned mind cannot prevent the production and proliferation of nuclear weapons, given the willingness on the part of certain nations to pursue such inimical ends.

Not only that, but how we distinguish between freely elected and purely involuntary ends can perhaps throw light on the meaning of a motive as distinct from what is fitful or unintended in its aim. For what we deem to be free is surely only the freely elected use of any means, whereas what we deem to be arbitrary or involuntary is surely only indifference towards the same. As instances of the latter we might cite malice or misanthropy at one extreme and negligence or self-abuse at the other. The basis for such discontent could be reckoned as undue distrustfulness or undue carelessness, indifference towards the weal and woe of others, indifference towards oneself. And that is because at the heart of evil what one frequently finds is pride and self-conceit—the separation of self from any concern about the consequences of its acts or concern about the welfare of those it might affect. What we mean by a *motive* on the other hand arises predominantly in situations where it is a question of (a) how others may be of use to us, and thus, what constitutes our own interest, or (b) how we may be of use to others, and thus, what constitutes the social good. Consider for instance the reason a person may have for keeping or breaking his promises, say perhaps, from fear of reprisal or the prospect of short-sighted gain. Here the value of an end pertains solely to the recognition of such and such a set of means. On other hand, consider a range of occupations and how the honing of skill may be made to work for the betterment of all. A teacher is the instrument for learning, an architect is the instrument for building, a pilot is the instrument for flying, and we could widen the circle to include acts of an even more philanthropic kind.

Where however it concerns the weighing of motives in connection with things that are not so dissimilar in their kind, then what this requires is a closer examination of the ends they are meant to sub serve. If for instance, we consider the sentiments of pity, felicitation, envy, and displeasure (i.e. teasing or fault-finding), then how we array or dispose these will depend entirely on our point of view. If we consider merely the stability or instability of an object, then it is envy and felicitation which will be coupled as one set of opposites and displeasure and pity as the other. If, however, we wish to consider either a direct or indirect engagement with the object, then pity and envy will be coupled in one way and displeasure and felicitation in another. That is, if there is indifference to an actual state then it is the latter that will apply, and if there is indifference to a *comparison* of states then it is the former that will apply. Or we might express it in this way. So far as there are grounds for separating the means and the end then this will proceed on the basis of a purely quantitative assessment of good and evil. We may for instance join the sentiments of displeasure and felicitation so far as there is a direct engagement with the object, and pity and envy so far as there is not, the comparison therefore being between more happiness to one person and more misery to another. The relationship between fitness and unfitness will thus exhibit itself in a certain economy or prodigality of parts—what is more or less commendable is only what is more or less direct, but the end itself will never be compromised or devalued to this extent. On the other hand, so far as there is any tacit agreement between pity and displeasure, it must surely be this, that another's misery is the object of their common and singular concern. In addition, however, there is also a sense in which the former is just as much selective as the latter is fixated. It may be possible to pity a person without knowing precisely what it is that is causing him distress, just as it is, to empathize with a person without any first-hand knowledge of his background or his friends. To be spiteful or churlish on the other hand is not only to exact pain but to reap pleasure from this as well, to give a person every reason to feel he has been put to the wheel. Therefore, in one respect pity and displeasure have no resemblance at all—or at least that is, if looked at from the viewpoint of a truly grateful or ungrateful reply.

Let us pursue this as follows. There is no way we ought to regard a choice between moral good and evil in terms of the positive snatching of a means and the indifferent apprehension of an end, or the positive snatching of an end and the indifferent apprehension of a means. In the one case, we are endeavouring to make a purely arbitrary end subordinate to a simple discrepancy in the means, in the other, a purely arbitrary means subordinate to a discrepancy in the ends. In neither case however does this point to any discrepancy between the motives which underlie the means, and the ends these means are intended to supply. Consider the argument that deliberation or premeditation is really only a certain oscillation that terminates upon a choice, or the requisition of such ends as will necessitate such and such a means (Hobbes). In this case, desire and aversion as a means are entirely neutral, since if what is done from desire could be called what is voluntary and if what is done from aversion what is not, then this must rest on the further distinction between what *might* or what must *never* be possible. But when desire and aversion are linked to the ends of our acts then this is different yet again, since we can both do and omit certain deeds based on a well-founded judgement of their likely effects. That is, we may both do and omit a certain deed if we apply this to the fear and confidence about an outcome, and thus if we adopt a consistently determinist point of view. A person who considers stealing another's car may desist from such action because he fears this could land him in jail. A person who considers avoiding his moral obligations may experience a change of heart if he fears this could damage his reputation or his good name. And so, there is a sense in which it is the ends of our acts which dictate those means for ensuring they will achieve their desired or intended results.

From our own perspective however it seems there are two key points which tell against this. Firstly, because what we mean by the will is not something altogether arbitrary but the means of achieving a certain *balance* where the ends of our acts are concerned. And secondly, because a moral choice does not rest on the clarity or obscurity of an end in relation to the clarity or obscurity of any means, rather, on both the clear apprehension of an end and the ready availability of any means. To begin with, let us consider what we mean by justice when we apprehend this as an end, and what we mean by justice when we apprehend this as a means. Consider the idea that in conjunction with the commission of wrong there must be a justifiable counter force in order that such a wrong be overturned. Here intendment or a motive has not been sufficiently distinguished from cancellation as an end, since in the way two forces may annul one another, this has no bearing on how any such relation may be viewed. There is a considerable difference between revenge as an end, retribution as an end, capital punishment as an end, and rehabilitation as an end. And that is precisely what we mean when we say that if the ends are right or wrong then the means are value-free, and that if the means are right or wrong then the end is value-free. Justice and injustice can only be distinguished as ends, not simply as means, but if it is proper to punish a wrongdoer then this concerns no more than a due apportionment of pain. In the same way, we do not regard the relation between sympathy and malice in terms of such and such a means but rather in terms of such and such an end. That is, we do not treat a good or a bad intent in the same way we do a useful or inapposite means. It is not inconceivable that an evil-doer could have the clearest presentiment of an end and be equally confident about the means, but we do not prize this more highly than we do the actions of a hero, simply because there is less certainty about what it is that might actually be achieved.

We have described a doctrine as being instrumental if it concerns (a) a comparison of means in respect to the same end, or (b) a comparison of ends in respect to the same means. The question remains however: Are there any grounds for distinguishing between these different approaches as such? That is, does the sense in which similar means may be joined to antithetical ends convey something different than that in which dissimilar means may be joined to consentient ends? The way we might approach this is to begin with the notion of justice, and work through the implications of regarding it in either an absolute or instrumentalist way. (Not however in the way we have just treated it from the viewpoint of either a purpose or an end). Let us represent a just state of affairs as one in which either (a) less gratitude for a favour will be met by more resentment for an injury, or (b) less resentment for an injury will be met by more gratitude for a favour. Now expressed in these terms the question that arises is whether this involves a comparison of means and yet no assumption about an end, or a comparison of means and its connection to some quite transcendental end. Of course, our initial reaction may be to settle on the latter, since we tend to regard justice (like prudence) as some divinely ordained precept and of which all competing virtues must simply be in awe. Frequently enough it is expressed as a mean between two extremes, as perhaps between acting unjustly and being justly treated (Aristotle). It may also be mirrored by the difference between perfect and imperfect duties, since such things as generosity and magnanimity, as more than what is strictly required, are not to be accounted duties in the true acceptation of that word.

Another way of raising it to some all-embracing standard is to compare it with benevolence and malevolence, or the prospect of a real disparity rather than just a balancing of pleasure and pain. If justice as a perfect duty cannot be made conformable to what is less so, then benevolence as what is 'imperfect' cannot be raised to what is more so. Let us consider a few examples. Suppose that two persons are applicants for the same job and that a staff member has been able to influence the outcome because one of them has been helpful to him in the past. Or let us consider another situation, where a person has been brought before the courts on a serious charge but receives a light sentence, because the judge, who is easily swayed, has been offered a sizable bribe. Now it seems that what we are dealing with here is ambivalence where it concerns righteous and benevolent ends; that so far as duty is beholden to helpfulness (or collusion) it is that much the poorer for so being. Having said that, what we also need to keep in mind is that so far as justice is not beholden to benevolence then it is not necessarily beholden to prudence, since to be a prudent man is to be an active man, and that may sometimes imply a degree of rashness in any action he undertakes. It may be reasonable to repay less gratitude with more resentment or less resentment with more gratitude, but what we mean by justice in this context is a hollow sentiment and not worthy of our esteem.

But if it is important to recognize the meaning of a qualitatively different end, then so is it important to recognize the sense in which the means may be contained or concealed in any end. That is, that what we mean by 'the instrument' may be relevant not only in the garnering but also in the ceding of such and such an end. Let us pursue this within the following framework. We do not wish to raise expediency to an all-embracing standard from which we should never depart, otherwise no distinction would be made between the appearance and the reality of affording someone good, or the appearance and the reality of affording someone harm. The kind of evil which we allow as the means of securing something good is very different from the kind of evil which is pursued under the guise, say, of benevolent intent. There is a particular argument that suggests we should always be steadfast in the face of a manifest hurt, since this is really no different from the pleasure we experience at the prospect of any communal gain. And that so far as we are truly impartial and fair, we should also be fair to ourselves—since not only will the good we do but also any harm we do ultimately redound on ourselves. It is precisely this sentiment which underlies the call of Epictetus to

Consider first what hurt is . . . for if both good and evil consist in choice, see whether what you say does not amount to this: 'Since he has hurt himself by injuring me, shall not I hurt myself by injuring him? (Discourses of Epictetus: Book II Ch. X—How we investigate the duties of life from the names which we bear).

And yet what is problematic about this and what it fails to address is how the nature of any means may be such that either it is or is not contained in any end. When a person acts kindly or is philanthropically inclined then the means will be contained in the end, since what the act does and announces it is doing is clearly augmenting the sum of good. And not only is this not harmful to the agent, it also kindles the warmth and esteem of his fellows. On the other hand, if the good to be sought can only be realized at some interim cost, then the means may be said to be concealed in their aim—as in the case of a strenuous medical procedure or the routine that a person practices in order to keep himself fit. Here, although the benefits may be genuine and of lasting worth, they cannot be realized without some proportionate effort. What we have in both cases is the promotion of good, but in the one case under the banner of meaning to do well, and in the other, of inadvertently doing harm. Much in the same way, if we do not separate the reality of doing harm from the appearance of doing harm, then neither can we separate the ground for being resentful from the ground for being beholden—we will be just as grateful to our assailants as we are to our protectors, just as angry at a doctor's diagnosis as we are at a romancer's lies.

Looked at in these terms what we mean by action of the most disinterested kind, be that benevolent or malevolent, is something that is reflected in its source, and so, if there is a bifurcation in the ends there must be a bifurcation in the means. However, an end which is extremely good or bad is not the same as an end which is only moderately good or bad. The real pith of a means-end relationship which is purely conditional can perhaps be best expressed as follows, that it involves either (a) quantitatively comparable means in respect to the same recognizable end, or (b) qualitatively comparable ends in respect to somerecognizably different means. In this arrangement we can see both what is and is not included, that there may be a connection between quantitatively different means and qualitatively different ends but not between means that are 'equal' and ends that are not. Let us pick up on our earlier discussion about the relation between pity and displeasure. The object of displeasure is delight at another's ill without the prospect of any gain, it may be to tease another, or to cajole another, or to raise another's ire. The object of pity is alleviation of another's suffering but not through any direct engagement, rather, through an indirect assessment and a willingness to assume pain in order that another's be allayed.

The real question that needs to be asked however is to what extent these ends imply distinct and yet not incommensurable means. In pity it is the misery of another which raises a greater despondency in ourselves; in ruthlessness it is the misery of another which raises a greater piquancy in ourselves. It seems therefore that in the one case we are connecting less pleasure with more pain and in the other more pain with more pleasure, and so, what could be more disproportionate than this? And yet if we examine it a little more closely then perhaps the discrepancy is not so much between the different quantities as it is the ends of pleasure and pain in themselves. That is, the means to the end of compunction is only a comparison of more and less ill (in the context of what is just); the means to the end of ruthlessness is only a comparison of more and less good (in the context of what is unjust). There is however no real exchange between pleasure and pain as such—the former has just as much an overriding value, and the other something always to be shunned. Yet if we were to suppose a different but no less conceivable relation than has herein been outlined, it may be possible by the sharing of pleasure and the excepting of pain (i.e. how we bear up to it) to admit the quite agreeable ends of felicitation on the one hand and courage on the other. And if we can connect these ends with means that are entirely diverse, then perhaps we have no good reason to deduce that internally consistent means must always be coupled with qualitatively different ends (just as we might say a grateful or ungrateful heart is not the same as the giving or denying of any pleasure).

Having observed a certain nicety in the way an instrumental doctrine may be expressed, the question that remains is as follows: How can we be sure that what we have is (a) a comparison of means in respect to the *same* end so far as a different means will be subjoined to the same end, or (b) a comparison of ends in respect to the *same* means, so far as there are different ends subjoined to entirely one and the same set of means? What makes this a little tricky is that although it is not unreasonable that different ends will be supported by their own particular means, where the latter is concerned it is not so easy to discern what is similar or dissimilar in itself. As we have already indicated, a situation in which less gratitude for a favour is met with more resentment for an injury may *appear* to be different from a situation in which less resentment for an injury is met with more gratitude for a favour, but since the two are only *formally* distinguished that is not to say they may not be *materially* just the same. Therefore, to resolve this, what we need to keep in mind is that there is a difference between the way the ideas of quality and quantity *may* be combined and the way the ideas of appearance and reality *must* be distinguished. If there were no difference between the appearance and the reality of an end then neither would we have the sense of a means as being *contained* in any end, as for instance, when we say that a callous act is reflective of a stony heart. But in other instances, what we are dealing with is a situation in which one thing may be formally but not materially excluded from another. This therefore will require a more tractable approach to the relation between quality and quantity.

In fine, it could quite plausibly be argued that what we mean by a consensus of interests and a contrariety of interests *must* be reflected in the means which conduce to them, and that this in turn will manifest itself in the difference between pity and envy, or displeasure and felicitation. In the case of the latter, it is the cheeriness of one person that arouses a certain pleasure in some other, just as with teasing or taunting, it is the misery of one person that arouses a certain pleasure in some other. Likewise, where pity is concerned, the misery of one person will arouse a certain sorrow in some other, just as with envy, the success of one person will arouse a certain resentment in some other. What this does not do, however, is address the question whether a difference is expressed in the *way* the means may conduce to their end, or, if it is only a comparison of means, and not any connection with those ends they are meant to sub serve. That is to say, it would surely be necessary to draw quite different conclusions if what we begin with are very different starting points. Congratulation and displeasure may well be connected so far as we assume a direct and immediate engagement with their object, just as pity and envy may well be connected so far as we assume an indirect engagement with their object. In salutation and congratulation, we enter directly into the well-being of another; in displeasure and fault-finding we enter directly into the misery of another, only in this case to reap delight from the comparison. In sympathy (or more strictly empathy), we make an indirect assessment of our own condition but without supposing it to be better or worse than any other. In envy, we make an indirect assessment of our own condition, only in this case by assuming it to be worse than what we are comparing it to. Thus, if we start with an end then what we have is something only qualitatively comparable, and if we start with a means then what we have is something only quantitatively comparable.

Chapter 4

Motives and Beliefs

To begin our discussion, let us address the broad question whether by a belief do we mean (a) a spontaneous mental act which arises in conjunction with some impression or idea, or (b) a settled state of mind which arises in conjunction with our wishes or desires. In respect to the first of these, what could be argued is that belief is merely the strength or vivacity that we have in connection with some idea, that if we observe a certain regularity in the behaviour of things we must assume they are connected, and thus, that what we observe or infer from the past will be strengthened and confirmed in the future. The problem here however is that to have a belief is not necessarily what it means to review or revise what we have always taken to be true. The belief that the earth revolves around the sun is very different from the belief that the sun revolves around the earth, but whichever we take as our starting point, that is not to say a person would have to engage in repeated mental acts to be convinced that what he believed was in fact true. Rather, this is done from an assessment of all the evidence, not a reasserting of what our 'common sense' suggests. In respect to the second of these, what could be argued is that beliefs are acquired not through reasoning or scientific testing but through simple intuition, in other words, what might be inferred from our experience and those events that shape our lives. The belief in a Supreme Being is a case in point—if a person has a strong moral outlook on life, he probably believes there is some superintendent agency as well. In the same way, a person who believes in euthanasia, or gay rights, is not drawing strength through any unshakable form of reasoning, but rather his commitment to some ideal that he considers to be just. Hence to believe in something does not necessarily mean it can also be proved or disproved.

So far as it concerns the relation between action and belief, then an account of moral behaviour that eschews all connection with the will could broadly be described as follows; in the first place, as a theory which is strictly *causal*, and in the second, as a theory which is strictly *linguistic*. To consider the first of these, there are those who would argue that the only real determinants of action are the conditions or the opportunities for such action, and that it is these which represent a certain disposition or settled state of mind. However, what it means for the agent to embark on a certain course may not always be so easy to explain, it may mean to set something into motion and be committed to this activity as an end, or it may mean to set something into motion but in a way that could be interrupted later on. For instance, an endurance runner who sets out to run the marathon must be steadfast in this pursuit; otherwise he will not achieve what he had originally planned to do. On the other hand, a person who places an egg in a saucepan, cooks it, removes it, and then places it in a cup, may have changed the object of the act but not his intention as well. (That is, he still intends to eat it but not in the original vessel.) To consider the second of these, there are those who would argue that language serves no other purpose than to reinforce a certain set of rules, that these rules are public, and that speech-acts that seek to mimic particular 'private' states are not really descriptive at all. Language therefore is not a means of connecting our intentions with our deeds; rather it is self-prescriptive in that you only know what move to make once you know the game that is involved. (Wittgenstein) "Being moral" therefore means acquiring a vocabulary, or a set of implements, which will specify such and such a particular *use*.

From our own perspective however, and leaving aside this kind of pseudo psychology, what we really need to know is what it means to inspire a particular belief, as when one says 'I guarantee it will rain tomorrow' or 'I'm sure he won't be long'. Here what we are doing is employing a particular word (*guarantee, sure*) to underscore the way we feel, but in such a way as engenders a degree of confidence rather than uncertainty. An air traffic controller is a good example of someone whose job it is to instill a degree of positivity, and whether this be right or wrong, sound or unsound, there is no question of a motive or reason why such directives have been given. That is, there can be no discrepancy between having the facts and stating the facts, or not having the facts and inadvertently stating what is false. But where there is the question of intent, then we need to distinguish between the raising or inducing of a belief, and the designing or proposing of a belief. What we mean by *proposing* a belief is either (a) claiming to be truthful in the matter of what has been stated, or (b) claiming to be faithful in the matter of what has been pledged. In the case of the former what we are dealing with is either lying or truth-telling, that is, disclosure or concealment of what is true. In the case of the latter what we are dealing with is a set of relations that are either symmetrical or asymmetrical. If for instance you promise your friend you will be a second at his wedding, you may well have the right intention, but if you suddenly fall ill and are rushed to hospital you can hardly accuse you of not being true to your word. Here a good intention may be coupled with a false belief. Or let us suppose your neighbour is going away and you promise to put out his rubbish, although you really have not the least intention of doing so. Unbeknownst to you, someone from the local council has set upon the task and when your neighbour returns he is happy to see it has been removed. Here a bad intention may be coupled with a true belief. Both these examples are asymmetrical, but in the case of the latter, if someone from the local council had not performed the action then it would be symmetrical.

When however, we say that a discrepancy may occur between the inner and the outer side of the act, what we are not saying it should be clear is that our utterances can only be descriptive of the former. Or at least that to the degree they are descriptive of the former they must also be indifferent towards the latter. As we have just seen, there are those who would argue that the only thing that counts is conformance between some utterance and its external gauge, that being the kind of rules that apply in the case of the game we call 'being moral'. And yet even granting this may be true in respect to the question of any general *consensus* that is not the same where it concerns the question of any relevant *intent*. As we have just seen, there are times when it is a good intent that may be matched with a false belief, or a bad intent that may be matched with a true belief. And if we are going to assimilate a false promise to something like the false move that a beginner makes at chess then we would have to commit the agent to a strict formula no matter what he says or does. But does it follow that a lie can never be told otherwise than in the context of 'I am lying when I say that such and such . . . ?' (just as a person who touches a bishop must move it, but the rules do not say he cannot throw it away.) Or consider the kind of question that a parent might ask a child (a) 'Have you washed the dishes?' and (b) 'Have you washed the dishes as you promised?' Now since both questions can be answered with a simple nod or shake of the head, on no account can we tell if it is a simple report that is being given, or quite specifically, the breaking or fulfilment of a promise. There is therefore no way to discriminate between what is strictly right or wrong and what is merely true or false, that is, the tacit consent to the doing of something and the *moral* consequences if one does not. Another point that needs to be made is that we do not say a person acts deceptively because his actions are not suited to his words, rather because his actions are self-serving or prejudicial to his fellows. We might think of inducing a belief in the context of inadvertently conveying what is false, but we might also think of it in the context of deliberately conveying what is false when this is done simply for amusement, not for illicit gain. A magician who entertains an audience may be engaged in various acts of misdirection but this is altogether harmless; we do not impute to him false motives when it is just a question of his cleverness or skill.

On the other hand, we may use the word *intent* in a weaker sense when this includes such things as affirming and denying, accepting and rejecting, liking and loathing, or what is not exclusively moral in its kind. There is for example a difference between the wish to sweep a footpath and the act of picking up a broom, or the wish to prune a rose bed and the act of putting on some gloves. Or we might consider the case where what we are doing is not so much inducing a belief as inducing a *response*, when our aim is wholly in the other, when we taunt or tease a person merely to gauge the way he might react. Thus, the word *intent* has a wide variety of meanings—it may involve a sign or gesture when it is a question of what is being conveyed, or it may be a wishing or willing at one extreme (indolence) and the complete joining of two selves at some other (love). Our ability to detach ourselves from any specific effect may also cause us to impute mysterious qualities to certain deeds, even if there is no evidence they do in fact exist. It may also make a person believe that what befalls him are his 'just deserts', not luck, and that a good or a bad 'effect' will always attend upon a good or a bad desire. Because our aims and preconceptions do not always work out as we might hope, this may sometimes cause us to imagine there is a dark purpose in even the most random of events. In the case of the untimely death of some high-profile personality or politician we often attribute this to a secret plot or some nefarious design. Thus, despite an extensive enquiry into the shooting of John F. Kennedy such has often been imputed to a 'conspiracy of agents', be that the secret service, the CIA, or the Russian mob. Or consider the case of an air traffic controller who inadvertently conveys false information which leads to the loss of many lives—in this case a small slip may not prevent a relative from believing there was something truly diabolical at work. A person's integrity may thus be compromised by the fact there is both a consciousness of what one is as the author of one's deeds, and a consciousness of what one deserves as the object of such and such a scheme.

But to return to our original discussion, we need to be clear about the difference between (a) having a belief and inducing a belief (b) having the truth and communicating what is true, and (c) having a sound as opposed to unreasonable belief that something is so. To induce a belief may mean to have a certain motivation but then again it may not, and there is a considerable difference between claiming that a woman has been cut in half and conveying the belief that the person you just saw is in the bathroom when he is really in the basement. Hence in the case of truth-telling, knowledge is allied to what is *actually* conveyed, while in the case of lying knowledge is divorced from what is actually conveyed. However, to be dishonest where this concerns one's relation to others is very different from what it means to be dishonest where this concerns one's relation to oneself. And that is because in the one case you may completely conceal what is true whilst in the other you can only partly conceal what is true. There are several ways of regarding this phenomenon of partial concealment, but in traditional psychotherapy what this means is that there is no single consciousness but rather only different strands of consciousness, that certain truths made accessible to our instincts (id) are not the same as others made accessible to our intellect (ego). (Freud)

Or there is the sense in which you might oppose a reasonable belief to what is capricious at one extreme or fixated at the other. To be true to oneself is also to be realistic in one's judgements about oneself, not to be persuaded by things that are altogether irrational in their nature. To a hypochondriac it is perfectly natural that he should be solicitous of his health; to a McCarthyite it is perfectly natural he should be suspicious of his friends; to a dieter it is perfectly natural he should be suspicious of his weight. At the other extreme there are those deeply held beliefs passed on from generation to generation, be that the effectiveness of herbal cure, the right to bear arms or keep slaves, the dangerous uncertainty about a Muslim or a Jew. On the other hand, where it concerns the question of our own temporality, then the choices we make should not amount to steering a middle course between impulsive urges on the one hand and deep-seated prejudices on the other. The future for us is both open and untested; hence, it is only by reconnecting with the past we can best realize who we are and what we could become. In other words, in order to attain maturity what is requisite that we both harness our emotions and learn from our mistakes, just as, for a person to seek reform is it requisite that he both know who he was, who he is, and what he hopes to become. We cannot realize a change in ourselves unless we can realize a change in our past, and we cannot realize a change in our past unless we can realize a change in our *projected* self, in our *ideal* self, not merely a series of isolated events or designs.

In terms of the relation between our motives and beliefs, then the former we might regard as entirely subjective whereas the latter we might regard as either subjective or objective. Thus, to act on a belief may simply be the *causative* aspect of inducing a belief, as when the forecast of rain will cause a person to carry a brolly or a coat. On the other hand, in the case of our motives then this more directly concerns the question of our *values*, as for instance, what is beneficial or prejudicial to our fellows. Given the existence of certain actions that we take to be inherently right and certain others that we take to be inherently wrong, the motives that attend a wide range of acts may colour our judgements as regards what they are in and of themselves. And so, a person who makes a large donation to a radical political party is considered less deserving than someone who makes a similar donation to the Red Cross, just as someone who steals because he has a large family is considered less blameworthy than someone who steals because he is a drug addict. There is a difference however in the way we might characterize certain actions as being 'upright' and the way we might characterize certain observations as being true. It is not a simple or self-evident fact that something is good or something is bad just as it is that something is yellow or something is blue, and that is because there is no form of absolute knowledge that corresponds to what we have called a *justified* or *warranted* belief. There are several ways we might approach the question of some alleged realm of moral truths, but if it does not pertain to the purely rational then neither does it pertain to the purely appetitive, otherwise anyone with some random desire could represent this as what was universally good. Or we might express this a little differently by saying that if our moral judgements are not always certain they do at least constitute a body of knowledge that can be consistently applied. To the naked eye there is a discernible difference between the colour red and the colour blue, but it may be difficult to say when orange becomes yellow or violet becomes blue, and that is because this is a change that occurs by insensible degrees. In other words, what we mean by 'good' and 'evil' are the extremes of what we judge about and there are many shades of grey, but because there is no absolute standard does not mean our assessments have no meaning at all.

The difference between motives and beliefs is also reflected in the fact that of the four ways we can conjoin proposing and inducing a belief, in only one case can this be said to be inadvertently right, and that is when a bad intent is coupled with a true belief. What we mean by 'intention' here is quite specific to the outcome or result—on no account does this concern the more general question of what we mean by a good or a bad *will* or a good or a bad *reason* And that is why we would not say that if a person proposes a true belief but induces a false one then he is inadvertently wrong, since in this case, we cannot connect the aim with any wherewithal at all. Hence, there may be a point of congruence where it concerns inducing a false belief and inducing a true belief, only in the first case where this concerns reporting the facts as one believes them to be true, and in the other, acting dishonestly but in a way that may actually not prove to be harmful. And of course, if there is a point of congruence in one respect then there must be a point of divergence in some other, that being where 'knowing the truth' is equivalent to representing oneself in a manner which only *appears* to be true. From the agent's perspective, the source of wrong-doing may thus be said to arise from a situation in which (a) if there is no outcome then at least one's intentions were good or (b) if there is an unfortunate outcome then one's intentions were not bad -they have simply been misconstrued. Hypocrisy, however, involves a further element, not only the question how one represents oneself to one's fellows but how one represents oneself to oneself. For instance, although we have argued that proposing a false belief and inducing a true belief may be construed as what is inadvertently right, we need to stipulate that this is only from the viewpoint of the recipient. From the viewpoint of the agent it is still *unconditionally* wrong. To return to our earlier example, suppose the person who has returned from his holiday decides to reward his neighbour for the deed he imagines he has done—then this may precipitate a condition that is not only illogical but self-deceiving as well. That is, the person who was dishonest in the first place may convince himself that he is justly deserving of what has only accidentally fallen in his lap.

Let us review what we have said about lying and truth-telling and the making or undertaking of a certain commitment. In the case of a promise what we mean by the 'objective' side of the act is what the act produces or what the agent has committed himself to do. In the case of truth-telling, what we mean by the 'objective' side of the act concerns only a standard of knowledge, since the intention *is* to inspire a particular belief knowing it to be true and not the opposite. Of course, we may also need to distinguish between acting on a false belief and inducing a false belief when the latter is not a mere addendum to the former. A student who responds to a question he is asked may be acting on what he believes to be true (even if it is true), but that is not to say he has the authority to *instil* what he believes to be true. On the other hand, an air traffic controller is someone who may not only be acting on a false belief but may also be inspiring a false belief. In neither case however would you say that the agent was acting deceptively, only in the latter case where this is somewhat double-edged—if the operator is a trusted colleague then this may save him from dismissal, but if he makes an awful blunder this may not save him from a lasting sense of guilt.

Now in a Kantian context let us consider what might be meant by the injunction to 'act on the maxim whereby one can at the same time will that it should become a universal law', in relation to (a) our moral duties (b) our legal duties and (c) our duties towards others. If we begin with the law of contradiction and attempt to apply this to human behaviour then what we are doing is grounding the prospect for lying in the *necessity* of being truthful, and in which case there are only two possibilities (a) if all statements are truthful then no statements are deceitful, and (b) if all statements are deceitful then no statements are truthful. And since what we are dealing with is a completely fixed starting point, although the statement 'all statements are truthful' must imply 'some statements are truthful', 'some statements are truthful' does not imply 'some statements are deceitful'. The problem with this is that if the origin of both lying and truth-telling resides solely in the ability to recite such and such a set of words, then it is difficult to say how one's utterances could be construed as anything other than formal. In other words, no matter what it is that men *ought* to do, it does not follow they can ever change what they have habitually done in the past, or be capable of any change in the future. If we assume that the basis for lying is *apriori* and not *aposteriori* then our language would be mired in complexity, and we would not be able to utter what was true or false but only what was trite or contradictory. To attempt to make a relevant statement would be like the scene in *Don Quixote* where a man, standing before a bridge, utters the words 'By the oath I have taken, I swear that I am going to die upon these gallows and this is my business and no other' in response to the landowner's demand that 'whoever crosses this bridge must first take an oath from whence he comes and what business he is about. If he swears true, let him pass, but if he tells a lie let him hang from these gallows'. Or at the other extreme it may cause us to formulate a sentence such as 'A man who is a man is also a man' which although not informative is at least not untrue.

If on the other hand we begin with the law of excluded middle, then what this commits us to is something like (a) if the statement 'this statement is truthful' is true, then it cannot be false, or (b) if the statement 'this statement is deceitful' is true, then it cannot be genuine. What it also enables us to do is consider a much wider range of outcomes, as when from a sample of statements, we might conclude that either (a) all statements are truthful (b) some statements are truthful or (c) no statements are truthful. Now even in the case where it is the last that applies it does not follow that such must always be so; rather, that this is only specific to the situation as it presently stands. Not only that, but what this indicates is that lying and truth-telling should not so much be joined through their origin as distinguished through their end. That is, that telling the truth presupposes openness, honesty, and fair dealing in the sense that it *produces* these things, just as lying presupposes suspicion, distrust, and uncertainty. So far as there may be any justification for the practice of lying, then we need to regard this not as a positive endorsement of that which opposes the rule but rather a negative deviation from that which supports it. That is, lying may be justified not when it is a question what is the most expedient thing to do, rather, what it is that is grossly inexpedient *not* to do. And this also raises the question of how we prioritize our duties. If your friend has been caught shoplifting and you are asked to supply a contact address then to mislead the authorities may be very convenient for your friend, if not yourself, but that is very different from a situation when it is a person's life that is at stake. To return to the difference between inducing and proposing a belief, to tell a lie may be to intentionally mislead a person, but the 'little white lie' that is intended to allay a person's fears is very different from the 'big lie' that is intended to deprive a person of his property or his good repute. An inveterate liar is someone whose actions will ultimately speak louder than his words, because at some point, others will come to see right through him, but that should not be compared to a situation where a person is forced to make a tough decision and he must prioritize his needs.

In respect to our legal duties, it is certainly true that if acts such as murder and suicide were widened to include all men and something that was willed by all men, it would destroy the very ground on which our civil ties are based. (Consider an extreme case such as the Jonestown massacre). However, we need to be careful about what it is that is actually in question—there is a difference between *how* a person may be treated as an 'end in himself' and *how* a means may be harnessed in such and such a particular way. So far as there is a difference between free or elective and forced or involuntary ends, then so may there also be in respect to the free or involuntary requisition of any means. In the case of an injurious act, it is not so much that one person is being treated as a means as opposed to an end; rather, that there is a forcible seizure of something that may be enabling in and of itself. In certain circumstances there may be an end which determines what particular means will be deployed, in other circumstances just the question of a means but no relation to any end. An eye surgeon may be the means to the recovery of a person's sight, a lawyer may be the means to the recovery of a person's wealth, but we do not say that it is 'wrong' to be used in such a manner. And if a person knowingly places himself in the hands of another he can hardly complain if things do not work out exactly as he might have wished. Thus, an end in this sense is very different from an end that has been fraudulently obtained—in the case of the latter it is not the end that really counts, only the means, or at least a means that does not recognize any sphere that is common to all men.

Or, consider that if one person takes the life of another then the state acting on behalf of the victim may well be disposed to take his. In this case it is difficult to say just how this relationship might be viewed—is the victim the means to the wrongdoer or is the wrongdoer the means to the state? There may also be the case of a free or volitional act but not in conjunction with a free or discretionary means. Suicide it has been argued is wrong because it treats the individual quite simply as a means, that is, not as the means to the good of any other, but as the means of avoiding something onerous in life. This account however is somewhat confusing, firstly, because it is not clear in what sense a means *might* be useful if it has nothing positive as its end, and secondly, granted that it is useful, why this might not apply to just *anyone* as an end. Rather might we say that in ending his own life is a person depriving another of the chance to use himself in a way that is supportive of human life, thereby do we preserve the 'assisting' nature of just such an act at the same time as conceding the negative import at its very most core. From our own perspective, the way we might describe this is an act that constitutes both an implicit means in one respect and an explicit means in another, or at least, how the removal of suffering for the agent must be balanced by the suffering that this engenders in his fellows.

On the other hand, in respect to the question of our duties towards others, then here at least would we give unqualified support to the injunction that you should 'act according to a maxim that holds good for all', but not so much because it constitutes a 'law of reason' as the natural affection all men should have for one another. To have a benevolent desire is not the same as to undertake a compassionate act but then neither is it opposed to it. On the other hand, how far it may be reasonable to perform a compassionate act does not exclude the question how far it may be reasonable to be apathetic towards oneself. And if we did not attend to the difference between a good and a bad will (i.e. benevolent and malevolent intent) then how could we draw the circle that encloses the origin of our acts with those ends they are intended to supply? By comparison, the rule 'Do unto others as you would have them do unto you' does not adequately specify how our ends *should* be joined, but only that like minds will be drawn to like sentiments or ideals. Of course, it is not inconceivable that the sphere of human happiness could be so ordered that no one would think fit to contribute to others, but that would be to deny there was anything outside those duties we are owing to ourselves.

Chapter 5

Of Justice: In Relation to Virtue and Vice.

To begin our study of the relation between justice and virtue, let us do so in terms of the traditional Aristotelian argument that there is always some intermediate state where our passions and our actions are concerned. Confidence, for instance, could be viewed as a mean between braggadocio and humility, bravery between rashness and cowardice, just resentment between envy and malevolence. If pleasure and pain are commensurable then they may be experienced both too much and too little. To seek the intermediate however, does not always mean to depart equally from both extremes; rather, it depends on our perspective and what it is we find pleasing as opposed to what it is we find repugnant. On the other hand, there is no intermediate where it concerns the bare expression of a pleasure or the bare expression of a pain; there is no 'mean' between being too cowardly and not being cowardly enough, between being too brave and not being brave enough, between being too malevolent and not being malevolent enough.

So far as it concerns the meaning of justice, then this could be expressed as an *amount* between two extremes, not expressed in terms of any qualitative difference, but rather in terms of what is qualitatively the same. In theory, what this means is that just action is an intermediate between acting unjustly and being justly treated, where it is neither active nor passive. In practice what this means is that acting unjustly and being unjustly treated are the extreme positions. In the case of the former, the agent has too much justice. In other words, looked at from the viewpoint of the agent there is too much justice, and looked at from the viewpoint of the recipient there is too little justice. Injustice proceeds from the fact that in one's own case there tends to be an excess of what is useful and a shortfall in what is harmful; in the case of others an excess in what is harmful and a shortfall in what is useful. From the viewpoint of the agent therefore to act unjustly means to act selfishly or without due regard for others, from the viewpoint of the recipient, to be treated with scant regard or to be punished more severely than is his due.

One of the major problems with this account is that it fails to clearly distinguish between what is meant by justice in a *legal* sense and justice in a *moral* sense. In terms of what it means to act unjustly in a legal sense, then this is what it means to act unlawfully and so be subject to the strictures of the law. But if the punishment is not proportionate to the crime, then there are two ways we might construe this, in the first place when it is unprofitable and in the second place when it is ineffectual. The punishment will be ineffective if it has not sufficient weight to constitute a deterrent in the future. The punishment will be unprofitable if it more than matches the crime, or causes the agent undue harm in comparison to what he has done. A just condition could therefore be said to constitute something between an excessive apportionment of punishment on the one hand and an inadequate apportionment on the other. In terms of what it means to act unjustly in a moral sense on the other hand, it is difficult to see how this could represent a mean or a midpoint in any true sense of the word. So far as it concerns selfishness, then this may be compared to generosity, but only so far as they are qualitatively comparable, not in terms of anything that represents a mean between the too. We do not say that being generous is being more than selfish and that being selfish is being less than generous. What we say is that being selfish is being less than generous and being generous is being more than 'just'. Another problem is that it is difficult to say if what we are dealing with is something prescriptive or rather descriptive in its kind: Are we saying that this is the way that men *ought* to behave because there is some 'golden mean', or is it just the case that experience teaches us that what is *generally* best is neither of two extremes? (Consider the wisdom of Solomon 1 Kings 3:16-28, when the best course is certainly not a mean between two extremes). Not only that, but rather than taking this conception of justice as affording the ground for a more general theory of virtue, we might perhaps take as our starting point something altogether different in its spirit.

Let us consider some simple situations in which there is a clear or explicit relationship between two things—as when one enters into a contract or negotiates a loan. We can conceive of a person as receiving more than his due under certain circumstances, but we can also conceive of him as receiving less, as when one worker receives a bonus in addition to his regular salary, and another, no compensation for any injuries or hardships he may have undergone. Here there is a certain standard which helps us calculate the difference between an input and an output, between the skill or expertise that is required and the remuneration that this attracts. It may be somewhat different, however, in the case of a promise, since if there is no legal requirement then the agent may deem there is no moral requirement as well. The degree of commitment that a person has may extend no further than his fear of chastisement or the distrust this engenders in either his colleagues or his friends. In this case, what we have may be a similar *motive* but in relation to two entirely different ends—fear of chastisement which will push a person in one direction, and the prospect of gain which will push him in quite another. What makes for a truly moral stance on the other hand is that more interest on one side will be matched by less interest on the other, and that what we mean by good is what *neutralizes* any harm. That is, it will be right to meet one's commitments not because doing wrong may issue in any harm to oneself, rather, because it is in the interest of both parties, not how these interests may be prioritized or assessed.

And this in turn raises the question whether by unselfishness or impartiality do we suppose a principle that precedes all question of interest, or one in which there is some implicit equivalence, as when it is said, to be indifferent towards oneself is necessarily to be partial towards some other, or to be partial towards oneself is necessarily to be indifferent towards some other. Thus, an attempt has been made to found the idea of impartiality on the difference between public and private good in conjunction with the difference between public and private ill. Another claim is that virtue and vice do not consist in the perception of just any pleasure and pain but quite specifically those pleasures and pains that arise when the object has no interest for us, or at least in situations where we are able to divorce ourselves from any question of our own short or long-term gain. And so, although the actions of an enemy may well be harmful to us, that is not to say we cannot appreciate the sense of what it means to be heroic. (Consider the case of Manfred von Richthofen, the infamous "Red Baron"). On the other hand, although the actions of a murderer may not directly affect us, that is not to say there may not be a sense of outrage or alarm at any suffering that has occurred. (Consider the Whitechapel murders in Victorian London).

However, the problem with this, and what it fails to do, is address the broader question of how we might *respond* to our enemies, and perhaps just as readily as we might to our friends. And this is the very point, that a proper response to evil does not revolve around any sympathetic regard at one extreme or a thirst for revenge at the other, otherwise to be cool and imperturbable may appear to be strangely apathetic on a person's part. This idea of a selfless response also has its equivalent in the nature of giving, as can be inferred from this passage in the Bhagavad-Gita;

That donation is known to be of the nature of *sattva* which is bestowed upon one who has not been a benefactor, in the simple conviction that gifts must be given, at the right time, in the right place, to the right recipients. A donation is of the *rajas* type, when it is made defectively, with the purpose of repaying another or with a view to a later reward. (39.17.20 trans. J.A.B. van Buitenen)

Here choosing or selecting out the person whom we deem a worthy recipient also means excluding other persons whom we deem less worthy in this regard. Hence what is bequeathed in one sense is also denied in a certain other. To view the matter any differently one would have to argue that either (1) the willingness to give must be founded on the willingness to gain, or (2) a refusal to accept what is given can only be mirrored in a readiness to return evil for something that is qualitatively the same.

However, even if by *virtue* do we understand a condition or disposition which is prior to all considerations of interest, it remains a moot point whether this is something entirely derived from our reason or also something in keeping with the way we feel. In the case of a promise, we have already suggested that impartiality consists in more interest on one side being matched by less interest on the other, but not when it is the recipient who has 'less' and the agent 'more' (that is, where it is only the agent's *motive* that really counts). What this also suggests is that moral duties must be distinguished from juridical duties, that there is a difference between ends that are in conflict and those that are the same. However, rather than choose to begin with the notion of duty, we may also do so with the notion of a bounteous as distinct from simply adequate reply. There is a certain assumption that what ungratefulness consists in is either a not receiving or a not returning of something good, or at least, that the doing of good should always be followed by a proper and seemly reply. In overall terms therefore, what we have is that giving is reflective of getting, either in terms of what a person is given and what suffices by way of a reply, or what is gotten and what may be shared in some 'fair' but nonetheless precipitant way. There is also the idea of an ingrate as someone who may actively dissuade another from his course of action, simply because he believes such action is an affront to his own self-conceit. In neither of these cases however is there any real attempt to distinguishing giving from getting, be it either that what is given signifies what is gotten, or that what is not given signifies what is not gotten. We might say that it is 'just' should a person feel aggrieved at any harm that is done him, but no less that it is 'just' should he feel grateful if he is the object of another's care and support.

On the other hand, this does not exhaust all the relevant possibilities in the way that a person might respond. Consider the case of a person who is wronged but who turns the other cheek, who is forgiving and not veangeful, who refrains from such punishment as is rightfully his due. Now in the upshot, if the same person were accorded a favour would it not seem reasonable to suppose he would be only too willing to requite it? Hence, in this instance would the person who both inflicts an injury and bestows a favour be forgiven and thanked. Or take the opposite case, a person who has been done a favour but shows no appreciation whatsoever, who demands more than is reasonable or is too hasty in his return. If in the aftermath the same person were to suffer an injury then how one suspects might he respond, would it not be with a show of distemper and a thirst for revenge? In this case it seems that the same person who has been done both a favour and an injury will not be the least bit put out, he will exploit both the opportunity for revenge and the opportunity for further gain. And so it should be clear that no matter what the ideal or the mean, circumstances may sometimes conspire to produce either too much or too little in the end; that either the deed will be outweighed by the consequences or the consequences will be outweighed by the deed.

This underscores the difference between treating justice from a legal standpoint and justice from a moral standpoint. What we mean by a person receiving more than his proper due can only be gleaned from a situation in which there is some implicit equivalence, as when a creditor receives more in repayment than is warranted by the size or the interest on his loan. Where it concerns a favour on the other hand, then we need to distinguish between what may be a fit or more than fit return, and a general unwillingness or incapacity for the enjoining of such an end. What ingratitude connotes therefore cannot be a one-sided but rather a two-sided approach, that is, it is no less a response to the doing of ill than it is to the doing of good. Ingratitude is characterized by the belief that we should always return more good and more ill than that which was given, and consequently, that there is a certain similitude between virtue and vice. Gratitude on the other hand is characterized by the belief that we should always return less good and less ill than what was given, and consequently, that there is a certain dissimilitude between virtue and vice. The difference between gratitude and ingratitude is therefore not based on a willingness or unwillingness to respond per se, but rather on *how* we respond to any action, no matter its kind or degree.

To pursue our enquiries, let us consider whether the requital of good can always be subsumed under the rule of a fitting or seemly reply. A suitable starting point might be to distinguish between an adequate and a more than adequate response, whilst not insisting that the latter conform to any strict equivalence as such. Punishment is based on the implicit right that each be given an equal share of what is for his own welfare. Injustice is a flagrant breach of such a right—the fact that the perpetrator deserves to be punished reflects a basic acknowledgement that there should be no harm given or received to begin with. Such punitive measures are administered by the community as a whole, since it is only from an admission of this whole that any partial or limited right can be derived. When we consider the notion of a kind or benevolent act on the other hand, what seems to be implied is not only that harm should be thwarted but that good should be promoted. Gratitude however should not be construed as a merely fit response, much in the way we have already suggested, since there is neither an original right to which it must conform, nor an original duty from which it might depart. And that is why the distinction between not-harming and helping is perhaps not so obvious as might firstly appear, since just as there is a helping which may sometimes be construed as a harming, so also is there a harming which may sometimes be construed as a helping. To the sick and the dying will we often refuse them things that could hasten their demise, and in the eyes of some this will be harmful, or at least undignified, whilst in the eyes of others this will be seemly, or at least bear witness to the unconditional value of human life. The point is, because there are so many different reasons why such and such an action could be chosen, the sorts of responses they elicit may not always be so proper or germane. The rationale for punishment however, unlike the rationale for mercy-killing, does not rest solely on a counting of costs, what it rests on is the implicit command that each respect that freedom he is owing his fellow man.

And that is why in conjunction with punishment do we have the idea of a 'just' estimation of pain—it is the proper appraisal of an action in order that it be more fittingly annulled or overturned. In the first place we need to address the effectiveness of such a punishment, whether it is justified not only on account of the wrong it combats but also on account of any good it might achieve. Thus, we will need to temper our judgement in the case of an immature child, an intoxicated driver, or a person who is simply mad. In the second place, we need to approach this from the viewpoint of the variability of the punishment in relation to the variability of the crime. If the crime admits of various degrees or is composed of various parts then there must be something in the punishment which corresponds to each and every part. A person who commits a simple murder has acted rather differently than someone who commits ten, just as a person who commits a robbery has acted rather differently than someone who commits a robbery but with aggravation as well. Another question is the equability of the punishment, or at least, the appropriateness of the punishment given the general nature of the crime and the circumstances of the agent. A good example of what was equable would be property confiscation in the case of a drug lord or someone trading on the misery of others. A good example of the opposite would be a pecuniary penalty for widespread corruption on the part of a public official or judge.

However, what we mean by a 'just estimation' in respect to pity or punishment is not necessarily the same as what we mean in the case of an emotion such as enmity or resentment. Spitefulness is something that may either strengthen or diminish with the passage of time, that may yield at one extreme or become quite implacable at the other. And that is not the same as any sanction that is self-adjusting, since in practical terms it is often left to a magistrate as to which of several penalties will apply. On the other hand, even if we do not allow that there may be a similar estimate in the case of what is good, we are not entirely averse to the idea that at least some good should be returned (only here, as in the case of punishment, what is invariably less if looked at from a strictly *moral* point of view). In itself will a good proffered lend weight to the idea that something greater could be shared, whereas to be strictly 'just' in the matter of punishment means to return what is strictly proportionate (in the case of a theft), or less in moral terms, or complete remission if one is fortunate enough to be exonerated and allowed to go free..

A spirit of true responsiveness therefore is very different from what we mean by a proper or seemly reply, or in other words, that gratitude is the proper response to a favour and resentment the proper response to a hurt. The strictures of justice—the fixing of blame, the righting of wrongs, the denial of clemency, are really no better than their opposites, revenge and reprisal, if we are seeking to address the real inconvenience here, that is, the circuit which encloses all bad and worse effects. Justice is based on the assumption that less gratitude can be matched with more resentment or less resentment with more gratitude, that both can be incorporated within some more integrated scheme. Where it concerns injustice on the other hand then its characterization is rather different—there may well be a collective sense in which the more and the less can be compared, but no consideration of these sentiments as what they are in themselves. That is, if looked at from the viewpoint of punishment, then this may simply be more or less than what the situation requires.

Consequently there is an assumed symmetry in the case of both justice and injustice, although in the former case where this pertains to a comparison of the sentiments in question (gratitude and resentment), and in the latter to what is greater or lesser on the whole (i.e. more or less pain) And that is why we would say it is more and not less resentment in the face of less gratitude that constitute a *fitting* reply, but more and not less resentment in the face of more or less gratitude that constitutes a *gainful* reply. It may be possible to distinguish between a situation in which it is the consequent that is superfluous but the antecedent that is not, or the antecedent that is superfluous but the consequent that is not. In the first place, so far as there is any general conception of justice then this must be reflected in both a resistance to evil and an inducement to good, such that, it will always be proper to express gratitude for a favour just as well as resentment for any harm. On the other hand, to consider that the response may be shaded and yet the action remain the same, what this implies is a qualitative relation which does away with the sense of what is 'proper' or 'fitting' as such.

Or consider this from the viewpoint of what it means to either withhold more good or withhold more ill. What we mean by gratitude or a show of goodwill must include not only a response to the doing of good but a response to the doing of harm, otherwise to respond to good would only mean enjoining a certain good, and hence, to be mindful of the consequences as well. The context in which we withhold or refuse good to ourselves is when we are measured and restrained in our desires. The context in which we withhold or refuse harm to ourselves is when we are steadfast and resolute in the face of any threat. But there is a critical difference, since the former is only an implicit concomitant to evil or unfettered desire, whereas the latter has some relevance for our common engagements as well. What we mean by withholding more evil pertains to the recognition of a state that we judge to be permanent; what we mean by withholding more good pertains to a state that we judge to be passing. That is, to be temperate may only be an expression of what is privately useful; to be brave and daring on the other hand may also imply a commitment to what is publicly useful. And that is the sense in which withholding more evil is the corollary of returning less good, and withholding more good the corollary of returning less evil. Looked at from the viewpoint of quantity there *may* be no discernible difference in the end; looked at from the viewpoint of quality there *must* be some discernible difference in the origin.

In the case of justice there is not one but rather two aspects to be discerned, it is a practical mean and a practical rule for the treatment of ill, but on no account a practical mean or a practical rule for the treatment of good. If we consider returning more ill for the ill we are done, then this may well be 'unjust' or disproportionate to the deed, but in the case of returning more good for good, we would not in a similar fashion say this was 'more' than what justice requires. And that is because requiting good with good can only bind the agent to more good—it does not prove there should be parity in each and every response; it only demands there should be parity in each and every *effect*. And so, if we are to be better informed about the meaning of a 'good will', we need to bring out more clearly the difference between extrinsic means or extrinsic commands and those ends on which all our actions *should* ultimately be seen to be based.

If we requite the harm that we are done with less good or the good that we are done with less harm then indeed we will have achieved a certain balance in their effects, assuming some starting point from which any comparison might be made. If we requite the harm that is done us with more harm, or the good that is done us with more good, then again we will have achieved a certain balance in their effects, only in this case where it concerns the strict relation between cause and effect. In the case of the former it is a different *quality* which engages our concern; we are endeavouring to achieve a result by removing or eliminating what is equivalent in its nature. In the case of the latter it is a different *quantity* which engages our concern; we are endeavouring to achieve a result by cancelling or eliminating what is equivalent in its strength. But if through the exercise of our wills do we withhold more good for the ill that is done us, or more ill for the good that is done us, then in this way will we return less of each, less ill for ill, less good for good, and the firmness of our resolve will obviate any need for a comparison in their effects. Requiting less where the disposition for evil is concerned ensures that the cycle of cause and effect will be disturbed if not destroyed—there may be no explicit disincentive to vice, but then neither will there be any prompting or any occasion for revenge. That a person may stand condemned in his own eyes is overridden by the fact that the response need not always be proportionate to the deed, that it may be 'just' to requite less evil and not merely repay it in like kind. Where it concerns the disposition for what is gainful or what is good, then again, by requiting less with less, can we see a disjoining in the effects, the recipient will be a little cooler in his praise, and the agent will be under no illusions as to what has actually been achieved.

Chapter 6

Of Justice: In Relation to a System of Deserts I

If justice be a reasonable and incontestable end as one might readily suppose, then the question that arises is as follows: What are the different and yet equally relevant means that might conduce to such an end? Or is it just the case that what we are dealing with is not really an assemblage of means but only the same means under the guise of what is variable or irregular? To begin with, let us consider whether justice and its opposite can in any sense be matched, that is, if there is both a point of agreement and a point of disaccord. Let us suppose that by justice do we mean a state in which less gratitude for a favour will be met by more resentment for an injury, and injustice a state in which more gratitude for a favour will be met by more resentment for an injury. What this enables us to do is express the relation between the two in purely quantitative terms, without any reference to an end that may be positively or negatively skewed. More resentment for an injury will be matched by either a greater or lesser means, and so, there will be nothing else apart from simple potency as an end.

Another way we might approach the matter is to argue that different means can be encompassed if we have recourse to the idea of a proper desert. That is, a person may be said to deserve good from those to whom he has done good, and evil from those to whom he has done evil, and thus that what we have are two entirely different but not discordant means for essentially the same result, that being a return to some initially 'just' state of affairs. The only problem with this is that in the sense in which a favour is really *more* than what justice requires, it is not only the case that any response may not be adequate to such an end, but that the agent may feel duty-bound to perform it again and again. On the other hand, where it concerns the administration of punishment or a due requital for wrong, then in this case is it by no means out of keeping with a just estimation of pain.

In *An Enquiry Concerning the Principles of Morals* [1] Hume argues that moral praise and blame reside in a certain sentiment, not in reason—that if there is indifference towards any end then there must be indifference towards any means, that reason can only indicate what is likely to produce such and such a result and not why that result should be preferred to any other. He then cites the state of being ungrateful and asks why we should account this blameworthy. The judgement we make cannot reside in any matter of fact or anything supplied by reason, since that only pertains to what is useful, and not necessarily what is moral. This is supported by the observation that there is a different sense if good offices are followed by ill offices than if ill offices are followed by good offices. Our evaluation therefore is not tantamount to that simple relation we call contrariety. The only problem with this is that Hume unwittingly assumes the very thing he is trying to prove, since there is already an implicit connection of which these cases are merely the extremes. That is, we can only discern what is praiseworthy or blameworthy if there is something that straddles this divide—the state of affairs that could be called 'fitting and just'. And that is exactly what is being assumed, that less gratitude for a favour will be matched by more resentment for an injury, or that less resentment for an injury will be matched by more gratitude for a favour. In other words, he does not explicitly deny that there is a relation that is proper and just, only that what is transposable cannot serve the end of what is also agreeable.

So far as it concerns the individual and society, then how we view this relation hinges largely on what we mean by equality and freedom—whether there is an implicit equality in all men concerning both their rights and their needs, or whether there is an implicit equality in all men but together with a certain disparity in their powers. If our immediate starting point is that benefits and injuries can be balanced or annulled in their effects, then there will be no difference between the pleasures and pains felt by one person and the pleasures and pains felt by any other. According to Bentham[2] we might consider this under several headings (a) The pleasures of amity and the pains of enmity (b) The pleasures of good repute and the pains of ignominy (c) The pleasures of benevolence and the pains of malevolence.

To consider the first of these, this concerns the pleasures of being on good terms with oneself and not being a nuisance to one's neighbour. The pains of enmity, by contrast, mean being hateful to others and the object of their ill-will. To consider the second, these are the pleasures that concern a sense of inviting the good will of others, and consequently, having the benefit of their steady and freely-given services. The pains of a bad name are the pains that concern a sense of being discredited and admonished in the world at large. So far as the agent is not accorded any esteem this may issue in either a refusal to perform good offices or a disposition to commit deleterious acts, in accordance with the kind he has already received. The pain of privation and the pain of requital are thus ultimately no different in respect to any outcome.

The important thing to note here is the line that is being drawn between the pain of privation qua the loss of good offices, and the pain that results from the return of ill offices. In the case of good offices returned for ill offices then this is not to be accounted as a part of justice, since the implication is that the rules of justice have effectively been waived. (This opens the door to the meaning of magnanimity). In the same way, benevolence and malevolence can be matched in their effects given that the spectacle of ill-will is just as much a source of pain as its opposite is of pleasure. On the other hand, since the noble or virtuous man can hardly act otherwise than honourably, and the bad or selfish man can hardly act otherwise than basely, the question must still be asked if there is any less reason to account the former's action as 'just' as there is the latter's action as 'unjust'. Hence equality in terms of a person's needs or rights is not the same as equality in terms of a person's aptitudes or skills.

Of course, that is not to say we would necessarily take issue with such a conception of justice—only where it concerns the question of extremes and these are taken to be conjunctive with something that straddles this divide. If a favour is deemed to be something more and an injury something less than what justice requires, then it seems that the 'more' and the 'less' can be compared, so that if a person were to receive more than what was rightfully his due then this could be offset by something less than what was rightfully his due. Thus, if good offices are followed by ill offices then this is really 'less' than what a person is due, whereas if ill offices are followed by good offices then this is really 'more' than what a person is due. And yet that the matter should not be so regarded should be obvious from the fact that to receive a seemly reply in one situation is not necessarily what it means to receive it in any other. An injury may be 'made right' if we consider that the punishment it attracts is self-adjusting, that is, that in order to be deemed 'unjust' the punishment may not only be too light but also too heavy. The connection which we forge between the act and our notion of justice hinges very largely on our sense of what it means to administer either an adequate or an inadequate reply. And yet how, by comparison, might we view nobility or any act that is self-denying? For if a benefit is more than what justice requires then so also should any response that attends it, and yet if we cannot allow any qualification in the way it is given then neither can we in the way it is regarded. Gratitude therefore must be based on the belief we should always return less good and less ill than that which was given, since in this case there can be no question about the commensurability of either an origin or an end.

What however we understand by justice in the sense of what is *commutative* is very different from what we understand by justice in the sense of what is *distributive*. So far as it concerns the former, we might describe this as any kind of exchange that assumes the equality of both parties, be that, an exchange of goods, an exchange of services, or an exchange of greetings. Even if the things exchanged are not the same, the implication is that the value of the one must be matched by the value of the other. So far as it concerns the latter, this is the apportionment of goods having a collective worth to those groups or individuals who merit our attention. Unlike commutative justice however there is no assumption about the equality of the recipients, rather the reverse, that due consideration must be given to their unequal talent or their unequal assets. Justice here is not based on any theoretical mean, as when we attempt to juggle things that are unequal in value, but rather on the equality of ratios, since a person of lower rank is surely less deserving and one of higher rank more deserving of our general esteem. In ancient times this mostly applied to valorous deeds and the distribution of honours; in more recent times it applies to a variety of things such as the opportunity for promotion, athletic strength and skill, theatre and the arts etc. Having said that, it is still a moot point how it should *ideally* be conceived. Should we begin with the question of society's most vulnerable members, or should we begin with its most talented members—those with the greatest needs or those on whom it most heavily relies? In the case of the first what we have could be called the egalitarian model; in the case of the second what we have could be called the conservative model.

And this leads on to a more general discussion about the relation between equality and inequality. Let us consider this in two respects (a) a natural or indissoluble right where this concerns equality, status, or personhood, and (b) a sense of fairness where this concerns equality before the law. The theory of rights has a long and distinguished history, but essentially what we mean is something deducible from man's moral or intellectual nature, a set of basic claims, independent of the characteristics which distinguish one person from another or one group from any other. As specifically moral they reflect the hopes and aspirations of men in their everyday lives, as specifically legal they reflect the fact that institutions may sometimes permit acts that are not always for the greater good. In more recent times these implacable rights have come to be known as *human* rights or a common standard for the assessment of all nations, and they typically include such things as the right to work, the right to an adequate wage, the right to free speech etc. So far as it concerns the expression 'rule of law' then we need to consider how, or in what way, the administration of law can be such that it is both transparent in its operations and even-handed in its aims. What we mean by a legal system is, according to Rawls 'a coercive order of public rules addressed to rational persons for the proper regulation of their conduct and providing the framework for social cooperation'.[3] Thus we need to appreciate what it is that men can reasonably be expected to do and what they can reasonably be expected to abstain from, and that includes not only obedience to the law but its administration as well. We could have no confidence in our legal system if we had no confidence in our judges and our legislators, together with a reasonable expectation they will perform their duties in good faith. In this connection it is also important that the law be clearly known and promulgated, that there be no offence without a law, and that legislation be not backward but rather forward looking so as to direct and not to ensnare the general populace.

Such considerations notwithstanding, to say that all men ought to be treated equally is not to say that all men must or will be treated equally. In reality it is much easier to recognize the differences between men than it is what makes them all alike. What we should really be saying is that in treating men equally we mean that they are deserving of equal treatment unless there are some relevant distinctions in any case that is presently at hand. Now let us consider this quite specifically in respect to equality before the law. One of the problems in determining what it means to be given equal treatment before the law is that there are two ways this might be construed (a) when we say that the law is unfair or unjust, and this involves an appeal to some higher statutory authority, and (b) when it concerns the *manner* in which the law is applied, that there should be no distinctions unless on relevant rather than irrelevant grounds. In the first case, we would not consider it just that a person who stole a loaf of bread should be branded with an iron when there were more reasonable ways the matter could be dealt with. In the second case, we would not consider it just that one person be given a lengthy prison term and another a community work order when it was essentially the same offence that has been committed. Thus, there are a number of issues to be considered here—we might say that the law has been administered fairly or to the letter but that a person has not received his just deserts, or we might say that a person has received his just deserts, but that the law has not been administered 'fairly', that is, that there has not been an equal distribution of what is right and proper.

And this is one of the reasons we would tend to take issue with Hume's overall argument, that whilst in the case of the social virtues, selfishness must give way to liberality, in the case of justice selfishness must give way to expedience. The problem with this is that whether we compare the application of a rule with something binding on all men, or with what may be of benefit to only some, ideally what we mean by justice concerns both the administration of law and the quality or characteristic of any law as an end in itself. That is, we cannot say in any fixed or invariable way that it is specific acts that are harmful but the system which is not, or the system which is harmful but specific acts which are not, rather, that regulation is important so far as it concerns those judgements that are *actually* made, and reform is important so far as it concerns those judgements in *need* of review. No doubt there may be a variety of motives for the way men behave, but the ends, be they good or bad, must always be distinguished from the means, be they generous or just. We do not deny that a benevolent man has acted well in providing relief to the poor, we do not deny that a parent has acted well in providing instruction to a child, but that is not to say a person may not perform an act that is simply just in itself, or that the law can be viewed no otherwise than as a disincentive to ill-gotten gain. On the whole however we would probably tend to think that 'equality before the law' implies that the law be administered fairly, that nothing irrelevant should have a bearing on judicial decision-making, and that the accused should be given reasonable access to those resources that ensure they have a fair trial.

Now let us consider how and in what way the notion of distributive justice may be influenced by a particular moral theory, and whether it is ultimately a question of how benefits should be distributed, or ultimately a question of how duties should be distributed. Moral theories can be broadly classified as either (a) teleological, where it concerns the ends of our acts and the value of those ends, or (b) deontological, where it concerns the ordering of our acts and their regulation as a whole. The first of these, what is good, we tend to connect with pleasure or well-being, while the second of these, what is right, we tend to connect with discipline or self-restraint. So far as it concerns the meaning of an absolute good then for an empiricist this can be expressed in either of two ways, as the acquisition of pleasure on the one hand or exemption from pain on the other. If further you were to argue that the only good that counts is your own, then such a view would be called egoistic, just as, if you were to argue that the only good that counts is that of others, then such a view would be called altruistic. But what if we were to ignore this distinction altogether and consider not what was in the interests of any group or individual, but rather in the interests of all? Then what we would have is universal hedonism. This in turn is the basis for the doctrine known as utilitarianism. A utilitarian is someone who argues that our actions should always be directed towards achieving the greatest *possible* good, that we should be strictly impartial in this regard, and that we should have no more a predilection for our own than we should for the good of any other. This doctrine contains a number of distinct features, some of which could be outlined as follows:

Quality vs quantity. So far as it concerns any individual pleasure or pain then this will depend largely on four factors, (a) its intensity (b) its duration (c) its certainty, and (d) its propinquity. As concerns the issue of their summing then we need to distinguish between the gross good and the net good. If all the consequences are good then we only need to sum this good, but since some consequences may be good and others bad this will involve not only addition but subtraction as well. And then of course, so far as there is a qualitative difference between pleasure and pain, it may sometimes be necessary to choose 'the lesser of two evils' rather than 'the greater of two goods'.

Objective vs. *subjective duty.* Sometimes we make decisions in our lives that will have consequences we could never have anticipated or foreseen. When a person is killed in a way that is particular tragic or horrific, it is not uncommon for friends or loved ones to ask themselves if there was something they could have done to prevent it. And that is because we have a sense that it is our 'objective' duty to protect those who are family members or our closest friends. But then if we cannot foresee all the possible consequences of our action is it really fair to blame ourselves if things do not turn out as we might have wished? Quite clearly, if what we *ought* to do is not always what has the best results then what is it—simply what we hope will have the best results? The difficulty here is that if we remove all reasonable grounds for the way we behave, we are in danger of going to the other extreme and absolving a person simply because he has the conviction he could not have acted otherwise. If we do not believe a person should be blamed because there was a train of events over which he had no control, neither should we say he is blameless if in fact he was exercising some control. The third alternative is that a person should be blamed if he has not made a fair assessment of the likely outcome of his acts, that is, if he has not acted judiciously. And that is what we mean by his 'subjective duty'—not something which is reckless, not something which is lucky, but a measured assessment of what it is that will most likely achieve the best result.

Act vs rule utilitarianism. The concept of a net good or a net gain implies that one can compare not just the happiness or misery of the agent but the happiness or misery of various people, that there is such a thing as interpersonal utility, or a calculus for determining how much of something has been attained. So far as it concerns the question of distribution, it is more important to know how much good has been realized than what is singular or what is plural of its nature. That is, if an act will affect two people and produce a net gain of ten units and the only other option will affect five people for a gain of five units then the former is the action one would choose. In a similar vein, although it may not be good practice to visit harm upon others, this may not always be the case if there are many lives at stake. In the case of a terrorist who has planted a bomb in a busy metropolis then here it may be necessary to weigh the endangerment of such a one against the safety of the multitude. On the other hand, how we treat the question of distribution could be quite different where it concerns relations that are much more cooperative in their kind. Suppose that in order to conserve fuel supplies the government introduces a strict quota system, and demands that all motorists adhere to this on a weekly or a monthly basis. Now a taxi operator might argue that he has more need of his car than does a shop assistant, and so, who could blame him if there was a little cribbing on the side. But since it is a burden and not a benefit that is being considered this also raises the question of fairness, and if it is not in clear contravention of the rule that what is onerous for one should be onerous for all? This then leads on to the idea that what we mean by a permissible act is one which is not prohibited by a rule to which conformity would in fact have as much net utility as any other at hand. Thus, it is not so much the net utility of the act but the net utility of a *rule* that determines how we should act. It should be clear however that what we mean by a rule in this case is not any particular rule but rather a set of rules, or something that constitutes a coherent body of rules. Otherwise we might still be left with situations in which it was unclear which action did in fact produce the best result. What makes one rule different from any other may also be something implicit in the very purport of a rule, as when the rule 'never tell a lie' becomes 'never tell a lie unless it is grossly inexpedient to do so' which then becomes 'never tell a lie otherwise than in circumstances X, Y, Z etc which could be described as what is grossly inexpedient' etc . . .

One of the objections that could be raised to this account is that it fails to distinguish between the kind of duties that are specifically other-regarding and the kind of duties that are specifically self-regarding. Retaining the traditional distinction between 'perfect' and 'imperfect' duties we would tend to think of justice as an 'objective' duty (because its sanctions are external) and benevolence as a 'subjective' duty (because its sanctions are internal). On the other hand, if we begin with the duty of self-preservation then justice may be no less an extension of benevolence than benevolence is an extension of prudence. A more serious objection is that utilitarianism tends to confound the meaning of the individual and the group, or at least that together with the theory of an ideal observer it creates the fiction of a group as any number of 'average' or 'common' persons together with an 'average' or 'common' utility. If every action has an equal and opposite reaction, then for every sentiment there must be an equal and opposite *response*. You might call this the billiard ball theory of moral sentiments. If we suppose an impartial spectator able to judge of the actions of others, then a kind of 'average utility' could be reached by simply cancelling out sympathetically imagined pleasures and sympathetically imagined pains. If a situation is perceived to produce more pleasure than pain it is good, and if it produces more pain than pleasure it is bad. What this fails to appreciate is that this imaginary spectator must himself be a self, and so, if not self-interested then at least self-defined. Thus, what is meant by 'an average utility' rather than eschewing self-interest actually presupposes it, or at least, by confusing sympathy with fellow-feeling, assumes that certain opposites can be matched. The question is, does a person exhibit sympathy because he is not self-interested, or is he sympathetic because he just happens to be a measuring stick for the behaviour of his fellows? We cannot say a person is sympathetic when he commiserates with others in the same way that he is when he shares in their joy, since in the latter case this assumes he is self-interested, whereas in the former, it does not.

And this is a point that has been made by John Rawls in *A Theory of Justice*. Rawls argues that there are two fundamental principles for our understanding of impartiality or fairness, and these are (a) 'Each person is to have an equal right to the most extensive basic liberty compatible with a similar liberty for others', and (b) 'Social or economic inequalities are to be arranged so that it is reasonable to expect that (i) they will be to everyone's advantage, and (ii) attached to positions and offices open to all'.[4] So far as it concerns the first of these, then primary goods are those that any rational man would wish for or desire. We must however distinguish between social and natural goods; the first includes rights and liberties, income and wealth, opportunities and self-respect, the second includes health, vigour, intelligence and imagination. The notion of liberty, however, will always be specific to a given situation or what is specific as a right, for example, the right to vote, the right to free speech, the right to property etc. So far as it concerns the second, then this might be understood as the principle of efficiency, meaning that it is impossible to change a particular configuration if to do so would make some persons (at least one) better off without at the same time making other persons (at least one) worse off. Or to express this more succinctly, an inequality is only allowed if there is reason to believe that the institution with the inequality will work to the advantage of every person engaged in it. So far as it concerns the relation between these principles then the former concerns essentially what is of benefit to the individual, and the latter, what is of benefit to the group. Although a primary good is something that can be secured by the individual and to such and such a degree, where it concerns the question of any economic or social standing this can only be secured by the 'representative man', or that person who embodies the echelon or office that is in question. The notion of a 'representative man' therefore is an attempt to obviate the difficulties that arise when we think of an 'impartial observer' as embodying certain aspirations or ideals.

As we have earlier argued, the relation between freedom and equality could be so regarded that there is either an equality of needs and rights but no inherent inequalities, or an equality of needs and rights in conjunction with certain natural inequalities. Rawls however would probably argue that although certain natural inequalities may be coupled with an equality of rights, this is not the case where it concerns what might be called 'equality of need'. This leads on to an examination of the relation between need and desert. There are many ways we might interpret the meaning of a need, as for instance when we say 'You need to be on your best behaviour' or 'You need to be careful about the facts', and we take it to be equivalent to the meaning of that which is *necessary*. However, we may also think of it as something that constitutes an impediment, say perhaps when one is penniless, the subject of abuse, or in a state of ill heath. A person may be in need of money, a person may be in need of advocacy, or a person may be in need of medical care. More precisely however, a need could be described as something that prevents a person from realizing some state defined by such and such a *norm*. Thus, in terms of our animal nature we have a need for food and water, in terms of our human condition we have a need for clothes and shelter, and in terms of our lifelong ambitions we have a need for tools and degrees. We may also have to distinguish between a public and a private need. In *TTG* Locke invokes the rather idyllic picture of a man in a state of nature who appropriates certain goods through the use of his hands, this then supplying the basis for what is private and exclusive in itself. But what we understand by a condition in which there is a scarcity of goods may be very different from what we understand by a condition in which there is an abundance of goods. So far then as it concerns the latter, we must approach this from a broadly communal point of view, otherwise a division may arise between productive effort as one kind of agency and the visible means of production as something altogether different.

What we understand by desert on the other hand is somewhat more involved, since it concerns not only some end that may be pursued but some rule that might be invoked. In the case of punishment, we have both the principle of common equity and the stipulation it must not be disproportionate to the deed. On the other hand, where it concerns something such as income distribution then there is both the specific issue, what is owing for the same kind of work, and the general issue, what is of benefit to the community as a whole. Thus, we need to know what is fair recompense for the kind of work that is being done, but we also need to know what occupations are more prestigious or have greater utility overall. In one sense a doctor has more value than a plumber, but under certain circumstances, if there is an oversupply of the one and an undersupply of the other, a plumber may have more value than a doctor. Thus, how incomes are distributed does not proceed from any ready-made formula, rather from certain relevant criteria such as length of training, degree of responsibility, hardship and danger entailed in the work. The question then arises, should we begin with equality in terms of what it is all men need or require, or should we begin with equality in terms of what it is all men are owing or due? If the former then we do not believe that it is a person's inborn talents that constitute his 'just deserts', if the latter, then we do not believe there are any natural obstacles that should prevent him from realizing his aims.

[1] *An Enquiry Concerning the Principles of Morals* Appendix 1 Concerning Moral Sentiment

[2] *Principles of Morals and Legislation* Ch 5.

[3] *A Theory of Justice* (Original Edition) Ch IV Equal Liberty p.235

[4] *A Theory of Justice* Ch II The Principles of Justice p.60

[5] *Two Treatises of Government.* Book II Ch.5 Of Property No. 28.

Chapter 7

Of Justice: In Relation to a System of Deserts II

Let us pursue our enquiries by addressing the issue of equity or impartiality as seen through the eyes of (a) Leibniz, (b) Bentham, and (c) Rawls.

Leibniz conceives the universe as having a certain moral dimension, and that if there is a government by men there must also be a government by wisdom, or a government by providence. What we mean by 'the will' in human terms is something that represents a kind of balance, it can act both hastily and foolishly on the one hand or wisely and prudently on the other. Not only that, but since God can foresee evil just as He can good a seemingly small blemish is something that must ultimately turn out for the best. Wisdom on a larger scale can be compared to art on a smaller scale, since what is ultimately "just" may not be so regarded if we view this more restrictedly. If we examine a work of art then what makes it beautiful will only be so if we regard it as a whole, not a mixture of shades and colours as appears in any part. Much in the same way, a composer will often mix dissonances with harmonious chords in order to achieve a particular effect. So far then as there is a problem with suffering or a problem with sin, this is because our vision is constricted and we tend to judge what is distant according to what is closer in time and space.

For Bentham, the supreme end of moral action can only be the pursuit of pleasure and the avoidance of pain. What he means by the Greatest Happiness Principle is that actions are right in proportion as they tend to promote human happiness, and wrong if they tend to prevent human happiness. But if we are going to consider what a pleasure is and how it has value in and of itself, then we need to consider this not only with respect to the agent but also to all those within his domain. That is, in comparing his own happiness and the happiness of others the individual is admonished to be strictly impartial, just as he would be if a purely dispassionate observer. Social arrangements therefore should put the interests of each individual as nearly as possible in harmony with the interests of the whole: and education must establish as close a tie as possible between one's private good and what is beneficial on the whole.

In the case of Rawls, he begins by postulating a state of nature in which the ends of men are not so much opposed as they are obscure, both in a private and broadly communal sense. This original position could thus be described as one of ignorance or mutual disinterestedness, since no-one is conscious of any advantage that might exist by virtue of his wealth, his intelligence, or his strength. It then becomes a question how those engaging in any joint activity might reach a consensus about the rules for determining their share in both its benefits and its burdens. The general idea is that in order to ensure the most extensive form of liberty it may be necessary to forgo one's interest in particular instances, even if the uniqueness of one's condition allows one to do so without being censured or disregarded. The underlying assumption here is also that there cannot be a balancing of gains and losses if this in any way undermines some original set of rights.

Now let us embark on a brief overview. As we have already seen, one of the major objections to utilitarianism is that it tends to confound the meaning of the individual with the meaning of the group, or at least to treat of the 'average' individual rather than those characteristics that are peculiar to any *specific* or particular group. For instance, if a government is forced to choose between two policies, one of which favours a narrower and the other a broader section of the community, then all that counts is the net value or the net result, not fairness or equity in the way any resources are distributed. Hence it is not inconceivable there may be a net benefit in servicing the needs of a smaller number of individuals even if it is clear that this smaller number is already better off from the outset.

In the theory developed by Rawls, part of the problem is trying to establish not only what things are available to be distributed but how or in what way they *might* be distributed. Where happiness is concerned it is easy enough to regard this as a ready-made commodity and something of which individuals may or may not be in equal possession, but in what sense are they equally free, or in what sense are they equally desrving of our esteem? Thus, when Rawls states that 'each person is to have an equal right to the most extensive liberty compatible with a similar liberty for others' then it is not at all clear how this might be estimated or assessed. Or consider the kind of proposal that there must be an equal distribution of 'basic rights and duties'. Duties are a set of rules which prescribe how people *should* behave but that is not to say they are the sorts of things that can be parcelled out in any lucky or purely ad hoc way. A similar doubt could be raised about the right to honour and to self-respect. The reason we are somewhat skeptical about the status of unlimited ends is that it is not expedience which is good or bad but our *relationships* which are good or bad. It is certainly true of a doctor that he warrants more respect than does a quack but a quack is just as much the means to a person's misery as a doctor is the means to a person's health. Respect and esteem therefore are things that stem from a web of relationships, not some intrinsic quality that pertains to all men, even if it could be argued that all men are equally entitled to a peaceful and trouble-free life.

We also need to consider the difference between justice as a set of observances, or what is *enabling* as an end, and justice as a set of precepts or what is *enabling* as a means. Perhaps we can illustrate this difference in the following way. The Ten Commandments are a good example of a set of rules which prescribe a particular morality, not a particular method. Likewise, in the case of Solomon, his decision was not so much politic as it was wise. On the other hand, the purpose or object of a rule may be not to so much to instruct, but rather, to supply the ground from which any activity may proceed. And this case, 'playing the game' does not necessarily mean playing it either rightly or wrongly. For instance, in the game of cricket a player who is caught behind may refuse to leave the crease even if he knows he is out. In this case we would not say the player was acting rightly, or in the spirit of the game, but then neither would we say that he was acting wrongly, or in contravention of the rules. If we attend to the rules just as they are and just as they apply then this is a purely procedural issue, not a question of what is proper in the boarder sense, rather only for those who are participants in the game. It may not be 'good form' to refuse to leave the crease when one is out, but that is not to say that such action is thoroughly unscrupulous, or out of step with any end that is just. (We could also imagine a player leaving the crease when he thought he was out but where the evidence proved otherwise. In this case it may have been the umpire who was at fault))

Where it concerns the idea of justice as the basis for social policy or institutional change then we need to consider this in both its milder and more extreme forms, or at least when it supports the end of what is essentially egoistic and when it supports the end of what is essentially collectivistic. In the first case, what we mean by social justice is inextricably linked to the wants and needs of individuals. Regardless of their different capacities or how they are raised, everyone has the right to a minimal level of subsistence and so also to the reliable delivery of things such as health, welfare, equal opportunity etc. Productive forces thus ought to be regarded not only as what is private but also as what is public, and redistribution may be justified on the grounds that surplus value should be relevant for the community as a whole. Having said that, private enterprise is something that should always be encouraged and never condemned. In a modern state there is no reason why the agent should not own both the means of production and that which he produces, or why goods should not be exchanged or tithed over for their equivalent in value. If the manufacture of goods is largely tailored to the needs of the consumer, then it is true that the latter may benefit in equal proportion to the supplier, but in a more versatile economy where there are not just owner-entrepreneurs but corporate entities as well, a tiered arrangement may arise consisting of shareholders, salaried executives, and foot soldiers on the floor.

On the other hand, where it concerns justice in a more ideal sense, then we are moving away from the idea of production to the idea of distribution, so that such should be 'from each according to his ability to each according to his need' (Marx). For the enemies of capitalism, the problem with free market economies is that they do not ensure a fair exchange between capital and labour, between the owners of equipment and machinery and the workers who mix their labour with their skill. Thus, in order that each individual be given his due what is requisite is that there be a return from the consumption of goods equal to that effort which each supplies. And of course, this may be taken to the extreme by suggesting that capitalism degrades the average worker, that it fosters profits rather than well-being and prevents the individual from realizing his true potential. Production has been divorced from the fulfilment of certain vital and indispensable needs, especially in the way these were supported by religious and social institutions in times gone by.

In terms of strictly procedural justice, the underlying assumption is that any action should be directed towards the advantage of those parties involved, and hence, that what this assumes is a set of rules adhered to by all. Impartiality in this instance means nothing more than what supports the objectives of that game we are in, and that an action is voluntary when it is directed towards the good of the agent in conjunction with the good of his fellows. However, this does not entirely exclude the prospect that those who are not team players may yet have a share, and some avenue to satisfy their needs, since equal opportunity is not the same as equality before the law. (That is, redistribution may be justified if there is a surplus value from such activity). Where it concerns the collectivist ideal, then it is not just a collaborative effort which supplies the ground for what is mutually beneficial but the aspirations of different individuals which supplies the ground for what is indispensable in itself. That is, individuals should be motivated to produce goods and services not for the sake of any differential rewards, rather, to the extent it enables them to remain true to their own aspirations and ideals.

As we have already stated, there is a difference between a need understood as what is needful (a duty) and a need understood as what is needy (an impediment). And so, if there is a particular index according to which different needs may be compared, so also must there be a basic subsistence level which is guaranteed by that agency we call the state. A need, however, in the sense of something acquired and not innate is more in keeping with what we mean by a taste or a desire. So far as it concerns their disposable income then the tastes of men may differ quite markedly; some may choose a hobby such as stamp collecting, some may choose a challenge such as mountain climbing; some may choose a pastime such as bridge. The concept of desert on the other hand is a little more involved, since there must not only be a rule but its relatedness to an end. In the more extreme cases, we would not say that a person who steals a bracelet 'deserves' to be rewarded, rather, that he deserves to be punished, that a labourer who works extra hours 'deserves' to be dismissed, rather, that he deserves to be compensated, that a fireman who rescues a child 'deserves' to be censured, rather that he deserves to be feted. We see this most frequently in the case of retributive justice: we may not agree that a good motorist is someone who should always be rewarded, but for the sake of public safety, we would certainly agree that a bad motorist is someone who should always be punished.

This also raises the question of what we mean by benefits and injuries on the one hand and benefits and burdens on the other. Institutions may well delimit the personal and proprietary rights of individuals (but not their right to self-respect) as well as the power to alter those relations in any manner they may deem fit. In addition, such institutions may provide for agencies which ensure these commitments will be met (e.g. the police, the judiciary, the tax office etc.), and the provision of services to which all are expected to contribute (e.g. gas and electricity supplies). Thus, what we mean by benefits and burdens only implies a change in that *aspect* we discern, whether it supports the kind of good which ensues from voluntary or the kind of good which ensues from involuntary arrangements. What we mean by benefits and injuries on the other hand is much more in keeping with the idea of a desert i.e. what is adequate or inadequate to such and such an end. We may need to qualify this to some degree however, since what we are really dealing with is the perpetration of a wrong, not the confirmation of any right understood in purely legal terms

As we have earlier argued, benefits and injuries are incommensurate in the sense that they cannot be balanced or annulled in their effects. However so far as they may also be said to be congruent, this can only be so if we treat the one as subordinate and not co-equal to the other. Hence, in the case of a benefit what we mean is remuneration to a *worker*, in the case of an injury compensation for any workplace *accident*. What should be clear is that what we mean by compensation in the case of hardship or injury is not what we mean by remuneration in the case of exertion or effort. And that is because in the case of the latter what we are dealing with is prudential desert, whereas in the case of the former what we are dealing with is moral desert, that is, harm unfairly visited upon another. There may well be a case for saying that a person who has a demanding or onerous job is deserving of fair remuneration, but that is only by comparison with what it means to be deprived of some more fundamental right. Quite clearly, market forces and not just social status will determine whether a plumber is paid more than a lawyer, a doctor is paid more than a cleaner, or a miner is paid more than a bureaucrat, since there is no simple index which corresponds to every trade or profession

Let us pursue this by addressing the meaning of a burden in respect to (a) natural inequalities, (b) involuntary arrangements, and (c) voluntary arrangements. Since Rawls argues that every member of society is entitled to the same liberty as every other, then such should not be countered by anything that undermines an equal distribution of deserts. In other words, no one should benefit or suffer through misfortune, and no one should allow his feelings to overrule the feelings of his fellows. Since health, vigour and intelligence are to be accounted as natural goods, and fragility, morbidity and stupidity as natural ills, there should be no less an endeavour to remove the one as there is to foster and uphold the other. But of course, by that we do not mean remove the 'botched and bungled', rather raise them to a level or a status which is in keeping with their need for self-respect. In other words what Rawls is saying is that so far as justice is concerned then (a) any person may be a player in the game and (b) the existence of certain inequalities should serve as the basis for a fairer distribution of those resources that are at hand.

Taking a slightly different tack, what could also be argued is that what we mean by a burden or constraint is not any actual impediment but those involuntary arrangements in which our lives are immersed, that is, those *actual* obligations imposed on us by the state. In these terms the only real players are those who contribute to the game, not those who derive a benefit from the generosity supplied by others. A system of taxation is something which may well support the disadvantaged, but that is not because they are the most deserving, rather, because they are the least unfit. Looked at from this perspective, involuntary arrangements are not the result of certain natural inequalities but the offshoot of certain voluntary commitments, and more specifically, those undertaken by capable and highly motivated men.

Where it concerns the question of voluntary arrangements, then we need to distinguish between the maximization of good through the agency of others, and cooperation as the basis for any system that is just. In the case of the latter, a person may well be prepared to accede to certain constraints provided there is due compliance on the part of those who are partners in any venture. What this also means is that a balance must be struck between sacrifices for the greater good and benefits derived from any efforts that are private. Inputs therefore in terms of effort must be matched by outputs in terms of reward. In the case of the former, this concerns the relation between efficiency on the one hand and sufficiency on the other. In any cooperative venture obtaining enough goods may not be matched by the value of those goods as they are in and of themselves. Hence it may be useful for one partner to specialize in a particular product, and then to trade this for others through a competitive system of bidding.

The question then becomes whether a distribution should be made according to those who contribute to the pie, or whether it should be made according to those who are non-contributory as well. We might take the more extensive view as Rawls does, and suggest that any person can be a player in the game, or we might take the more restrictive view as Nozick does, and suggest that only useful members can be a player in the game, that rewards should only be allocated to those who have actually earned them (prudential desert). We might illustrate this difference by citing the following example. Imagine a situation where there are three possible outcomes (a) you can lose seven dollars (b) you can lose six dollars (c) you can gain twenty dollars. Now consider another set of circumstances, where (a) you can gain four dollars (b) you can gain eight dollars (c) you can gain ten dollars. In this case the least risky course would be the second, since at worst you might gain four dollars and that would be better than losing seven. Roughly, this is what Rawls calls the maximin rule, that is, it is a way of maximizing the minimum possible gain. However, let us consider another scenario. Suppose that the possible outcomes were (a) you can gain seven dollars (b) you can gain six dollars (c) you can lose twenty dollars. And in another set of circumstances (a) you can lose four dollars (b) you can lose eight dollars and (c) you can lose ten dollars. As was the case before, the least risky choice would be the second, since you can only lose ten dollars rather than twenty. This then might be called the minimax rule, that is, the best way of minimizing the greatest potential loss.

The possible response of a utilitarian to this might be that it is only relevant if we assume no distinction between ethical egoism and ethical altruism. For if we take ethical altruism (or at least venture capital) as our starting point then what could be argued is that our aim should be the maximizing of any *possible* and not just certified good, so that if there was a chance of gaining twenty dollars then this would be better than the chance of gaining ten. Since the agent is not the loser whatever the outcome, affording others the opportunity to make gains may also involve taking risks on their behalf. In the case of universal hedonism on the other hand, the rule of distribution might be as follows: for x number of persons, subtract the smallest from the largest quantity and then divide this by the sum of all combined. The smallest fraction will then produce the best result. In this instance we are only considering the manner in which any quantity may in fact be distributed, hence the total good must include all parties, those both directly and indirectly involved. From our own perspective and as a rule specifically *for* distribution, we would probably prefer a solution not connected with either ethical egoism or universal hedonism. That is, rather than subtracting the bad from the good to achieve a net gain, we would probably prefer if the agent wore the bad consequences and all others achieved an outright gain.

Or we might approach this not by speculating on any original or 'pre-civil' condition, but how a problem might arise if the ends are discordant and there is no consensus about the practicality of any means. In his inaugural lecture as Professor of Moral Philosophy R.B. Braithwaite asks whether 'the philosophical moralist can give any advice to people with different aims as to how they may collaborate . . . so as to obtain maximum satisfaction compatible with fair distribution' [1] He then goes on to outline a problem in which two musicians living in adjoining rooms have one hour to practice each day and at precisely the same time, but that they cannot avoid a certain cacophony because of a lack of insulation in their common wall. The most sensible way to resolve this would be by reaching some agreement about the distribution of their time, such that each plays half an hour a day or each plays a full hour on alternate days. But what if the situation were such that each party had its own priorities—how then could you settle the issue and in a manner that was agreeable to both? Say perhaps that their first preference was to play solo or be silent whilst the other played. But additionally, that person A would prefer they both played rather than remain silent, whereas person B would prefer that both remained silent rather than that both played. In these terms, the idea that each might be given equal time does not appear to square with their wishes or desires.

In seeking a solution there will be a considerable difference if we assume (a) that different outcomes can, or (b) that different outcomes cannot be, achieved on different days. In the case of (a) we do not begin with any specific point of non-agreement but only some equivalence between playing all the time and being quiet all the time. What it therefore means is that any departure from this will result in one person being better off at the same time as the other is worse off. In the case of (b) since we cannot solve the issue by a mixing the roles then there will be a clear point of non-agreement, and that is if they are playing all the time. In this case what we mean by the optimal outcome is one which incorporates a certain standard of efficiency; such that neither party will be better off in any other circumstance. (Calculations suggest that this might be somewhere around the 90 percent mark for person A). By contrast, since in (a) there is no basic incompatibility between playing and not playing, the solution consists in a gross distribution of time, that is, how many days one person should be playing and how many days the other should be playing. (Of course, this also requires that the same person be playing on successive days.) From a strictly utilitarian point of view the only aim of such an approach should be the maximization of good, and this in itself does not indicate how any good should be distributed, or how any need should be met. Fundamentally, there may be no more reason to exclude either party than there is to include both parties, but where it concerns any conflict in the rules then it is only the consequences which determine which is right. Thus, in this instance the only real solution is to have person A playing all the time and person B not at all, since any alteration would make A worse off, and to a greater degree than it would make B better off. Such may also be the stance taken by either party if he judges that the other's interest will be out of kilter with his own. The implication is that it may be better to know what constitutes a minimal gain rather than not knowing how the other will respond in that exact circumstance where one does or does not choose to play.

Even allowing for these different permutations, one of the reasons it seems natural to give both parties equal playing time is because of the way this ties in with a system of correlative right and duties. That is, person A has the right to play his trumpet and person B has the duty to respect that right, just as person B has the right to play his violin and person A has the duty to respect that right. On the other hand, this is perhaps not quite what we mean by a system in which the elements are logically or organically bound, since in the case at hand it is really a question of priorities, not so much one of rights. It would be a different matter if the situation were such that person A chooses to play his trumpet but that person B prefers to read a book. In this case, person A would have the duty to desist from such activity if this infringes on B's right to be at peace. Since reading a book does not infringe on a person's right to be musically active, a person's right to be musically active may well infringe on a person's right to be reading a book. Here we have a clearly defined set of rights and duties that are organically bound i.e. a situation where a right precedes a duty. In the problem we have just been dealing with, it is not unreasonable that person B should sacrifice his happiness for the sake of person A, and that is because it is the preference and not the *right* of B which should yield to the preference and not the *right* of A.

If there is a general observation that might be made about utilitarianism it is that it tends to regard rules as being subordinate to the realization of certain ends, and not ends as being implicit in the implementation of certain rules. That is, it does not take rules to be susceptible of any independent measure but rather regards them as self-adjusting or self-delimiting according to our ever-changing needs. That is, either they will point in entirely different directions or they will be more or less useful to the degree they are more or less specific. For instance, a person's willingness to tell the truth may be tested if he is asked to inform on a friend whose long-term prospects could be ruined through such an act. However, to weigh up the options does not mean to compromise on a result, rather, to choose the rule that is most efficacious on the whole. In the same way, the general rule 'always tell the truth' might appear to be less useful than the more restrictive 'always tell the truth unless it causes embarrassment to one's family or one's friends', when we can retain both the general purport of the former and the basic requirements of the latter. There may also be a rule which stipulates that the individual should sacrifice his own good for the sake of others if this will issue in a net gain, but again, only when there is the complementary rule that a person should seek his own gain when this has no impact on his fellows

On the other hand, there is much to be said for an approach which begins with the concept of equal liberty, and then proceeds from a distribution of goods to the basis for a distribution of burdens. That is, if we adopt the view that every member of society is entitled to the same degree of respect, then what this implies is not only the maximization of good but also the minimization of harm, or at least agreement about the way a system of burdens should be distributed just as much as in the case of what is good. By giving equal weight to benefits and burdens what this also means is that we can have the widest application of a rule, or at least, that we can incorporate a variety of rules within a system which is proper and fitting for all. In the aforesaid problem Braithwaite's solution appears to satisfy both these requirements – or at least in a way which is conformable to either end. On the other hand, there is a problem if we treat these as though they were opposing sets of rules, and thereby rejecting the one at the same time as affirming the other. If the utilitarian is committed to the idea that one good may be traded for another then he is also committed to the idea that one burden may be traded for another. In the case of a set of traffic laws for instance, there is a difference if we say that since the burdens *must* be borne equally the benefits *cannot* be shared equally, or, that if the benefits *need not* be shared equally then the burdens *may* be borne unequally. If it is the case that burdens may not be borne equally, then a policeman or a public official who is caught speeding might argue that he is well within his rights, and that others should sacrifice their good simply because this was an adjunct to his own. Thus, a utilitarian is caught on the horns of a dilemma if he is going to argue that burdens should be distributed in the same way as are benefits, and that the consequences as they pertain to the former are of no relevance in comparison to the consequences as they pertain to the latter.

[1] Later published as 'Theory of Games as a Tool for the Moral Philosopher' (Cambridge University Press 1955)

Chapter 8

Of Justice: In Relation to Nature and Artifice

In broaching the relation between nature and artifice there are two conceptions of justice that we need to attend to, and they are (a) an innate quality that might be deduced in some purely *apriori* way and (b) a contrivance or expedient by means of which the unruly passions of men may be checked or constrained. Reason is the starting point for natural law theory, since it posits this as an innate quality that separates man not just from other creatures but the way this is characterized in the early part of the Bible. Human consciousness is taken to be so imbued with the capacity for reflection it can discern with perfect clarity the necessity of living conformable to the law of nature. What we mean by the law of nature is a dictate of reason which indicates that an act has the quality of being either good or bad so far as it does or does not conform to the social nature of man. In the case of the latter it is forbidden and in the case of the former enjoined by the will of God. This also suggests that in their natural condition men are duty-bound to respect one another and be so united that none has reason to harm his neighbour, rather, seek a common set of goals and purposes. If, however, there ever be any reason to punish an offender this power should reside not in the hands of one or some but rather in the hands of all.

We also need to distinguish between right reason and impaired reason. Right reason consists in principles which agree with things upon an exact examination, or anything that may be fairly deduced from such principles. Impaired reason, on the other hand, consists in principles that are either false in themselves or wrongly deduced from principles that are true from the outset. Natural law must also be contrasted with positive law i.e. the law that *in fact* holds good at any given time and place. A law that is voluntary is one that proceeds from the will of the legislator who instigates such a law. But in this case, there are two aspects to be discerned, firstly, observance of a code, and secondly, enforcement of a code. On the other hand, natural law derives from reason, and since reason is common to all men, the law that one obeys is also the law that one prescribes. In saying that we are not suggesting that what is meant by positive law is feckless or unfounded; rather that to be true law it must meet the test of what has been deduced from principles inherently just. If it can be so deduced it is a rule of natural law whether or not it is embodied in any specific law of the state. The law of the state may well reflect the natural law, but if it does not, then it has more the character of what is malleable and hence as something constantly under review.

The claim that justice is not natural, on the other hand, stems from the belief that (a) there is no inherent characteristic by which one action can be distinguished from another in regards to its moral status, and hence what is or is not a duty in itself, and (b) that there is no necessary nexus between the good of the agent and the good of others, in fact quite the reverse, that to be partial to oneself is to be indifferent towards others, and to be partial towards others is to be indifferent towards oneself. There will therefore be a presumption in the weighing of various claims—we are more likely to trust a relative or a friend than we are a stranger when he solicits our support. And since every vice as well as virtue derives from the passions, it is a serious matter if we refuse to countenance other viewpoints simply because they are not in keeping with our own. In order therefore to overcome this deficiency what is requisite is an artifice or expedient for the regulation of desire, something which makes men sensible of those common interests that are binding on them all. (Hume).

There is ample evidence to suggest that what makes for any association of men is in fact not anything singular but rather a multiplicity of things, be that a common language, a common currency, or even a common cuisine. In particular, strict rules will be necessary where it concerns the transfer or exchange of goods in order that a person not be denied the benefit of those things he has acquired through his labour and his skill. The strictures of justice therefore concern largely the question of what is mine and what is thine, and this in turn presupposes a distinction between the rightful obtainment of goods through effort and industry, and their wrongful obtainment through deception and guile. But when there is a question of the suspension of justice, we need to be careful not to confound scant or exiguous means with a state of nature that is bountiful in its ends. There are certain circumstances when the rules of justice will be rendered useless, and they are (a) when there is no legitimate authority for a determination of what is fitting and just, and (b) when there is insufficient means for the maintenance of human life. For example, a person who is set upon by robbers does not have the time to consult with others if it is his life that is at stake, and so he must defend himself, no matter what the final judgement of those who may be in charge. Or consider the case of a person who finds himself on a ship and it is rapidly sinking; here again, he may well have the right to save himself even though there are others with better claims. There are also rare occasions, as during war or a lengthy depression, when men may be so desperate, they will feed on dead carcasses or the remains of those who were formerly their friends. On the other hand, when nature has rendered us such bounty as is more than a match for our needs, then this does not, according to the same logic, render justice useless, rather, it raises the prospect it may simply have been surpassed. That is, in a situation where the resources are so abundant their ownership would never be in question, then neither would there be the issue of their division to begin with..

Quite clearly a sense of justice or a sense of what it means to be fair-minded cannot be discerned when there is partiality towards the self, partiality towards one's family, or partiality towards one's friends, and so it is only by a common initiative or a common agreement that men will assume certain responsibilities in exchange for certain rights. In the context of a set of laws to prevent something such as littering on the sidewalk or parking within certain zones, there is a difference between the recommendation of certain practices and the strict penalties that ensue from any breach that may occur. If individuals were merely *advised* to operate within a certain set of strictures, then self-interest would take control and there would be only mayhem in the streets. Therefore, when it concerns a question of public safety, considerable importance must be attached to any agreement that is binding on all. A similar observation may be made about entrenched poverty, when the distribution of wealth is so unequal that certain sections of the community may be denied basic amenities such as sewerage or adequate drinking water. Here, however, we are not so much concerned with the question of what is generally advantageous as what is not disadvantageous in any single case.

Up to this point we have had little reason to address the issue of a state of nature otherwise than as some primitive condition that implies either equality or inequality in the status or welfare of men. But properly speaking a state of nature is a pre-political state used to explain the derivation of the state, or at least, that particular set of institutions that has come to be known as the state. This is a slightly different debate than that which concerns our conception of justice, since in this instance there is both a point of agreement and a point of divergence. When we say we have a conception of justice as being 'natural' then it is very easy to appreciate how our conception of the state may be 'natural'. And that is because there is an easy transition from our concept of individuality to any arrangement in which the individual may be housed. We do not only have an ideal conception of the individual when he is fully developed, we also have an ideal conception of society when it is fully developed. It is quite a different matter however if we regard justice as an artifice, since in these terms how we conceive of any situation which is *civil* is not necessarily how we conceive of any corpus that is *grown*. A convention in these terms may only be an implicit agreement to raise a system which *tends* to the general good, but not necessarily something that is useful in all its applications. And that is not quite the same as a contract or compact, taking that to mean that in any cooperative venture every member is *strictly* bound by any undertakings he has given.

Apropos this hypothesis, we need to distinguish between what could be called (a) a state of nature (b) a right of nature and (c) a law of nature. By a *state of nature* what we mean is that original condition prior to any civil arrangement or any consensus of aims. The basic condition of men is such that although they may well seek happiness for themselves, in their mutual dealings they are so consumed by ambition and envy it is impossible that there could be any general accord, in fact just the reverse. The true mark of virtue would be to acquire and maintain one's possessions, to remove any intruders, to be vigilant and wary at all times. Such a situation might be described as one that pits all against all, a condition in which there is no equality or peace, where the general practice is to appropriate what one can, and then defend it to the very death. What we mean by a *right of nature* is the power to do and to forebear in the absence of physical constraint, to act with discretion when there is no directive or commandment from above. Such liberty however, is not a licence to do what is simply within one's power; it is not the right to wage war, but rather, to counter any aggression, to use whatever is necessary when it is one's liberty or one's life that is at stake. It is also important that our judgements be based on circumstances that are actual, not what we imagine, and that even if we were forced to abandon our neighbours we can never be forced to abandon ourselves. The right of nature in this sense is not something that raises us above a certain wangling but what makes us more skilful in the way we resolve any threats. Even in a state of nature prudence will direct us towards the making of promises and pacts, but this will be only in the short term and in no way for our common good. What is lacking therefore is some explicit body of rules enforced by an agreed upon executer. Such practices and recommendations as can be crafted into a body of laws are precisely what we mean by the *laws of nature.*

The pith of such an idea can be expressed in the negative injunction *not* to do unto others as you would not wish to be done to yourself. In these terms what a person is being asked to do is accommodate himself to a system of needs and expectations without involving others in his machinations or designs. It may therefore suggest a certain ambiguity with respect to our rights, or least that there is some part that must be maintained just as there is some part that must be let go. We can never be forced to relinquish the right to maintain ourselves, but there may be a case to be answered where it concerns more vehement or fulsome desires. To renounce the right to all things does not therefore mean to renounce the right to all claims, rather to delegate or appoint some authority in whom such claims can be weighed and assessed. The artificial man, or what we call the behemoth, is not a whole whose efficiency is mirrored in each of its parts, rather in only those that are active, in those willing to lay claim to what they believe to be fitting and right..

Where however it concerns a discussion about the relation between equality and inequality, then it is very much an open question how this should proceed, whether, in the context of how men are to be treated (a) there should be no distinctions otherwise than on relevant rather than irrelevant grounds (Aristotle) or in the context of what is meant by a *state of nature,* (b) there is or is not equality prior to any clearly promulgated laws. (Hobbes vs Rousseau) We have already addressed the first of these in an earlier chapter, that is, a sense of fairness and equality before the law; now let us turn to the second. Supporters of Hobbes would argue that by nature man is not an amiable or sociable animal, but rather a creature of habit or a creature of vice, driven by his instincts and subject to desire. If Hobbes had lived in the present age, his 'state of nature' might resemble something such as price fixing, road rage, or militant unions acting in defiance of common conventions.

Supporters of Rousseau would argue that to be in a state of nature is to be at one with nature, and that we can achieve this much better if we are less self-conscious rather than define ourselves through our income or our wealth. As the book of Genesis says, it is the knowledge of good and evil that is the *root* of good and evil, not what proceeds from our instincts or desires. The virtue that comes most naturally to us is the virtue of compassion—generosity in relation to those who are weak and clemency in relation to those who have erred. The aim of reason, on the other hand, is to increase self-esteem as well as resentment for any wrong; it is less likely men will forgive than be bloodthirsty, since every injury will be seen as an affront to their dignity and something that needs to be undone. Hence, it is this that causes men to remain cool and aloof—they are so concerned about the 'welfare of humanity' they do not see the suffering at their very door. Rather than applying the golden rule that we should be considerate to our fellows we are more inclined to be considerate to ourselves—just as long as we do not do harm to our neighbors. The words *weak* and *strong*, *idle* and *robust*, *helpful* and *harmful*, have no application in a situation where men live singly and there is nothing that sets them apart, as we have said earlier about any association of men (e.g. rupees and roubles). And yet, the instant one man becomes of use to any other, the instant one man is forced to bear allegiance to another then there arises the notion of property, there do we have the denuding of land, the razing of forests, the depletion of the oceans and the seas. The upshot of all this is that men will be divided according to their clumsiness or their skill, their shortcomings or their talents; a system of wants will arise through the subjoining of certain ends, and they will become a slave to their accomplishments, the victims of their own designs.

The controversy over whether justice be natural or artificial also raises questions about the meaning of natural law, or the relation between a set of divine sanctions and the kind of sanctions that are implicit in any social or legal code. What we mean by an injunction or a law can be viewed in either of two ways (a) from the viewpoint of a ruler or a law-maker, and (b) from the viewpoint of a subject or recipient. But there is a difference between the right that a person has to command and another to obey when this proceeds from the *will* of the commander, and the right that a person has to command and another to obey when this proceeds from the rectitude or propriety of the order. Although God may be the efficient cause of his creations and able to prolong or shorten life as He sees fit, nothing that exists in its formal nature can ever be changed by an act of the will, for if that were so, we could never distinguish between essence and what was a purely wavering expression of the same. We have already seen this in the case of natural and positive law. Something that is directed by the will of God is only valid so long as it reflects the nature of man; something that is directed by the will of man is only valid so long as it reflects the true nature of society, that is, the *potential* for an alignment of all interests and aims.

So far as it concerns a distinction between what is positively or naturally good and what is positively or naturally evil, then what this hinges on is a distinction between what our intellectual nature obliges us to do unconditionally, and what we are obliged to do accidentally, or at least, according to some act by which things initially indifferent acquire a value in and of themselves. When men embark on an activity such as the exchange of goods, then what was initially a quite casual affair may come for a time to command their complete and undivided attention. The word *natural* however, unlike the work *specific* has certain connotations which are not so helpful where it concerns the qualities and characteristics of different men. And that is because we sometimes confuse a skill acquired through practice with a lack of skill when this stems from what is simply defective to being with. We sometimes use it in the context of what a person is *predisposed* to do and sometimes in the context of what he is *inclined* to do, as when we say that a person is predisposed to an illness because it runs in the family, but not inclined to poetry if this is more than what his talents will allow. It may for instance become evident that a person has a natural talent for music or the theatre, but that is not because it can simply be read in his genes or gleaned from his parentage.

There is also the way we connect what is natural with what is necessary and what is natural with what is accidental. An event such as landslide or an earthquake is not a necessary event, nor does it presuppose a necessary as distinct from accidental cause. If on the other hand we define an equilateral triangle as a three-sided figure with sides that are equal, then it is perfectly 'natural' any figure whose sides are equal should be just so regarded. (Or at least, that there might be a similar description for something having four sides as in the case of a square). Where however it concerns something such a s man, it would be difficult to say from any given definition how we might deduce that all men were equal, be that equal in courage, equal in strength, or equal in intelligence etc…And it is precisely this that has led some to believe that if we do not know what makes all men the same, then there must be some explicit convention before they can be joined in any association or guild..

The sense in which a system may be artificial (or the result of planned initiatives) has sometimes been contrasted with the sense in which an act may be involuntary (or instinctive and not pre-planned), as for instance the urge that a person has to help another no matter what the cost to himself. A spirit of true disinterestedness has thus the same relation to egoism as class-consciousness does to a society founded on strictly egalitarian principles. But if we are going to argue that certain actions are inherently 'natural' and certain others are not, then we need to be clear about the context in which this occurs, whether in connection with a rule that is based on reason or a rule more in keeping with desire. In the Kantian context what we mean by a rule of reason is something couched in the form of a test for universality, as when it is asked 'What would happen if everyone did that?' For instance, what would happen if everyone did not vote in a general election? Does that not mean that democracy would simply become a byword for sloth and indifference to the political process? Or what would happen if it was made compulsory for everyone take up smoking? Does that mean that hospitals would be overcrowded and be forced to close their doors? Thus, if the consequences of everyone doing something is better than their failing to do it then it *ought* to be done, and if the consequences of everyone failing to do something is better than if they did it then it *ought* not to be done.

Of course, in these terms we are taking the view that it is the consequences that matter, not adherence to any given standard or rule. No one can force a person to give up smoking, just as no one can prevent him from taking it up, although it should be obvious which of these two one would prefer. And similarly, no one can force a person to vote in a general election or to prevent him from voting, but again, it is much better to act from a sense of duty than it is from a lack of due care. There is a difference when one says: "What I judge to be right for myself must be right for anyone else provided his station and his circumstances are the same" and "What I judge to be right for myself must be right for anyone else provided his aims and objectives are the same". In the first case, its validity hinges on certain facts that are in no way skewed towards the agent. In the second case, its unfitness hinges on the existence of certain loyalties that may well be unreasonable or misplaced. There is a difference between telling a lie when it is a friend's reputation that is at stake and telling a lie when it is another's life that is at stake, and so, although we might regard the consequences of lying as being generally deleterious, such action could be justified if due restrictions are applied. In other words, it is not the case that lying is self-defeating under all circumstances, rather, that a change in circumstances may require that we reassess our aims.

What we mean by a rule that is based on our instincts can be viewed as either (a) the right to our own safekeeping, or (b) the right to the fulfilment of a more idealistic set of needs. In the case of the latter, this is the instinct that a mother has for the nourishment of a child, that a benefactor has for a stranger or friend, that a patron has for the cultivation of the arts. In the case of the former, this is the instinct for self-preservation or the right to retaliate when all else seems lost, broadened to include sympathy for the suffering of our fellows. Thus, what we mean by a system of justice or benevolence is a series of acts which will hit the right mark. An act in the context of a rule that is given by our reason may be seen as an exception to that rule; an act in the context of a rule that is given by our instincts must be seen as an extension of that rule. So far as we may distinguish between a rule of reason (impartial) and a rule of justice (retributive), then what we mean by the latter is the righting of a wrong and by the former what is fair or even-handed. When we say that a person has a duty to tell the truth or to keep his promises, what we mean is that it is reasonable to do so because the consequences will be generally advantageous, and only rarely will certain considerations compel us to pursue a different course.

In the same way, although occasionally there may be a discrepancy between duty and interest, on no account can we accept that this also reflects a difference between public and private good. When a paedophile is returned the community but in a location that affords him access to those who are vulnerable then it is the public which is the loser; just as, when a breadwinner in unable to repay his gambling debts then it is his family which is the loser. What this proves under certain circumstances is that there may be a conflict between duty and interest, not that sympathy towards others *must* also make us neglectful towards ourselves. It is true that excessive self-regard may at times cause a person to be indifferent towards his fellows, but that is not to say self-love cannot support a system of mutual gain, or that we have just as clear a conception of what it means to be 'publicly hurtful' as we do what it means to be 'publicly helpful'. It is only a matter of degree how far a person may choose to augment the public good or how far he may choose to place himself at risk. There is no set rule for how a person's acts may militate against his ends, or how far his own interests may be prejudicial to his fellows. A person who enters into a contract for the supply of goods may not be acting from the same spirit as someone who makes a donation to a charitable organization, but that is not to say that both may not contribute to a system that is useful, or at least in the case of the former, to a system that is fruitful. We do not chide a person for being philanthropic simply because he has not laboured all his life, nor do we deny a worker the right to strike even if this places a strain on his family or his friends. In fine, a system of public benevolence can only be established if there are at least a number of propitious acts, just as, a system of public justice can only be established if there are at least a number of deleterious acts.

Chapter 9

Of Rights and Duties I

In treating of the relation between rights and duties, then the first thing we need to recognize is how these terms may be viewed in and of themselves, and how they may also be viewed in a more complex set of arrangements. In the main, and in terms of what any society affirms, we might regard the relation between rights and duties as such that it is the former which is contingent upon the latter and not the latter which is contingent upon the former. Or at least, that it is our solemn and foremost duty *not* to infringe upon the rights of others, and from this might we deduce what it is fit and permissible to do. A duty however is not necessarily the same as what is meant by a law, since a law is a separate entity which expresses what it may only be usual or customary to do. What we mean by a law is the translation of a right from the realm of what is subjective into the realm of what is objective—a specific injunction which is sanctioned or supported by the state. The breach of such an injunction is what we call a crime or an act of refusal, but such things as homosexuality and euthanasia, whilst under certain circumstances deemed to be criminal, are not in themselves the breach of any specific duty that we are owing to others.

Looked at from a simply relational point of view rights and duties may be regarded as what is logical not legal, since it is merely a question of how two things are related, not what constitutes the one and as distinct from the other. That James has the right to walk his dog means that John has the duty to respect that right—but there are not two things here, only the one, the act of walking one's dog. We may also construe this as the outward condition that reflects the development of one's inner personality, or what is private rather than communal in its kind. The right for instance that a person has to acquire a house or a car make these his exclusive possessions—it corresponds to the duty that any other has not to deprive him of such procurements. We may also consider the sense in which rights and duties belong to a realm that is suprapersonal, as in the case of international law, or that relation which the community has to those individuals that make it up. It may be a matter of choice whether a person is a smoker, or a drinker, or a drug taker—society nonetheless has some responsibility to ensure that a person does not stray too far from what is in his own true interest. And in the case of smoking or drinking this is by no means a misguided concern, given the additional strain it places on hospitals and public health facilities needed to address it.

Or we might approach this from the viewpoint of public and private good in relation to public and private ill. To begin with, consider how we might form the idea of a private injury or the kind of injury that has harmful and deleterious effects. In the contract theory of government, the foundation for justice might be regarded as the willingness on a person's part to cede certain rights at the same time as retaining certain others. The difference between a stable and a ceded right might thus reflect the difference between our own desert and that which is owing to others. That is, it creates a formal duty not to interfere in any good that is the procurement of others. However, that such a rule will for the most part be adhered to does not mean it may not also be breached, and this we would say is what constitutes a wrong. The important question however is whether by 'injustice' do we mean something outside of or included under this general rule. To the degree that we might regard justice as something more than simple non-interference (that is, as what may also be merited or deserved), it might appear to be not the least 'unjust' for a person to be thoughtless and careless as well. On the other hand, if evil or injury at a private level bears comparison with the public good, then it may also complement it, and so be reflective of what could be called our 'common ill', as is broadly alluded to in this passage by Hobbes:

> And so in commonwealths private men may remit to one another their debts, but not robberies or other violences, whereby they are endamaged, because the detaining of debt is an injury to themselves, but robberies and violence are injuries to the person of the commonwealth.
>
> (*Leviathan*: Of Other Laws of Nature Part 1
> Ch. XV)

The question that needs to be asked however is this: How far *can* the remission of punishment be likened to the remission of a debt? The rationale for punishment is surely to prevent further acts of wrongdoing, because from the viewpoint of the victim evil is something unwillingly borne, and for the most something that cannot be readily undone. The rationale for exacting a debt on the other hand, is something altogether different, since if the creditor chooses to waive the payment this can hardly be said to constitute an injury to himself, any more than it does to the debtor. There are those on the other hand who would argue that so far as there is a 'disinterested' regard of society there must also be a perception of what is both publicly 'useful' and publicly 'harmful'. What this assumes but without any clear evidence, is that a reasonable regard for others must imply a complete disregard for the self, and that so far as one is conscious of the former one is necessarily indifferent towards the latter.

And yet from our own perspective it seems that self-love may equally prompt a person to the doing of good and the doing of ill—it should not be assumed that all good, and specifically that of the social kind, must spring from indifference towards the self. We do not object to philanthropy because the person in question is very wealthy and may remain so; neither do we deny that in certain cases criminal conduct may be tied in with an abusive upbringing. But there is a considerable difference when we say that sympathy is 'disinterested' and malice is 'disinterested'—in the former case we mean not at all engaged with one's own good, in the latter case excessively engaged with another's pain. It should be clear that any indignation a person feels at something done in the public arena is no more extensive than any indignation he may feel at what is done to himself. If someone learns that a stranger has died in a traffic accident this may arouse a certain fellow-feeling, but that would be nowhere near as strong as if it were a relative or friend. And that is why the difference between a 'public' and a 'private' hurt surely concerns the question of how this is *perceived*, not what these two things are in and of themselves. You might well say that damage done to a public school was more extensive than damage done to a student's locker, or that the swindling of a corporation was more extensive than the swindling of a private person, but that does not alter the fact that whatever has a specific effect must also elicit a quite specific response.

On the other hand, where it concerns the relation between public and private good, then we might be more prepared to countenance such a distinction, looked at from the viewpoint of what was either qualitative or quantitative in its kind. Quite specifically, we might argue this on the grounds that it is possible to achieve an alignment of all pleasures and pains, both in terms of addition and in terms of subtraction. This harks back to what we have previously said about the difference between a gross and a net good (Ch.6). Sometimes a difference may be expressed in terms of the 'greater of two goods' and sometimes in terms of the 'lesser of two evils'. This, however, is altogether different from what we mean by a principle of distribution, since we would tend to regard this as conjunctive with ethical altruism and not ethical egoism. Another way to broach the difference between a public and private good is to consider that in the private sphere there is something called a civic duty, and that in the public sphere there is something called a societal duty, or at least the duty society has to ensure a minimal standard of safety and welfare for all of its members.

The way we have handled the relation between rights and duties could also be compared with something much more speculative in its kind, as when it is argued that the two are indistinguishable if looked at from a certain point of view. In these terms, a right and not a law is the objectified expression of a person's will, and therefore what is legal and what is moral are two things effectively as one. From this perspective coercion has both a positive and negative acceptation—there is both its 'fit' application in one set of circumstances and its 'unfit' application in another. The miscreant is not someone who wills the means to the destruction of another but someone who wills the means to the preservation of all—by embracing any punishment that befalls him in the course of events. And yet the reasoning here is somewhat unclear, since it seems to confound the means for wrongdoing with the means for bringing it to an end. In the game of tug of war there are not just two forces but a piece of rope as well—without the latter there would be no gain or loss since there must be something to be neutralized as well. And in exactly the same way, we do not regard punishment and evil as what is qualitatively different yet quantitatively the same, but rather, as what is qualitatively the same, since the former no less than the latter is an impediment to what it means to be both happy and free.

Let us address this a little more closely. The purpose of punishment must surely be (a) to restore the rights of the victim, and (b) to deter others from acts of a similar kind. And that is why in order to be fully effective it should be administered neither too lightly nor too harshly, in the first place, because otherwise it would not suffice to prevent any recurrence, and in the second place, it would be no better than what it was intended to combat. To suggest however that punishment may in some sense constitute a criminal's *right*—or that a person's life is a merely conditional gift of the state, is a somewhat meaningless assertion. It is a little like saying that if you give up smoking after twenty years then your health will be better than if you had never smoked at all. Or you might also consider how this argument could be used to justify suicide or self-harm. In the way we might characterize suicide as the negation of a negation (that is, the removal of pain) then we do so by connecting it with antithetical ends or one end to be garnered and another to be let go. But on no account would we wish to suggest it has any positive value withal—that what we have here is a perfectly fit end, only in conjunction with the snatching of a somewhat inapposite means. The fact that it is within a person's power to terminate his own life does not mean that the *right* remains intact—as if the act destroys a life but not the value of any available means.

The way in which we might regard a person as an end in himself, unconditionally shall we say, rests entirely on the presumption he has a domain of personal freedom that cannot be impinged on. That is, we recognize that a person not only has a duly sanctioned right, but also the capacity to influence his fellows for their betterment or ill. The 'division of interest' implied in the latter however should not be confused with the 'consensus of interest' implied in the former, although neither should they be regarded as entirely discordant in their aims. In the final analysis it is really only individuals who make the laws and individuals who enforce them, individuals who obey the laws and individuals who ignore them. Thus freedom under the law can only mean freedom from the arbitrary rather than legitimate constraint of others,* the question of a motive is not something that limits due compliance but rather adds to it, since to fear punishment, quite naturally, is to be displeased with this as a result. On the other hand, if obedience to the law were invariably accompanied with a degree of severity, then what might be inferred is that men should be just as ready to share their disappointments as they would their hopes and dreams. Rights and duties therefore should not be divided along the lines of what is pleasurable and what is painful—or at least not in such a way as to invert the natural order of things. If there is a duty to give pain to oneself then this must surely correspond to the right to give pain to any other, or to be a willing participant in such an enterprise. And that still leaves open the question whether any *specific* law satisfies the standard of improving public welfare or augmenting public good. Injury to a person involves constraint; depriving a person of his property involves constraint—we do not wish to confound what is a violation with due respect for the law, any more than we do what is freedom *for* the public good with what is freedom *from* a public hurt.

That is why we also need to be vigilant about the difference between 'perfect' and 'imperfect' duties, since in the case of the former we must be clear in what sense it will always be an advantage to us. A 'perfect' duty it has sometimes been argued, concerns the doing or omission of an act that is of such and such a *sort*. It thus seeks to promote or proscribe certain acts, but only when this has universal application no matter what the time or place. The implication here is that where there is a duty so also must there be a right, and that it is the latter which draws its sustenance from the former. What the legislator does in framing such and such a law is to protect the rights of the community by establishing the boundaries within which any individual may act. By contrast, what is meant by an 'imperfect' duty is something for which no correlative right exists—the individual is nonetheless tacitly obliged to achieve the best result. Thus, an act of beneficence does not stipulate *who* it is that should be the recipient or *who* it is that should be preferred—this is left entirely to the discretion of the agent. Or we might turn this on its head by suggesting that there are certain rights or claims not yet recognized because they are seen as morally objectionable, as in the case of homosexuality. Essentially there are certain rights that could be regarded as specific and certain rights that could be regarded as general, the former arising from a sense of what is distinctive and the latter from a sense of what is simply due. There must always be a special right or claim to justify a limitation put on others; otherwise what is good for one must be good for all. An advocate for gay marriage might argue that there is nothing that prevents two persons from entering into a loving union, even if this upsets the sensibilities of those who would prefer to stick with the prevailing mood.

So far as it concerns our general understanding of duty, however, it is very much to the point whether pursuing the welfare of others should or should not be seen to include the welfare of the agent. It has been routinely argued by those of a Kantian persuasion that although we may have an obligation to promote the happiness of others, we do not have such a duty to ourselves, but rather, only the duty to realize our capabilities and our skills. The reasoning behind this is that where private happiness is concerned it can only be an indirect means of securing something good, or at least, of removing pain and adversity, since these may well be temptations to the transgression of our duty. However, if we attend to this with the seriousness that it deserves then it is perhaps not nearly so clear as to which is the means and which is the end. Is misfortune the means to vice or is vice the means to misfortune? It makes a considerable difference if we say that a person *chooses* vice, and misfortune is the consequence, or that a person *experiences* misfortune, and that evil follows in its wake. But no matter how you look at it neither is invariably true. There is no good reason why a vicious person may not also be healthy and wealthy, or why adversity and poverty should not be the occasion for a virtuous display.

Another issue we might wish to address, and one that has already been touched on, is the question of punishment, and from whence derives the need to punish those who have done us any harm. According to Mill it seems that this may have its origin in the instinct for self-preservation in one way, and sympathy in another. We can generalize from our own hurts to those hurts that are felt by society, and from this construct a set of rules built around justice rather than willful or spiteful revenge. Looked at from this viewpoint, what we mean by social engagement is not necessarily incompatible with 'private duty' or any duty we are owing ourselves. We may only be thinking indirectly when we mete out punishment for wrong, but that does not mean there is any conflict between public and private good where it concerns any act that is hostile in itself. On the other hand, in the way we might describe any act as 'disinterested' rather than simply fair or just, then this may not be on account of its agreement with duty but rather with something that surpasses it. We do not insist that a person put at risk his own life for the sake of preserving another's—it may be meritorious but we would not say 'dutiful' in the strict sense of that word. And this is particularly so in times of war—we do not demand that a person lay down his life because he ought to; rather, we make a legitimate distinction between calculated and reckless behaviour, even where this concerns a hazardous or uncertain end. The reason we place such weight on spontaneous acts of courage and valour is because the individual has does *more* than what is asked of him, but that does not include pointless bloodshed or pointless sacrifice when all is well-nigh lost.

Where however it concerns the relation between happiness and freedom then on no account should the latter be made subordinate to the former—it is just the case that we might restrict the latter, but the former we would not. A person is not free to avoid paying taxes or dishonour his pledges, and that is because the gain to one person must necessarily be offset by the loss to some other. Happiness on the other hand affords no such ground for its provisional pursuit, and if there is any right to receive it then there can be only the duty to return it. The conviction that happiness must always be circumscribed has sometimes been expressed in terms of a purely qualitative difference between public and private good, and an unqualified command that the ends of humanity be furthered, no matter what the cost to the agent. In order that the individual be afforded the dignity that he deserves no-one should be made subordinate to the end of any other; rather all partial and purely private ends should be subordinated to those which embrace the collective well-being of all. Such reasoning would appear to underlie the remark by Kant that. . .

> it is not enough that he is not permitted to use either himself or others merely as a means (which would imply that he might be indifferent to them) but it is in itself a duty of every man to make mankind in general his end.
>
> (IX What is a duty of virtue? Preface to
> *The Metaphysical Elements of Ethics*)

The only problem with this is that there is a subtle difference between doing wrong when this implies the appropriation of another's end, and a willingness to be instrumental for the sake of another's gain. Certainly, to act virtuously implies more than just preventing oneself or another from being used in such and such a way, but there is also a valid distinction between allowing oneself to be of use to others and preventing men from realizing their own illicit ends. To restrict another in the exercise of his freedom may well be a subversion of justice, but to maintain one's own end under certain circumstances may also be evidence of what is reasonable and just.

So far as it concerns the concept of a right, as in some sense derived from law but not what it is that shapes it, then what this hinges on is the claim that the law obliges us not only to be even-handed, but upright and seemly as well. What we feel obliged to do, and what, if we disobey it fills us with guilt and remorse, that do we call a *law of nature*, something whose purity is absolute and undiminished. Compliance to the law in the best sense should not be fixed in any external authority, but that involuntary urge, that immutable command, which contains the very kernel of what is fitting and just. In historical terms, this was first expressed by the Greeks as a canon for the equality of all men; that the civil or mutable law prescribed by men should conform to that 'higher' law which is universal and unchanging, burning brightly in the human heart for evermore. Later it came to mean something more pre-political, a golden age which existed prior to any social or legal system. All individuals have the right to equality, self-preservation, and the fruits of their labour, and no government or institution can ever withdraw or take this away from them. A law of nature in this sense would remain true even if every positive command disowned it.

Whether however there really are any such higher order rules from which lower order rules may be derived is very much a matter for debate. What were once called 'natural rights' are now broadly what we mean by human rights, but even here, although we may be able to prescribe a uniform standard of behaviour for all people, this is very far from proving there is a blueprint for how this might be done. Discrimination comes in many forms; it may be racial, it may be religious, it may be economic, and this is precisely the kind of evil that law-making is intended to combat, but that is not to say we can simply deduce 'by the light of reason' what it is all men should routinely aspire to be. Of course, a case could well be made for saying that what seems reasonable for most men is indeed what is reasonable in itself, that if such things as human trafficking are condemned by most nations then they are indeed, intrinsically evil, just as debt relief is intrinsically good. But this is very far from proving that from a 'consensus of interests' we might deduce a body of laws that should be binding on every nation..

Another argument in favour of natural law (proposed by Locke) is that power vested in any country to punish aliens who transgress its laws testifies to the fact that there is a power in all men to punish transgressions that are done to their persons, and thus, that there is an antecedent right in respect to injury no matter what the time or place. However the fact that a person who sets foot on foreign soil is subject to the law of the land does not prove (a) that there is a body of laws and hence a right that is common to all nations, or (b) that there are any sanctions other than those enforceable through such and such a legislative will. That is, the right that a country has to punish foreigners who violate its laws is due to its own sovereignty, not because it does or does not adhere to any universally agreed upon charter or *jus gentium*. If there is a right that is antecedent to any body of laws then there must also be a law that is common to all nations, or a law that is binding on all men. But whether this is or might ever be so is beside the point, since to achieve autonomy is all that is necessary to be effective as an end, and different countries or principalities do not need to give reasons for defining the law as they see fit.

There is a difference also in the way we might conceive of a natural and a legal right as distinct from a natural and a legal duty. From a traditional perspective, there are those who would argue that what we mean by a natural right, no less than a natural duty, must proceed from something called a natural law, but this depends entirely upon the way we regard the matter, i.e. whether by a 'right' do we take this to mean something backward or forward looking in its aim. By the former, what we mean is some quality or characteristic which exists prior to the founding of any association or group. By the latter, what we mean is the expression of an end or ideal towards which all men might strive. It concerns not the fulfilment of particular needs but the furtherance of society as a whole. In other words, a right is that which pertains fundamentally to our social consciousness, and only ratified or endorsed through the state. Thus, it needs to be clear that what we mean by a duty is something external, not internal, and that what we mean by a right is something internal, not external. The balance that exists will always be influenced by the kind of agenda that we set, not in any sense the necessity of the one and the contingency of the other. The institution of slavery for example, was a long-standing practice before it was abolished in many countries, but that was because of a certain change of heart, not because there were any ineluctable forces at work.

Or in respect to our purely physical state consider the strict injunction that we are under to pursue pleasure and avoid pain. If we are duty bound to avoid pain in our own case, then why it might be asked, should this not extend to the realm of all sentient beings? This then creates a problem so long as our own needs are at odds with the needs of other species, even species that are domesticated and what we call our 'pets'. Campaigners for animal rights frequently find themselves acting on the fringes of the law, unsure of how the state will react to any initiatives they may undertake. Yet it is not inconceivable that in the future what was originally a 'moral' right may gain some legitimacy and legal status as well. That is, that animal experimentation may be outlawed on the grounds that the costs exceed the benefits, or there were some other more practical and palatable means for achieving the same result.

Another point that needs to be made is that although we would never accede to the claim that might is right, neither would we accede to the claim that right is might. For although it may be difficult to conceive of a law that is not supported by any sanction, in the case of rights these may altogether prescriptive and not descriptive in their kind. In other words, although we might argue that a person's rights should always be respected, it may not always be clear where autonomy begins and heteronomy ends. A patient with a terminal condition for instance, might well argue that he has the right to know the truth, but a doctor is hardly likely to be disbarred for being less than frank in this regard. There are many occasions in life when we feel we have a natural and indispensable right to certain things, to be told the truth, to have access to loved ones, to choose the circumstances of our death, but we should not expect the law will always be so helpful or forthcoming in this regard. There is a considerable difference when we say that a specific right is grounded in a more general right, and that a specific duty is grounded in a more general duty. It all depends on whether we take the view of what it means to be more restrained or what it means to be more unrestricted. Moral rights, the right to life and limb, the right to free speech, are surely more inclusive than civil rights, the right to vote, the right to marry, which in turn are more inclusive than legal rights, the right to form associations, which in turn are more inclusive than welfare rights, the rights of the disadvantaged etc. The perspective that we take with respect to duties, on the other hand, is not so much the question of what is more or less specific as what is more or less peremptory. Hence, we would not say that a person has a duty to marry or to hold political office, but we would say that he has a duty to respect the life and liberty of his fellow man.

* For a discussion about the rule of law see Locke, TTG Second Treatise Ch. XI

Chapter 10

Of Rights and Duties II

In addressing the relation between rights and duties, we have suggested there is a line of demarcation between what it is permissible to do and what it is obligatory not to do. Hence, although in the one case this implies a certain capacity rather than incapacity, in the other it implies a certain limitation. And this raises the question of what we mean by a *sanction* for certain forms of behaviour.

So far as there can be a binding force together with the different modes of conduct, then there are six that need to be reckoned with (a) Physical sanctions i.e. the dictates of prudence or the obligation one has to oneself (b) Legal sanctions i.e. the dictates of justice or the obligation one has to the law (c) Social sanctions i.e. the dictates of benevolence or the obligations one has to one's neighbor (d) Religious sanctions i.e. the dictates of faith or the obligation one has to one's creator (e) Moral sanctions i.e. the dictates of authority or the obligations one has to one's superiors (f) Natural sanctions i.e. the dictates of conscience or the obligation one has to an elective will. The word *sanction* in its original sense meant a solemn ratification and hence was much the same as what it meant to *sanctify* an action. In its broader acceptation it means any consequence stemming from the abuse or observance of a norm which motivates men to conform to such a norm. Thus, sanctions can be said to be either positive or negative, and looking at it from the perspective of the agent either internal or external. Legal and physical sanctions we might regard as what is *external* in their nature, religious sanctions as both *internal* and *external*, moral sanctions as *external* in their origin and *internal* in their end, and natural sanctions as *internal*. Physical, religious, moral and natural sanctions could be said to be either positive or negative, social sanctions primarily positive and legal sanctions predominantly negative. In the case of this latter we say predominantly negative because this typically involves some infraction of the rules, but that is not to say the state may not encourage a particular practice when it deems it may be useful to. The state may encourage owners of commercial crops to destroy vermin such as rabbits by placing a bounty on their head. Or it may encourage consumers to return disposable items such as bottles and cans so as not to pose a threat to the environment. In such cases however it is a moot point whether these should be deemed sanctions in the strict sense, since a sanction is something *added* to a rule, and that does not mean it is always right to shoot rabbits or that it is always right to return items simply because they have become a nuisance.

In respect to a division of duties we might approach this from the viewpoint of (a) what involves external constraints and by that we mean our legal duties (b) what may or may not involve internal constraints and by that we mean our duties to others, and (c) what involves both internal and external constraints, and by that we mean our moral duties. Legal duties as an end correspond to legal sanctions as a means; moral duties as an end correspond to moral sanctions as a means; social duties as an end correspond to social sanctions as a means. As for the remaining sanctions we would not regard these as altogether binding, or at least not a necessary element of any society or social group. Of course, it can hardly be denied that there are such things as religious observances, but these occur within a framework of something freely chosen, not enforced, or, in countries where there is no clear separation of church and state, what pertains to the legal system as well. As for physical sanctions, what is a duty to oneself may in no way be inconsistent with a simple will for survival, thus, as the duty *not* to abuse, debase, or destroy oneself. (There are also acts that do beyond the call of duty, as in the case of heroism or self-sacrifice). What we mean by a natural sanction is a person's sense has that he has acted either rightly or wrongly (conscience), but so far as it concerns respect for the law this may be no more a relevant factor than sympathy or self-concern. What is important is that a person be duly compliant with the law, and this cannot be discerned through the reason for its doing, rather, through its visible effects. (That is, we do not regard a feeling of shame or complacency as the basis for what is right and wrong). Now let us furnish a more detailed account of these principal duties.

Legal Duties. The correlation of rights and duties means that (a) the right that one person has to the free exercise of his powers corresponds to the duty that all others have not to interfere with such a right, and (b) the right that one person has to certain specific claims corresponds to the duty that some other has to satisfy these claims (e.g. the payment of a debt). So far as it concerns the question of a set of visible sanctions then those at work here are the clearest and most demonstrable of all, since the state never rests and it never ceases to function as a warning to the herd. A sanction such as this however does not rest simply on what is efficacious as a means; rather, it is something promulgated by the legislature and which may be tested through the courts. In this context, the way that a person's behaviour may be shaped by pleasure and pain does not presuppose any ideal or ulterior end, only that the good of some must be subordinate to the good of all, and that purely private or partial aims must be incorporated within those of a more comprehensive kind. (That is, we do not see happiness in ideal terms unless it is accessible to all.)

Duties towards others. The kind of duty for which there exists no correlative right is what we call an indeterminate duty, that is, when the question of its purport or aim is left entirely in the hands of the agent. So far as it concerns the question of a *motive* or a *means* then we have chosen to characterize this as internal rather than external, and that is because a person cannot be compelled to assist his neighbor, even though he may be buoyed by any response that he receives. The feeling or instinct that a person has to help others may not always arise spontaneously, it may also to some degree be the result of what he anticipates in the end. Or at least, it is not so much a love of reputation as a sense of inner peace, knowing that one has acted as one should, in both a caring and considerate way. To that degree it must be distinguished from the pleasures of amity or the pleasures of a good name, since although it is a caring it is not necessarily a sharing, that is, what is mutually advantageous in itself..

Moral duties. So far as there is a duty that is acquired and not simply innate then this we might describe as what is strictly moral in its kind. We have already seen how juridical duties are connected with external constraints, and how benevolent duties are connected with internal constraints, but what do we mean by a duty that is neither of these? What we mean is something external in its origin but internal in its end, that is, the kind of broader influences that shape the way we think and act. The training that a person receives from an early age will stand him in good stead when he enters the world of his equals—and he will imbibe a set of values that are proper for that social circle in which he moves. Moral etiquette might be regarded in much the way that we would table etiquette, since just as you learn to hold a knife and a fork in the proper manner, so do you learn to read and respond to a person's behaviour in a way that is best suited to that end.

In contrast to the way we have handled this question, there are those who would argue that since there is no real difference between a moral and a legal right then neither should there be between a moral and a legal duty, that the right to be told the truth corresponds to the duty not to lie, just as the right to remuneration corresponds to the obligation not to steal. However, the reason we have approached this the way we have, is because although a legal duty incorporates the idea of what is *permissible,* in the case of a moral duty it does not. What we mean by a moral duty or a moral sanction is not what immediately connects a motive with an end, but rather, what, by repeated practice, enables us to internalize a set of rules that were already there from the start. A legal sanction is something that may be administered by a magistrate or an official; a moral sanction is something that can only be administered by a guardian or an elder. It is not therefore the simple acknowledgement of a law that causes us to act lawfully but rather the kind of means that might apply in this situation or in that. A child who commits an act of arson would not be treated like an adult even if the results were just the same—and that is because we regard the child as being susceptible to training whereas in the case of an adult we do not. (In the case of the adult we might say that he is less culpable if he has had a poor upbringing, and hence, if he was not properly instructed to begin with). Or we might consider this from the perspective of what is and is not morally binding and what is and is not legally permissible. It may be legally permissible to smoke and to drink, but it is immoral to break a glass and threaten a person by thrusting it in their face. It may be legally permissible to commit adultery (or at least in most Western countries) but you would not on that count say that what was strictly legal should ever override what was strictly moral and just.

Another reason we might have for regarding moral duties as unconnected with either internal or external constraints is that it enables us to avoid any discrepancy between the two, or at least what we sincerely believe to be our duty and what it is objectively right to do. It is only an assumption that compliance with the law should never run counter to respect for the law, since self-regard is surely just as much a reason for acting lawfully as self-neglect is for anything that runs the other way. So far as there is any discrepancy this is not really between the fulfilment of law and any likely or possible spring, rather, between what the agent perceives to be dutiful and its relation to any actual laws of the state. For instance, it may not be easy to say whether a person who practices polygamy is acting rightly or wrongly even if this stems from a sincerely held set of beliefs (as in the case of a Mormon). Likewise, it may not be easy to say whether a person who avoids military service has acted rightly, even if he is following his conscience or acting out of fidelity to some newly instilled beliefs. And then of course there is the question how, or on what grounds, any present law may be repealed or set aside. The realization that such and such a law may not be just does not proceed from questions about the autonomy or heteronomy of the 'will', rather, from the evidence of a widening gap between those who are privileged and those who are not. Slavery in the southern states of America would never have been abolished if one had to rely solely on the self-determination of plantation owners in Louisiana or Georgia. It matters little if God-fearing whites kept slaves because it was lawful, or because they were teaching them the value of Christianity—what matters is whether the law is *in touch* with the present agenda or is tied to outmoded ideals.

As we have already argued, a person's primary duty to himself is to ensure he maintains a degree of self-respect, but that does not mean he may not advance his own cause or open the door when new opportunities arise. In this case what we mean by a set of rights and duties are not something in conflict, rather, in perfect accord. There is an argument that states that duty is 'objective' when it produces the most fortuitous outcome and 'subjective' when it produces the most foreseeable outcome.(Ch.6) The only problem with this is that it does not address the question of what it means to be a good role model or act against the ostensible interests of those of whom one has charge. After all, a teacher quite rightly believes he should discipline her pupils for their own good, just as a person who is overweight quite rightly believes he should diet in order to maintain a degree of self-respect. Thus, it is not unreasonable that individuals should come to decisions they would not otherwise make for their family or friends, and that is because private gain and public duty are not always in general accord. Neither would we wish to confound the meaning of a moral and a natural sanction. Moral sanctions pertain to moral duties, and they quite clearly are external sanctions that attend the development of a rational and conscious being. A natural sanction on the other hand is merely a feeling or sentiment one has, but that can never raise the action to what is truly good or just. Only through self-love can a person be motivated to behave in a way that is thoroughly consistent, and that objective is only attainable through the guidance and good example of his fellows. When a person is issued with a set of directives then eventually these may become part of his routine, but not if they are inflexible, only if they can help him realize his aims. One has not done well simply because one experiences some 'inner glow', some 'inner light', otherwise any kind of feeling could be good, be that pity, conceit, amity, or envy.

We have defined a legal right as something that concerns either the equality or the special claims of individuals, but let us pursue this in terms of a distinction between public and private law, or those rules on the one hand that serve the interests of the state, and those rules on the other hand that serve the interests of its members. What we mean by public law is a concern about the public interest, and what is directly affirmed through the officials and functionaries of the state. What we mean by private law is a concern about the rights of individuals, but only through the actions and initiatives of the citizens itself. Another way of saying this is that there are certain duties that are directly or *implicitly* obliged, and others that are indirectly or *explicitly* required. Thus, in the case of a self-regarding duty we would say that this was implicitly obliged, that is, an obligation on all the members of society irrespective of their colour, creed, or race. On the other hand, in the case of the Law of Contract then this is something that is explicitly required, that is, it only takes effect when someone voluntarily agrees to some arrangement, which may or may not concern his colour, creed, or race. Private law and its attendant duties can be further divided into those that are general and those that are particular. An instance of a particular duty would be the obligation that a person has to render a service if that service has been advertised and is conditional upon a fee. An instance of a general duty would be the obligation to provide an adequate degree of safety, as in the case of a fairground operator, who is obliged to ensure his facilities are up to date and well-maintained.

It is an altogether different matter however if we wish to assert a distinction between absolute and relative duties, or those that do and those that do not imply any correlative right. It has been argued that a self-regarding duty is also an absolute duty because its breach does not impinge on anyone else, but that is only to confound the way in which a moral injunction may underpin a legal injunction with what is *specifically* a legal requirement as such. To take a simple example. Should a person refrain from homosexuality because he has an absolute obligation not to do so? Whilst it may certainly be regarded as a moral injunction (Leviticus 20:13) that has no bearing on the question of its legal status, since what it means in Sweden may be altogether different from what it means in Ireland. Not only that, but it is important we do not confound the meaning of a legal duty with the duty that a person has say, to be benevolent— that is, where there is some question about the specificity of such and such an end. Legal duties are predominantly negative, that is, they oblige us to desist from specific acts. Benevolent duties, on the other hand, are entirely positive; a person may not be compelled to behave generously, but a benevolent heart can express itself no otherwise than through beneficent acts. The notion of an absolute duty or something for which there is no correlative right would seem to hinge on the idea of an absolute order, or the belief that the state is not only the guardian but the creator of rights as well. This however is a somewhat doubtful conjecture, since there is no reason why the state cannot also exist as a legal person, cannot own property, and hence why its actions should not be scrutinized just as keenly as those of its members. No doubt there is some sense in which it may be said to have rights, just as it does duties, but even the right to levy taxes or raise troops is something that may be challenged through the instrumentality of the courts.

Not only would we not accede to a distinction between absolute and relative duties, we would prefer to begin our discussion with a distinction between absolute and relative *rights*. We have already argued that a legal duty differs from a moral duty by virtue of the fact that it does not attest to what is morally binding, and we might strengthen t The fact that a person is free means he may be disposed to do a wide variety of things; and that could be as simple as walking his dog or as complicated as solving Rubik's cube. This however is not quite what it means to enter into a certain arrangement when it is opportune, as for instance the right to marry, to start a business, or to make a will. So far as there is something binding in all these cases this could only be called the 'sanction of nullity', since there is nothing that compels a person to make a will that is valid, start a business that is successful, or be in a marriage that is lifelong. To have a power therefore and not an inability could be termed an *absolute* right, just as, to act freely without the intervention of others could be termed a *relative* right.

This then leads to a twofold a division into (a) relative duties in relation to absolute rights, and (b) absolute duties in relation to relative rights. So far as it concerns the former (a), then what this underscores is the idea of a right that is perfect or imperfect, equitable, private, positive, and proprietary. So far as it concerns the latter (b), then what this underscores is the idea of a duty that is perfect and neither private, positive, nor strictly proprietary. Let us consider this in a little more detail. We have already addressed the difference between a perfect and an imperfect duty, but what do we mean by the difference between a perfect and an imperfect right? A *right* might be described as the reasonable pursuit of an interest in conjunction with the use of something otherwise than through its acquisition by force (what is perfect). But there are some things in the nature of a *legal* right that may not satisfy this at all (what is not perfect). In the case of a crime such as rape, the victim may not be able to gain redress because the authorities had not been notified within a time that would allow them to act. This is what we call the statute of limitations. Or there may be the case of a contract that is witnessed and signed and yet is inadvertently lacking some important detail, thus rendering it null and void. Finally, there is the question whether the right that is vested in any nation-state is the same as the right that is vested in a majority of nation-states given the existence some originally binding compact or accord. As we will later see (Ch.21) claims against foreign states could be described as imperfect if looked at from the viewpoint of municipal law.

Rights are equable in the sense that legal imperatives may sometimes have to undergo a trial by fire, or be tested by the broader community when certain differences are brought to light. Such rights however can only be claimed by certain sections of society (e.g. the disputants of a will) and fundamentally concern the reward that a person receives in relation to any input or contribution that he makes. Rights are positive in the sense that a positive right corresponds to a positive duty, and the duty that a person has to perform some act favourable to the person in whom that right resides. The wealthier members of society have a duty to help those less able with their responsibilities and their everyday needs. Rights are private where it concerns the intercourse between individuals in their private and not their public capacity, but as we have already seen, the law that applies may be either general or particular; it may concern the duties that are incumbent upon different individuals, or the duties that are incumbent upon different institutions in relation to their supporters or their members. Rights are proprietary in the sense that they concern a person's estate or his earnings but not any status or privileges that this might bring. The lawful acquisition of land, securities, stocks and bonds, form the nucleus of a person's holdings and are altogether incontestable in and of themselves.

On the other side of the coin we have absolute duties in relation to relative rights. Rights are relative in the sense that a relative right corresponds to a positive wrong, or at least, what is harmful or abusive in itself .Thus, a parent who unduly beats a child is guilty of a positive wrong, just as, at the other extreme, a child who is unduly disobedient is in breach of a certain directive, that is, the directive not to misbehave. Rights are public in the sense that a person is not acting for himself but in his public capacity or as an official of the state. The state itself could be described as a public person, so far as the law it enjoins is the means of regulating both its agencies and its members. Rights are personal and not proprietary since they concern his general welfare but not his goods or his chattels. There may also be the question of a person's rank or status, but we need to be clear about its application in a wider sense - not simply the power this might afford him in relation to his fellow men.

A person who enlists in the army has a duty to obey his superiors, but he also has the right to claim a pension when he leaves. A person who marries has a duty to provide for his offspring, but he also has a right to their support in the autumn of his life.

So far as it concerns the meaning of an absolute duty, then not surprisingly, we would tend to connect this with the relativity of any right, but not in the same way we would an absolute right in connection with the relativity or specificity of any duty. A specific duty to pay one's taxes for example, does not correspond to the absolute right to avoid just an end. The point about an absolute duty is that it does not correspond to anything that could be called an absolute right, be that the right of a prosecutor, the right of a jury, or the right of the constabulary. Rather, we would prefer to consider how a range of actions might have implications for the efficient running of the state, and not where its overthrow was the immediate object of our concern. Treason, for instance, is certainly something injurious to the state, but that may be no less so where it concerns financial mismanagement or a Ponzi scheme, and clearly, where there is the undermining of certain basic rights. Likewise, we do not distinguish between crimes and misdemeanours on the assumption that the former is 'public' and the latter is 'private'. It just so happens that the state may sometimes remit the punishment it imposes for certain crimes. It just so happens that the injured party may sometimes pardon his adversaries even when this involves the tarnishing of his character or good repute. But a private person does not have the authority to pardon a serious crime and the state does not have the will or wherewithal to pardon a simple indiscretion. Thus, what we mean by an absolute duty is conditional upon the relativity of certain rights, those on the one hand that may be attributed to the state and those on the other hand that may be attributed to any citizen. When we say that a person has committed a serious offence, we do not mean that he has threatened the very life of the state; what we mean that his actions will have consequences for its efficiency and for however long this may last.

So far as it concerns the meaning of an absolute right, or what is empowering in itself, then we take this to be conjunctive with the kind of duties that are either broader or more specific in their ams. In the case of the former, a contract between two persons may well involve a readjustment of their rights, as for instance the right that a person has to sell his services, the right that an employer has to sack a worker, the right that an adult has to adopt a child. In a narrower sense a contract may be something that requires one person to be inactive in order that this be of benefit to someone else. The creation of a set of rights *in personem* is thus dependent on both the form of the contract and that end it has in view. (An harassment or restraining order might be a good case in point.) For the most part, a written contract is much more binding than an oral one, and that is very much the case where it concerns the right to prosecute or sue. Likewise, a promise made in the heat of the moment is very different from a promise that requires some recompense or reward. If one person agrees to mow his neighbour's lawn but then is lacking the necessary means (a stolen lawnmower) there may no liability if he fails to deliver, but that may not be the case if he performs the service so poorly it causes damage to his neighbours' fence. There may also be certain circumstances where a contract is not enforceable at all, and these include the issuing of threats, misrepresentation of the goods, death or incapacity on the part of the parties concerned etc . . .

Chapter 11

Of Civil Law

As we have already seen, there is a considerable difference in the meaning of a 'law of nature' if this derives from a divine will or contains an implicit command, and something such as a recommendation or a practice that can be crafted into a body of laws. A law of nature in the first instance is an axiom which is invariable for all men no matter what the time or place. And accordingly, it is some inherent characteristic which exists prior to the forging of any agreement or any consensus of wills. Such things therefore as liberty and equality are characteristic of men's nature and are universally valid no matter what a person's religion, his social status, or the colour of his skin. Given a completely different set of assumptions on the other hand, then a right of nature means only the right to protect or defend oneself against undue aggression, the basic assumption being that the relations between men can be no otherwise than inimical. A 'law of nature' thus becomes the means of removing oneself from some pre-political state and transforming what is hostile into something altogether more benign. However even if we allow that men are not by nature reasonable and amiable beings, this does not address the question what we mean by a *civil la*w, that is, how law should be instituted once it is agreed what rights are to be abandoned and what rights are to be retained. And this leads inevitably to the question of the form or the composition of any government.

Let us consider in the first place the classical or Hobbesian argument for a monarchical system of government. Individual or specific contracts may enable men to reach an agreement about the things that concern their particular needs, but where it concerns a collective interest can only be achieved when there is at least some majority which decides what end is to be contracted for. And this ultimately can only be the quietude and security of all, that a person will have no reason to fear others so long as they have no reason to fear him. It is not enough, however, that there is agreement not to harm one's neighbour, or to steal from him, or to slander him, since the motive for these arrangements may be nothing more than personal gain, and this may be as fickle as a summer storm. What is requisite for the maintenance of peace therefore is a system of punishments which ensures sufficient provision will be made against the doing of wrong, and that, given men will always choose a lesser to a greater evil, there is ultimately less reason to do wrong than there is to desist from it. Since everyone who contracts for this end agrees not to harm his neighbour he must also agree to transfer the use of the sword from the private to the public domain, and admit a supreme power in keeping with this general resolve. He who by right punishes entirely as he deems fit can be conceived no otherwise than as absolute, able to compel men to all things just, to raise arms, to unite and mobilize them for their common defence.

Not only that, but since the right to employ force exists by virtue of a single and not diversified act of the will, any judgement about its use must also derive from such a will, since if the power to make and execute a judgement were in various hands, nothing effective could or would ever be done. It would be pointless to reach a decision if you could not act on that decision, or assign power to those not so easily persuaded by your views. Neither can the ruler in any sense be obligated to keep his word, since a party is either he who compels or he who obeys, but it cannot be both, and if sovereignty were embodied in a common will then there would be no power to command nor any duty to obey. Whence it follows that to whatsoever any citizen is bound there can be no other for whom it constitutes a right; all men are bound by the same laws and no one is free to dispense with them just because they are burdensome. Of course there may be such a thing as natural justice which excludes the right of the sovereign, i.e. the right to life and limb, but in the main, men are beholden to the civil laws, that is, those general directives that give to each what is his due and limit him in any extra rights to which he may lay claim. And so, although the sovereign does not have the right to demand that a subject kill its own child, he does have the right to decide if he has been unfaithful, has stolen any property, or is conspiring against the state. In fine, the supreme authority is that which is able to make and repeal laws, to defend itself from attack and insurrection, to settle disputes and appoint ministers for cases not within its immediate scope.

One of the problems with this account of a pre-political state is the assumption that it makes about the meaning of a state of war, since 'war' is indiscriminately applied to any state that is hostile, and the right to defend tantamount to the right to attack. Within a more cautious framework, the meaning of war should not be taken or applied indiscriminately to both the right to defend and the right to attack—it is a unilateral act rather than a contest between roughly equivalent powers. If this were not the case, then nations no less than individuals could justify their actions based on simple expediency, they could argue they were goaded into war, just as a person who steals or bullies might argue he was provoked by a greedy vendor or a simple slip of the tongue. And if our immediate assumption is that a state of nature can be no otherwise than inimical, then this must also involve some territorial aspect, that is, some relevant question about the allotment of goods and resources. This however would not necessarily apply in the case of distinct territories, understood as those in which there were no cultural or linguistic ties. There is surely a considerable difference between the force that is needed to quell an insurrection or a riot, and the force that is needed to invade a foreign land. In the first case, there may well be ground for the exercise of a certain reasonable or limited force, in the second case scant regard for any specific treaties that had already been put into place.

We need therefore to distinguish between the right to make war or the necessity for war when the relations between men can be no otherwise than inimical, and the right to self-defence in conjunction with the desire or the wish to remain at peace. We also need to be clear about the difference between a set of written conventions that guide the conduct of nations and the kind of morality that enjoins them to engage in war for whatever ends they deem fit. When we say that men have formed an association for their common good what this implies is that they have created a mechanism for ruling on their common complaints and their common concerns. But since in the League of Nations (or what has become the United Nations) there is no such common or legitimate power, what this indicates is that there is a natural right to be at peace, and only then, the prospect for any hostile designs. Even if we were to take a different view about a state of nature (as does Locke) it does not follow that the force of any individual is equivalent to the force of any nation.

Another objection to this is that it affords no basis for a distinction between public and private good—that there is reliance on a solitary will even though this may not always be to the benefit of all. Thus, the sword of justice is something that both commands and obeys, and for which the question of its proper use extends no further than those decisions that it actually takes. But again this is somewhat problematic, since the question that it raises is to whom a judge or a magistrate is finally accountable- and hence a difference between the public and the private good. If the supreme commander did not have the power to execute his designs there would only be bedlam and disorder—citizens could simply bribe the judges and judges could ignore any limitations on their power. There is a difference between the notions of *will* and *force* where this concerns the power to do and to forbear on the one hand, and the means to realize one's ends on the other. Hence, the issue that needs to be addressed is whether force is anterior to will or will is anterior to force. Since he who has the power to command has more compass than any of his subjects, what he commands can and must remain the expression of his inviolate will. On the other hand, if there is a legislative will that reflects the will of the majority then there will be no more force needed than for the attainment of just such an end. When we say that the will of the legislator is in keeping with the will of the people this is altogether different from what we mean when we say that the will of the people is in servitude to the will of any ruler. If force then is not the basis for the will then neither is it the basis for any mandate or any right. One of the conditions for a social contract is that there must be some parity between the parties concerned, or at least, that what is assigned must have a positive rather than a negative acceptation. What is given freely therefore can never be the surrender of any undivided self, or at least the self in its capacity as an independent agent. A prince or a ruler who demands the loyalty of his subjects has nothing by way of a written agreement, and security is a double-edged sword if it merely binds one to one's master.

This belief in an inviolate will is thus very different from that approach which involves the forfeiture of such and such a right. Social cohesion, according to Rousseau (1712-1778), derives from the creation of a popular will which is not the command of any actual superior, but rather the formal requirement for what is lawful, and which preserves the equality of all men by ensuring that what is enacted is general in both its essence and its object. Thus, the exchange that men make is not the renunciation of freedom for the sake of peace, but rather the renunciation of what is arbitrary for the sake of what is moral.

This meaning of a general will however should not be confused with the meaning of a strict imperative that derives solely from the intellect, and in no way from the affects. The so-called Categorical Imperative (Kant) is by no means a true injunction, since it is entirely ambiguous with respect to both its origin and its end. Assuming it does not have a divine or other-worldly origin then it is by no means incompatible with some singular yet nonetheless unruly will. Moreover, since it can in no way be aligned to any true or proven interest then neither can it be said to have specificity as its end. The general (or popular) will on the other hand is something that treads a finer path between the universal and particular, and whilst it does not altogether eschew the question of private interest, neither does it endorse any aggregate or assemblage understood as a majority of wills. And further, since the general will is concerned only with the equity and good of all its members, it is necessary that there be a separate body to apply the law when circumstances indicate that all the basic conditions have been met. This body, which concerns the particular and not the universal, is what we call the executive. Taking impartiality in the broad sense what this means is that one should render to each what to each is his due - but taken in a stricter sense what this means is to act without fear or favour, not to allow personal feelings to interfere with one's overall judgement. And so, the role of a magistrate or official is to administer the law as best he sees fit, as well as checking any considerations of a purely personal kind. If by 'government' do we mean the administration of law but not the making of law, what it means to create such a body is to elect or appoint those persons best suited to this task. Thus, although the general will is something that bears directly on the question of a common welfare, the executive on the other hand, is something that recognizes the need for an elite or ruling class where it concerns the letter and not so much the spirit of the law. It should not however be thought to exist in its own right, but rather, a commission which always remains subject to the will of the people, or in certain cases the will of the legislature.

There are two ways we might regard the role of government (a) to mediate between the sovereign and the state, and (b) to exercise an influence in and of itself. So far as there are numerically more citizens then so does each have a proportionately smaller say in the drafting of any laws, just as, when there are numerically fewer citizens then so does each have a greater say in the drafting of any laws. But since the multitude also represents a quantum of force that may be used in any way that it pleases, the government has a role in ensuring that any outbreaks or insurrections will be rapidly put to rest. The government's measures to offset the force of the people may also be checked by the sovereign, thus ensuring stability at both ends of the spectrum. In absolute terms however, if there is a change in the size of the populace then there must also be a change in the size of the government, just as in the constant proportion A: B as B: C, if A and C are the extremes then the product of A and C must equal the product of B and B, so that, given the indivisible sovereign(A), then the number of citizens(C) must be the square of the number of intermediaries (i.e. the number of officials or bureaucrats.)

To understand the reasoning behind this, we need to attend to the difference between force when it is concentrated in the hands of a single individual and force when it is concentrated in a body of wills, and that is precisely what we mean by the sovereign will. Although it is preferable that the sovereign be more effective than the government, the natural tendency may not always be so consonant with this outcome. Let us consider this in terms of the relation between the sovereign and what could be called the corporate will. If we admit the sovereign will within the corporate will then the government will be at its strongest, since then it will be government by a single person. On the other hand, if we admit the corporate will within the sovereign will, then the government will be at its weakest, since in this case the power of the people must usurp the power of the bureaucracy, and hence order will swiftly disappear. Thus, striking the right balance means that if there is a greater populace there will be a proportionately smaller bureaucracy, and if there is a smaller populace there will be a proportionately larger bureaucracy.

So far as it concerns this notion of a *general will,* then there are two objections that could be raised to it, the one formal and the other material (to use a Scholastic expression). In the first place let us consider how the idea of a general will might be arrived at by distinguishing it from both a particular will and any consensus of wills. In the relation between any two persons there are three possibilities (a) they will have all their interests in common (b) they will have some interests in common and (c) they will have no interests in common. So far as it concerns (a) and (c) then it is highly unlikely either will ever occur, but in terms of

(b) we also need to distinguish between a majority vote and a range of diversified interests. When the community votes on a particular issue it does so in the expectation that the majority will always override the minority. On the other hand, if we take just those interests that are peculiar to each, then a sum of interests on the one side will be cancelled by a sum of interests on the other. For instance, if John has interests a, b, c, d, and Simon has interests d, e, f, g, then a, b, c, will annul e, f, g, and we will be left with d as what is common to them both. Thus, a common interest is not only what joins two individuals, but also, what separates them from any third. What we mean by the 'common interest' therefore is neither (a) a private interest which ties the individual to purely private concerns, nor (b) a collective interest in the sense of any majority vote. The only problem with this is that in the way we have formulated our ideas about the individual*, the interests of two people *must* incorporate the interests of some third (*principio individuationis*). No doubt there is a difference between an interest which is 'common' and an interest which is not—between exclusive and common interests in the strict sense—but this nonetheless only remains true from a numerical viewpoint; it does not suppose any matrix or any conjugate set of forces. On the other hand, if we take the view that where there is a coincidence in number there is not necessarily a coincidence in kind, then the dynamic that underlies the agreement of any interests must differ from the dynamic that underlies their opposition. Interests that are opposed are not necessarily interests that are annulled; rather do they suppose a logic that is peculiarly their own.

There is also the question of what we mean by a 'common good' and the relation that it bears to the state. As we have elsewhere argued (Of Rights and Duties I) although there may be some basis for comparing public and private good there can be no basis for comparing public and private ill, since although we may discern some conflict in the case of an allotment of good this cannot be so where it concerns any allotment of ill. That, however, is not to say that because we can conceive of a 'common good' that excludes what is good for the agent then it must also be real, rather that individuals in union make for what is collectively their good, not any 'collective good' which encapsulates what each of them desires. It is only when we are considering any method for the distribution of goods, or the distribution of deserts, that we may exclude the agent from any calculus. There are thus different ways in which we might conceive of the relation between public and private good. We might say that if a person is compelled to obey the law for the reason he might otherwise be penalized, then this is justified because it serves the public good. Or we might say that what counts is not the good of any individual but only the good of any association, adjusted nonetheless to meet the end of what is beneficial on the whole. We might also say that private good at one level corresponds to public good at another, or at least that the duties we impose on ourselves correspond to the rights we are granted by our fellows.

How we see the relation between an allotment of good and an allotment of evil may also have implications for the way we regard the relation between the criminal and civil code. The distinction between civil and criminal law has often been linked to the distinction between a public and private wrong—the latter is an infringement against individuals qua individuals, while the former is an infringement against the state, or individuals in their capacity as members of the state. The problem with this is that what we are dealing with is not really any discernible object or end, rather only the kind of remedies that may be applied once certain actions have been brought clearly into the light. Thus, the same act in its criminal character may have both a public and private acceptation; because a person is punished by the state does not mean he cannot be sued by the victim, nor does it mean the state cannot remit that punishment once it has been imposed. But then neither would we accept a definition of civil law that equates it with the enforcing of rights and a definition of criminal law that equates it with the righting of wrongs. Given the sense in which rights are the obverse of duties then quite clearly this cannot make for any real distinction, since a 'right' in the strict sense is not something enforceable but rather only *permissible*. On the other hand, we would certainly agree (not to be too pedantic) that civil law is concerned with the enforcement of *claims*, given that what corresponds to a claim is a non-claim, and that this is exactly what we are dealing with when one person has no direct involvement with another. To be engaged or liable is however something that spans a very broad divide—there is the sense in which a person may be immune from liability (e.g. the status of a foreign diplomat), there is the sense in which a person may be under a certain legal liability (e.g. to obey the conditions of a restraining order) and there is the sense in which liability may also imply a certain criminality (e.g. when a person breaches the moral code and is penalized by his peers). Or in common parlance what we mean by liability is a simple predisposition to behave in such and such a way.

In saying however that there is no such thing as an enforceable right is perhaps not altogether to the point, since there is a sense no doubt in which a right *may* be coerced if we connect it not with duties but with a certain wherewithal or skill. A single mother has the right to claim for alimony if we connect this with the capacity or benefit that her husband derives once he has become a parent. A patient has the right to sue for negligence if we connect this with the capacity or benefit that an intern derives once he has become a doctor. A relative has the right to contest the contents of a will if we connect this with the capacity or benefit that a person derives once he has become a testator. A politician has the right to sue for libel if we connect this with the capacity or benefit that a person derives once he has become a newspaper editor. In all these instances we might broadly describe this as the enforcement of a right or the enforcement of a claim. But perhaps the best way to bring out the difference between a right and a claim is in terms of the difference between a strict and a purely remedial form of liability. Consider the case of a person who is seeking to sue a tobacco company for the damage caused by a lifetime of smoking. This is a case where compensation is something a person could be said to have more a claim than a right to. And that is because even if the smoker were to win his case that would not prevent tobacco companies from continuing to advertise their product and profiting from the trade. The kind of liability involved here therefore is clearly remedial and not so much penal. On the other hand, in the case of something such as welfare fraud, then there are two ways a person may be punished, firstly, he may be required to make restitution, and secondly, he may be sentenced to a lengthy prison term. In this case therefore we have both the protection of a right (i.e. the right of the taxpayer) and the enforcement of a claim (i.e. the claim of the government).

* "The Limits of Knowledge"

Chapter 12

Moral Imperatives vs Legal Restraints

One of the more positive features of the contract theory of government is that it lifts the individual out of a state of servitude and turns him into the master of his own ineluctable fate. Obedience or compliance is something that no longer resides in some iron-cast law or the divinity of kings, but something which may be achieved through bartering, and the ceding of a certain license in exchange for certain basic rights. However, in the way this theory has been formulated we need to distinguish between (a) retaining a certain right in the context of *transferring* a certain power, and (b) acquiring a certain right in the context of *surrendering* a certain power. One of the main objections to the notion of a social contract is that it does not conform to the general requirement that there be some parity where the respective parties are concerned. A right of nature, which at the most rudimentary level must also involve the right to act freely, does not appear to be commensurate with a civil right, which only permits one to act within the bounds of what is deemed reasonable and just.

A contract is something that may broadly be regarded from two viewpoints: either it expresses what is positive in relation to one and the same act, or there is the surrender of a partial good for the sake of some more comprehensive gain. A gift for instance, is something that implies complete affirmation from one viewpoint and complete negation from another. It is only the value of the object, not the relation between the agents, which indicates that what is given is also of the nature of what is gotten. And this is altogether different from a situation where there is some precondition, as for instance, that something be given for such and such a time, upon maturity, or in exchange for what is equivalent in its value. However, although a contract is something that implies a certain 'give and take', what we mean by the duty to desist from wrong is not a harnessing of ends but only the recognition of such and such a *rule*. In regard to non-interference, there can only be the ceding and not the staking of any claim—it is the idea of what is permissible against the backdrop of what is proscribed, and within those bounds of what is deemed reasonable and just.

Under certain circumstances however, the ceding of a right might also suggest there is something to be retained, and hence a discrepancy between what is and what is not to be let go. That is, it would be difficult to say why a person would return a gift if it had been freely bestowed, or why the pact between two parties should not be of benefit to them both. On the other hand, any rule that proceeds from a struggle over just the one thing, or a mutual affection for one and the same person, is surely very different from that which is based on the need to restrain or control our desires. The state or commonwealth may well be able to vouchsafe certain freedoms in exchange for certain checks, but this unshakeable right extends no further than what it may *prevent* a person from doing, and so, does not encompass purely private dealings or the trafficking and trading of goods for their mutual use.

We might also express the difference between a 'right of nature' and a 'right by decree' in terms of the difference between some initially changeful state of affairs and the creation of a fixed or determinate power. Whatever we imagine or conceive to be an equal right to all things, it is surely an open question what the relation might be between any two parties and at any given time, or to express this a little more succinctly, who would be the predator and who would be the prey. Suppose, say, you had a number of billiard balls placed in a row, then if you strike them from one end, what results will be one kind of reaction, and if you strike them from the other end, what results will be another kind of reaction. Thus, it would be completely indeterminate which was passive and which was active, and hence, on what grounds any individual might choose to abandon one right in order to create a certain other. In many instances, when it was perfectly clear which was the stronger, then it is obvious who would prevail, but that would not be the case if both were the same in their stature or their strength.

Thus, the way we might approach this question could well be through a series of progressive changes rather than in terms of any singular or sudden 'leap of faith'. The nub of this would be as follows. In a state of nature disputes may arise in connection with any number of things, if for instance, there was a stronger or more incessant craving for a particular delicacy, the gathering and collecting of things for a specific use, the uncovering of rich forests and fertile tracts of land. It behoves men therefore to reach some compromise about these various claims, or more precisely, which should be retained and which should be let go. In the making of a compact, each individual would agree to the limits of his freedom and the propriety of his claims, thus the rule of what is good for all overriding the rule of what is good for some. Initially these arrangements would be valid so far as they stipulated what a person was *not* entitled to do, that he was not entitled to appropriate any private tenure or holdings. There would also be pledging of private property as surety against the violation of any other's. However, in order that there be a complete vouchsafing of all such rights, what would further be requisite is a compact binding each to the *protection* of his neighbor, and to a degree of vigilance on his neighbour's behalf. At this point each promises not only to refrain from doing harm but also to be an instrument for the doing of what is good (Fichte).

The further question that this then raises is how far the recognition of a moral duty can be applied in a way that is *binding* and not just what is *opportune* as such? In the kind of compact where there is nothing more than the injunction to refrain from doing wrong, and the conditions for this can be stated quite explicitly, then at least we have something that can be tested by the law. However, in the case of a simple promise it may not be so clear how far we can guarantee the good this is intended to supply. Are we not in danger of confusing the agreement to keep an agreement with the process that is initiated through such an oath? In the event that both parties were attacked and at the same time, then neither could come to the aid of the other, and so, one would still need to be convinced there was due fidelity at all. In other words, if there is always something that frustrates the chance to realize our aims, then what is to say there were any aims at all?

In order to address this rather awkward solecism, we need to consider not only how society may be regarded as a cluster of interests but as a totality as well, that is, not just a consortium but what in some sense constitutes an *élan vital*. Whilst it is true that no one can be sure if he will ever be the target of aggression, the realization that there could be a threat also implies this might be a threat against all. The contribution that each make is thus based on the assumption this could also be for their own protection, and that if there is a certain indeterminateness about the means there can be no indeterminateness about the end. The fact that all members of society may be subject to attack means that any member of society may be subject to attack. It may be pertinent to compare this to the order exhibited in a plant or a tree. The soil or materials that provide the growth for a tree are subject to separation and recombination, depending on each part's function in relation to the whole. The bark, for instance, has the function of protecting the cells which form the trunk, the laburnum carries nutriment from the roots to the leaves, and the leaves provide the phloem which carries food to every extreme. Or we might adopt the view that it is not the parts that are subordinate to the whole, but the whole that is subordinate to the parts, that is, that the parts are parasitic upon the whole. If you graft a scion from one tree onto the trunk of another then it will retain its own characteristics rather than adopt those of the stock. What we mean therefore by the 'whole' may only be a number of independent parts surviving on the nutriment they receive in a purely adventitious and not systematic way.

This also raises the question whether what we mean by 'society' is simply a set of rules which allows individuals to pursue their own self-initiated goals (as in the case of Hobbes), or whether it is the welfare of the parts that must be subordinate to the welfare of the whole. For centuries writers have speculated on the meaning of the state, and most especially, whether it concerns something natural or artificial in its origin. In the *Politics*, Aristotle argues that the social whole must be taken as analogous to the physical whole, or that what a person is in terms of the function of the person is what a state is in terms of the function of the state. According to Aristotle, if the parts are not lost along with the destruction of the whole then it is an *artificial* whole we are dealing with, whereas, if the whole is not lost along with the destruction of a part then it is a *natural* whole we are dealing with. And quite clearly, although the state may survive the loss of some of its parts, the parts can never survive in the absence the state.

In more recent times this has been given a boost by the proponents of natural selection (e.g. Spencer), since they would argue that if the human species has evolved gradually to where it is today, then it is logical to suppose that any changes in a social sense could not predate any changes in a physical sense. We are thus urged to consider more closely the resemblance between society and single organisms. The first thing to note is that both organisms and social wholes exhibit the characteristic we call growth, that is, there is a significant increase in their size, and that just as a germ or a seed grows into a tree, so do communes grow into cities, and tribes into mass migrations. The next point to be made is that in both cases there is an increase in structure and definition as their parts multiply and differentiate. This is particularly evident in the case of arms and legs, of aids to respiration (the nose and mouth), and in a separate alimentary system. In human societies an obvious parallel to this is what we call the division of labour, arrangements that support particular needs such as the supply of money, of food and of clothes. And of course, it goes without saying that so far as there is a greater differentiation of functions this will make the parts more subservient to the whole, or at least the life of any part more dependent upon its coexistence with all the rest.

Now let us consider some of the theories that would appear to be in keeping with this conception of civil society. As we saw earlier, one of the problems with the notion of a right of nature is that it does not make clear in what sense one thing is to be surrendered and something else is to be retained. One possible solution is to suggest that the act of association does not involve a reckoning of rights abandoned and rights retained but a double commitment between the public and the private 'self', between the sovereign in its active and the sovereign in its passive capacity (Rousseau). For others of a more Kantian persuasion there is no such thing as a natural right but only that which devolves from a moral personality or that which is perfectible in and through the course of time. Membership of any community is also simultaneously membership of all communities looked at from the viewpoint of freedom and not repression, of what is empowering and not disabling, of what binds men universally. The right to be free is more important than the right to be fettered, the right to be a family member is more important than the right to be a derelict, and the right to be accorded citizenship is more important than the right to be expatriated. But although it does not follow that the state creates a particular right, neither can there be any right against it, since the state is just that complex to which men are bound, just this implacable force which nurtures their ambitions and helps them chase their dreams.

Or again, we might view this in terms of the relation between whole and part such that (a) it is the part that is subordinate to the whole or (b) it is the whole that is subordinate to the part. Whether we regard the whole as comprising the sum of its parts or quite specifically what is greater and what is lesser, any addition of specific interests cannot account for what is binding or common in istelf. On the other hand, to understand what we mean by a 'sovereign act' is it necessary not only that any law be willed by all but also that it be equally *applied* to all. There is no distinction with respect to the spirit and the letter of the law, since what is good for one must be good for all and what is obeyed by one must be obeyed by all.

What we mean by 'free will' may therefore be understood in two ways, (a) when freedom is conjunctive with force, and (b) when freedom is opposed to force. The general will can only be effective if men are in some sense made to obey the law, if they are in some sense forced to be free, if the laws are in some sense a testament to the pertinacity of their wills. On the other hand, the freedom that a person exercises in riding a bike, or taking a walk in the park, is quite clearly one that is opposed to force, since although he may be open to persuasion, he cannot be compelled to behave in just such a way. This, likewise, may be said for the punishment that ensues upon a crime—there is a point beyond which the duties of the subject are not the same as the duties of any self-respecting being. If a person is physically bound or imprisoned, then this does not mean it is something for which he has formally contracted, or that he should be only too willing to face the firing squad if there was any chance he could escape. To submit to the law is not also to be enslaved by the law—no rule or edict can oblige a person to abandon his own safety or ignore his most basic of needs. There are two ways therefore that the individual may undertake a contract; he may contract with himself for the sake of his freedom, or he may contract with the state for the sake of being obliged. In the case of the former, the state is the protector of rights that are inalienable, or those bequeathed by virtue of a person's status or rank. In the case of the latter, the state is not merely the protector but also the creator of rights, since if the relation between such parts suggests there is 'enlightened' self-interest in one respect, there must also be 'enlightened' public welfare in another.

Or we might consider this in the context of the kind of theory that posits not a state of nature but certain historical phases (Hegel). To view the individual in his initial phase, we need to consider him within the framework of the family, since this is the most obvious form in which different lives are connected and ultimately also, from which they are disengaged. The universality of individual being does not consist in the actions of a conscious mind but in the process of nature, which takes the individual from an accidental origin (birth) to its ineluctable end (death). Consanguinity therefore is important because it disrupts this process and ensures that our loved ones will be both remembered and revered, that there will be a single and unbroken line from the home of our ancestors to the burial grounds of the dead. The movement to a more ethical standpoint however, can only be achieved when there is not so much a division as a confederacy of families, a banding together of men for the sake of their common protection and their common ideals. The rudiments of civil society can be found in a condition in which particular persons or particular groups are so related that they establish themselves through and in conjunction with one other, and there is a system of mutual dependence which provides for their mutual good. Through diligence and toil, the specific materials of nature are moulded and adapted to serve a variety of needs. It also supposes a partition into groups and classes, the most important of which are: (a) the agrarian class; (b) the business class; and (c) the class of public servants.

Whilst the end of civil society is the protection of personal freedom and property, at the next level what we have is complete unification of both individual and universal being. To better appreciate the meaning of the state it is necessary that we consider this not with respect to its origin but rather with respect to its end. The state is the culmination of a process that begins with a simple collective, then proceeds to a specialization of its parts, and terminates in a truly universal will. Let us track this through the idea of a system of rights in which there is: (a) some semblance of form but no content; (b) some semblance of both form and content; and (c) complete identity of both form and content. At the most rudimentary level a person who has no rights can have no duties either e.g. a slave is someone who may have an abstract understanding of freedom but is not actually free, and hence has no duty to behave otherwise than what his initial condition will allow. At the next level there is a division into rights and duties which implies similarity in content but not necessarily agreement in aim. A son's duty towards his father must differ from his rights against him (these different 'moments' could be expressed as respectfulness on the one hand and irreverence on the other), or, there is a difference between a servant's duty towards his master and those rights he has against him (these different 'moments' could be expressed as loyalty on the one hand and disobedience on the other). At this stage what we mean by 'duty' is nothing more than the neglect of particular interests, that is, a person may be said to be acting less dutifully so far as he is acting more selfishly, and less selfishly so far as he his acting more dutifully. But at the highest level, and in its most concrete expression, duty reveals the moment of particularity as itself essential and not merely as some purely adventitious means. Thus, every opportunity the individual has to realize his duty constitutes for him the moment of self-fulfilment and the realization of all his needs.

Now let us address the question of what we mean by a compact or a promise in the sense of some arrangement that is helpful, but more in terms of what is morally rather than legally binding. We might also approach this from the viewpoint of what is purely conditional or what is strictly unconditional of its very nature. A conditional arrangement is one in which a person contracts to do something if someone agrees to do something in return but at a later time. Consider for instance, the payment to a builder in relation to the construction of a house. We could either say that the payment was conditional upon the product from the viewpoint of the purchaser, or that the product was conditional upon the payment from the viewpoint of the builder. A difficulty may arise however if neither is sure the other will honour his commitments, and a half-completed house is not a fit dwelling just as part payment is not a full settlement. In terms on the other hand, of an unconditional pact, then what this means is the complete fusion of both word and deed, so that when a person' gives his word' he binds himself to all its consequences as well. At the highest level, to be true to one's word may also in a sense to be true to oneself- as occurs for instance in a marriage ceremony when two selves commit to both a caring and a sharing life. We also need to be clear about the difference between private intentions and public avowals. To say that a promise is connected with some implicit set of rules does not mean it must also be connected with some specific set of outcomes. A person who promises to repay a loan may not have the least intention of doing so, but that is not to say he is not liable or really did not commit in the first place. The only qualification is that it not be done under duress, since as rational beings it is clear we have an unconditional right to our own survival. And this may at times cause us to divulge things we would not otherwise be inclined to.

This also raises questions about the relation between legality and morality, and whether the ends of society are strictly moral or a mixture of the moral and the legal. When we say that rights and duties may be correlated what we mean is that there is a sense in which they may also be opposed, or at least, opposed in the way that force and freedom are opposed. Thus, even where it concerns our specific duties (e.g. parent to child or manager to worker) there can never be anything more than resemblance in what they connote. On the other hand, to suggest that rights and duties are correlated in the sense of being perfectly identical, seems to raise the spectre of a larger whole in which they are either completely immersed or completely let go. There is a difference however, when we say that a right or a duty is implicit, and what we mean when we say it should be severed from the purely affective part of our being. In the case of the latter what we mean is that impartiality should be raised to a level where there is an equal allotment of good, not simply what is good for our family or our friends.

Let us pursue this through a comparison of moral rights and moral duties with negative duties and positive rights. As we have stated elsewhere (Ch.10) what we mean by a *moral duty* is something neither exclusively internal nor external—it is that code of conduct we imbibe through instruction and through training. This however, is something that pertains to only a certain period in our lives, prior to a state of full maturity and responsibility for what we do. Additionally, what we mean by a 'sense of commitment' is not so much a settled outlook as a response to those challenges that arise in the course of our lives. By a *moral right* what we mean is the good sense of the community, not something predetermined but effective nonetheless. We might also regard it as something that is customary for us to do, not only in our private dealings but in our public commitments as well. From this viewpoint, law is merely the objective side of a subjective condition when it reaches a certain point, rights supplying the ground for that end we consider fitting and just. By a *negative duty* what we mean is the kind of duty that arises from a condition in which a community of men is at least evident or discernible. In the first instance individuals must agree or make a collective determination of what it is they would wish for themselves and what it is they would wish for their fellows. In these terms the will is only effective so far as it concerns its own possessions and not the possessions of others. By a *positive right* what we mean is the kind of right that arises from a condition in which protection is just as necessary as any obtainment at the outset. Since such protection is not possible so long as there is no awareness apart from the self, there must be a further commitment that each will defend the rights of his neighbour so far as his strength or capacity will allow. That however does not mean that right has been replaced by might, it simply means that limited force may be reasonable in the case of any outstanding or uncalled-for attack.

The relation between negative duties and positive rights also leads to a discussion about the relation between positive duties and negative rights. We might begin by reminding ourselves that in the way rights and duties are correlated this means there must be a 'division of interest', neither complete separation on the one hand nor complete coalescence on the other. In plain terms, what one person has the right to do someone else has the duty to refrain from stopping him from doing. On the other hand, where it concerns positive duties and negative rights then the implication is that these are altogether active, in the one case on behalf of others and in the other in respect to just ourselves. A positive duty could be defined as the duty to assist others when need and circumstance dictate that one should, that is, to act from a spirit of brotherly or filial love. (A good example during the Gallipoli campaign (WW1) would be Simpson and his donkey). That of course is not to say it is a strict duty we should do no matter what the circumstances, as in the case of keeping one's promises. A negative right could be defined as the absence of a right in conjunction with the absence of a duty (i.e. the duty to preserve oneself) understood as a certain permission or indulgence but not in the way this might normally apply. There is a difference between what it means to be permitted to do certain things in the course of one's life and what it means to perform a meritorious deed, to become a hero or a saint. To become a hero or a saint is not to go beyond the call of duty, but rather, in some sense, to make a virtue out of self-denial.

Ordinarily it is negative duties that are coupled with positive rights, but under certain circumstances the forfeiture of a right is something the agent may feel he is simply duty-bound to do. In this case what we have is the simple *negation* of any right. Consider the following examples: (a) A soldier becomes aware that a live grenade has landed in the midst of his platoon. Without thinking he jumps on it and as a result saves many lives, including that of his commanding officer; (b) A person standing on a cliff top sees his friend thrashing around in the surf, and realizing he is in trouble, jumps in to save him. But because of a strong tide and not being a good swimmer, he only manages to drown as well; (c) A person protesting civil rights contravenes an official order to vacate a particular site and is shot by the police. Now in all these instances, if you take the view that the value of the act resides solely in a counting of its consequences, then you would surely say there was a world of difference between what these actions betoken and any good they actually achieve. On the other hand, it is perhaps the mark of a truly mature society that it is able to countenance and treat equally such diverse acts, irrespective of their differing motives and their differing effects. What these acts symbolize is the strength of a common identity, the strength of a common commitment, and the strength of a common comradeship.

Chapter 13

Of God's Existence

Perhaps the best way to broach this subject is to consider the work of two very influential men, the somewhat unorthodox Dutch thinker Baruch de Spinoza (1632-77) and the German polymath Gottfried Leibniz (1646-1716)

In the *Ethics,* Spinoza begins with a formal distinction between a necessary being, a chimerical being, and a contingent being, on the assumption that in the first case what we have is something whose essence cannot be conceived of without its existence, in the second case something which cannot be conceived of as having either existence or essence, and in the third case, something which cannot be conceived of without an essence but not necessarily existence. This also ties in with the distinction between causes that are internal and causes that are external; in the case of a necessary being this is something that has both internal and external causes, in the case of an absurdity something that has neither internal nor external causes, and in the case of a possibility something with external but not necessarily internal causes. God, therefore, is something which can be conceived of from the viewpoint of either internal or external causes, that is, from the viewpoint of what it means to be either essential or existent, whereas contingent beings can only be conceived of from the viewpoint of external causes, and chimerical beings not at all. (That is, they are only possible through our linguistic constructions)

We also need to distinguish between the idea of a cause which is immanent but also external, and the idea of a cause which is external but also transmutable. Thus, when Spinoza says that nothing can be destroyed otherwise than by external causes he means causes of an intermediate kind or causes derived from a material and not mental substratum. An immanent cause may also be said to be external, but an internal cause cannot also be said to be efficient. However, if we allow for the prospect of free will or some discretionary power then there seems no reason why something cannot be destroyed by internal means, or the simple disposition that a person has to behave in such and such a way. Of course, it is true that outside pressures may sometimes cause a person to contemplate his own demise, but the real question is why different people respond differently given entirely the same set of circumstances. Such notwithstanding however, the idea that everything endeavours to persist in its own being, that every man pursues necessarily what is good for him, is by no means an untenable one. The real question is whether something is to be accounted good simply because we seek it, or seek it because we firstly *judge* that it is good.

As we have seen in our discussion about the relation between virtue and justice, it is sometimes necessary to distinguish between an approach that is strictly descriptive and an approach that is strictly prescriptive. In the *Nicomachean Ethics,* it is clear that what Aristotle is doing is establishing a standard of excellence and then defining virtue as what is intermediate between two extremes. On the other hand, there are many situations when the word 'mean' conveys not what is excellent but rather what is average, as when we say of someone that he is an average swimmer, or an average golfer, or an average bridge player. Given a sample of the general population there would be a certain percentage who were good bridge players, a certain percentage who were average bridge players, and a certain percentage who did not play bridge at all. Thus, our approach here is entirely descriptive, since we are not saying that a person who is an average bridge player *should* become a good bridge player, merely, that this is how he sits in the overall scheme of things. Virtue on the other hand is something we regard as a recommended course, that is, something that a person *should* aspire to. Spinoza's approach to this question is not altogether in keeping with the Aristotelian model, since it rests on the distinction between adequate and inadequate knowledge, not excellence and mediocrity, but there is also a sense in which this represents a kind of mean between self- improvement on the one hand and self-destruction on the other. However, he does not deduce this empirically but rather logically, since if no existent has a cause which enables it to destroy itself, then what pertains to its finitude must proceed from without, taking care to distinguish between what is transitive in the case of destruction and immanent in the case of creation. Hence, it follows that if something that exists does not have the capacity to destroy itself then it can do no otherwise than preserve itself in whatever state that might happen to be.

Another consideration is that we sometimes regard an action as being inherently good or bad, no matter how this is represented on any particular index or scale. Thus, as Aristotle quite rightly points out, passions such as envy and malice together with certain action such as murder and theft, are inherently bad. Once we have determined the mean or the recommended course, we need not quibble over an excess or deficiency in what is palpably a good, just as we need not quibble over whether there is an excess or deficiency in what is palpably an evil. In terms of our own axiology however, we might approach this somewhat differently, since it ought not be assumed that because insufficiency represents something fixed this may not also be so in the case of its opposite. Nor that there cannot be discordance between those ends we pursue and those means we employ. Consider the situation where a person is overly self-conscious to the point where he is neglectful of his fellows, or overly concerned about others to the point where he is neglectful of himself. And also, where the value of the act may not be in keeping with the end it enjoins. In the case of suicide, a person may only appear to be somewhat neglectful when in fact he is overly self-conscious, which in turn leads him to be neglectful of others. Such action might therefore be described as the arbitrary or indifferent application of a means. What we understand by supererogation, on the other hand, is a form of behaviour that is deemed to be meritorious or praiseworthy because it shows an undiminished love for one's fellows, but again, in a way that may or may not imply due modesty towards oneself (The agent may simply be seeking fame or a lasting good name). Such action we might nonetheless describe as the measured application of a means. And this leads on to the third alternative, a simple observance of duties that are either self-regarding or other-regarding. A person who fulfils his moral and legal duties has acted rightly, but no more so than someone who pursues his welfare within the bounds of what is reasonable and just.

So far as it concerns Spinoza's political theory, then what is distinctive about this is the way he treats the relation between *jus* and *lex;* that there is no law other than that which is dictated by one's carnal nature, and that there is no right other than that which is dictated by the need for self-sufficiency. In the case of Hobbes he is careful to distinguish between *jus* and *lex,* together with 'blameless liberty' in respect to moral imperatives, and 'urgent necessity' in respect to the will to survive. There is however a considerable difference between *perseverance* as Spinoza sees it, and *self-preservation* as Hobbes sees it. Since Spinoza holds that everything has just as much right to act as it does the power to act, either from instinct or reason, there is as much a right to be dissolute as there is to be virtuous, to be ignorant as to be wise. So far as it concerns the question of a *state of nature*, then although he follows Hobbes in this regard, his account is somewhat muddled, since if the power of man and the power of God are as one, as he elsewhere maintains, this does not explain how or on what grounds the attributes of the one appear so removed from the attributes of the other. Neither can this be accounted for in terms of any inherent sinfulness, since in a state of nature man does not really sin but merely obeys the promptings of his innermost drives. And yet what we are also being asked to believe is that if there is a 'free cause' in any sense, this can only be the Almighty Himself, the original source of all goodness and virtue, the wellspring from which all perfection proceeds.

It is true that Spinoza does distinguish between the *naturans* and the *naturata,* but this is altogether formal, since what is a mode or attribute of the divine essence is also just an image or reflection of the divine will. Thus, it is not entirely clear why men, rather than having a perfectly docile nature, do in fact have just the reverse, or why, as autonomous beings, they might not be accorded some free election withal. Not only that, but since there is no more a distinction between 'right' and 'might' than there is between intellect and will, and since men do in fact display aggressive tendencies, so are they equally justified in pursuing their discordant aims. Such a doctrine however may not be so serious where it concerns the question of any original right, but it does assume a more sinister guise if we consider its implications on a much broader scale. Since individuals when not checked by social bonds are constantly at war, then it may likewise be perfectly lawful for nations to go to war provided this is conformable to the will of the majority, or the citizenry as a whole. In order for a state or a commonwealth to secure peace, on the other hand, it must enter into some alliance or compact, and this will be binding only so long as there is the prospect of invasion or the prospect of being overrun. Thus, what for Hobbes is merely a state of disorder, in the hands of Spinoza becomes an instrument for global oppression and fear.

On a more positive note, the account that Spinoza provides of our civil arrangements is both perceptive and wise. He begins with the general observation that since men are governed by appetite as much as they are by reason one should not deny they will sometimes be motivated by treachery, deceit, or foul play. On the other hand, where it concerns the relation between short-term and long-term good, preference should always be given to the latter, and hence, a person is 'freer' to the degree he follows his reason and not simply his instincts. This however does not alter the fact that what constitutes the standard for each individual is what he judges to be in *his* own best interest, rather than what he judges to be in the interests of others. For instance, if one pledges or give's one's word on a certain occasion then this is binding only so long as the situation or the circumstances remain the same. It is not unreasonable therefore that each should be the judge in his own case, and that prudence should direct him every step along the way. Of course, this will be viewed very differently in a pre-civil state than when there is a joining of ends, but the principle remains the same, what is right or just is the greater and not the lesser of two goods or the lesser and not the greater of two evils.

The art of government therefore is the ability to convince a person that what is in his best interest is not *always* what he believes to be so, that discrepancies may arise between civic duty and a person's private good. It might therefore be described as the art of persuasion rather than the hammer of command. As he further points out, there is a difference between slavery or bondage in the sense of enslavement to one's desires, and slavery or bondage in the sense of enslavement to any command. It may be in the interests of a citizen to offer due compliance to a ruler, but that will depend on whether the ruler is self-seeking or acting largely for the common good. Spinoza recognizes that a sovereign's motives may be no less venal than those of his subjects, and thus, that there must always be some expedient for the return of power to those who were originally vested with it. This is different from Hobbes, who seems to suggest that a contract is really nothing more than a *fait accompli*, and that the installed sovereign is in no way beholden to his subjects, since there will always be need of a public and not merely a private means of enforcing the law.

Since for Spinoza what he means by the will is little more than the actualization of power, he does he not seek to distinguish these powers, since everything is living, and everything is moving, and everything is subject to the strict necessity of its being. For Leibniz, on the other hand, there is a profound difference between the way that nature may be viewed as either a mechanism or an organism, and hence between a simple conatus and a true entelechy or form. One of the most striking differences between a living entity and any artifice is that in the case of the latter the parts must always be subordinate to the whole, whereas in the case of the former they are interdependent as well. For instance, a battery is the driving force behind a radio, a microchip is the driving force behind a computer, but it is not at all clear what the driving force is behind an animal or a plant. Hence by the 'whole' what we mean is something betokened or represented in each and every part, the basic unit of substance in this case being what Leibniz calls a *monad*. A monad is defined as something simple and without parts, that is, something without extension, shape, or divisibility. And since only simple things are real, it follows that unless there is a change in simple things there can be no true change at all. There is no means, either natural or artificial, by which a monad can be created or destroyed, only perfect spontaneity in respect to itself and perfect conformity in respect to its environs. Looked at from the inside, we might regard this arrangement as a series of well-ordered dreams; looked at from the outside, we might regard this arrangement as a certain regulating or harmonizing of ends. The series of states which embody our knowledge of the universe are called *perceptions;* those powers which ensure the transition from one state to another are called *appetitions.*

In keeping with Spinoza's distinction between adequate and inadequate knowledge, Leibniz holds that the transition from one state to another is really only the confirmation of two states that are antithetical in their kind. A monad's *actions* are those changes by which it proceeds from a less to a more perfect state; its *passions* are those changes by which it proceeds from a more to a less perfect state. A monad's degree of perfection therefore could be described as the degree of distinctness in its perceptions—there being a graduated scale from what is more obscure, on the one hand, to what is more pellucid on the other. Or we might approach this in dynamical terms by comparing passive force in the sense of matter or mass and active force in the sense of entelechy or form. In the first case, what we have is something that resists not only permeation but also motion, since one body cannot be moved by another unless it opposes its initial force. (This implies that inertia is not only the disposition of a body to remain at rest, but also to counteract any force that proceeds from without.) Active force on the other hand is not merely the propensity to action but something which involves effort or striving. In addition, active force must be separated into something original and something derived; the former pertaining to essence or quiddity, the latter pertaining to permutation or change. So far as it concerns the relation between body and soul, Leibniz rejects the idea that there can be either any causal connection or any divine intervention, rather, that they are like two clocks that chime together in keeping with their original constitution. There is therefore a kind of pre-established harmony; souls act according to the laws of final causes and bodies act according to the laws of efficient causes, these being both separate domains, and different perspectives from which the whole may be viewed.

Now let us consider Leibniz' account of the traditional proofs for the existence of God, treating of the more recognizable ones, firstly, the Ontological argument, secondly, the Cosmological argument, and thirdly, the Argument from Design. The Ontological argument has been professed by a number of thinkers (principally St Anselm) and seeks to demonstrate the existence of God from postulates which require no independent or objective verification. The argument can be couched in a variety of ways but is roughly as follows. Whatever can be demonstrated from the concept of a thing must also be said to be attributable to that thing. And since whatever is the greatest and most superlative of beings contains all of its perfections, God must exist as the underived source not only of Himself but of everything that results from any action He performs. However, since there is a clear distinction between analytic and synthetic truths, Leibniz adopts the view that God's existence is contained only in His possibility and not his actuality, but that this will suffice, since even if it is not necessary it is at least not self-contradictory.

But whether you approach this from the viewpoint of a logician or a theologian, there are major objections that cannot be addressed simply by an appeal to the subtleties of language. Rather than demonstrating the true relation between existence and essence what this appears to do is confound them, since if something exists, then by that very fact it must also have a cause, whereas if something has an essence, then by that very fact it may or may not have cause. And what it means to have a cause is precisely what it means to exhibit such and such a set of features—something we are not afforded in the case of a perfectly Necessary Being. As an example, consider the definition of a triangle as a figure whose sides are equal to two right angles. Now no matter how precise may be this conception it does not contain all the features that a triangle could or might ever possess. That is, when presented with a certain figure our knowledge will be quite useless in identifying this one as isosceles or that one as scalene, or some other in any other way.

The Cosmological Argument has traditionally been handled from the viewpoint of a principal or primary cause, and that any activity implies not only an end but some initial condition as well. Since whatever is finite has a cause, and whatever mobilizes it must also be finite, then eventually you will reach a cause which is the originator of every possible train of events. However, Leibniz does not call this a primary cause but rather a metaphysical substratum, a reason which *inclines* but does not necessitate. From the very fact there is something rather than nothing it follows there must be a certain need to exist, and that for things expressing a possibility this will be either a quantity of essence or a quantity of form. And so, although the world is only a metaphysical possibility it is nonetheless a physical necessity, since if it did not exist then this would involve an imperfection, as well ultimately as a moral absurdity.

A major difficulty with this is that it is not altogether clear what is meant by a reason that *inclines*, since what is sufficient to produce a particular effect may only be what is *known* to produce a particular effect. Anyone could argue that the Big Bang theory was a sufficient explanation for the creation of the universe; that all science does is fill in the gaps in our knowledge, and that beyond that there is really nothing worthwhile to be known. In the same way, anyone could argue that an atom, by comparison with a quark, was an insufficient explanation for the constitution of matter. The idea that God acts freely and not just physically harks back to Aristotle's fourfold distinction in his treatment of causality. In the *Physics* he argues that causality may be used to explain not only the form and content but the origin and purpose of a thing as well. This unhappy coupling of an agency and an end has convinced some philosophers that there is an immanent or final 'purpose' and not just some active or energizing agent.

The Argument from Design states that although there is a palpable order in nature this cannot have arisen in any purely fortuitous way, that there must have been some wisdom or goodness by analogy with the causes at work in purely artificial things. This is a little more promising, since apart from the criticism of Kant or Hume, it does allow us to posit efficiency or adaptability as an end. For Leibniz the pith of this is that there is a fixed relation between substances, a mutual resonance as though but not *because* they are acting upon one another. God has so created the soul that everything that proceeds from it must do so of its very nature, and accordingly that each of these substances mirrors the whole universe in its own way, even if it does not transmit this as we would ordinarily understand by the transmission of any species.

This however is somewhat solecistic since although there may be some pre-established order where it concerns a composite i.e. the union of body and soul, this is not necessarily the case where it concerns the monads themselves. Simple substances may be analogous to composite substances if the universe is a plenum, but that is not the case if it is a void, or if what we mean by action-at-a-distance (gravity) is different from what we mean by action as a physical effect (collison). In that case, there might only be one atom in the whole vastness and emptiness of space. And if the monad knows only itself and its inner state, then how does it know if there is anything apart from itself, or that what it *thinks* is outside is really only the result of its own artfully constructed dreams? (Descartes grappled with the same question in his original conjectures)

Hence a solution can only be found if there is not merely some logical or metaphysical framework but some inter subjective relationship as well. And this leads on to some further considerations.

What we mean by a monad is a particular conception of the self. Stripped of its logical apparatus what this embodies is the belief that the individual must contain once and for all everything which will happen to him, that it is the present that is 'big' with the future and not the future that is 'big' with the past. We must nonetheless distinguish between the sort of connection which could be called *necessary* and that which could be called *ex hypothesi*. A necessary connection is one that is formed in the realm of pure ideas, that is, in the realm of logic and mathematics. An accidental connection is one in which the opposite does not imply a contradiction. As an example, Leibniz cites Julius Caesar as the master of Rome but also as the destroyer of personal freedom. Here what we mean by the concept of the person is that which includes all its attributes, but also, that there is a fixed relation between past, present, and future.

The fundamental question that arises here is not whether it is accurate but rather whether it is complete. In other words, if there is a present which is 'big' with the future why should there not be a future which is 'big' with the past? And that is why we have sought to introduce the idea of modeme. What we mean by a *modeme* is something in which the present is contained in the future just as the past is contained in the present, that is, that in order to create the future is it requisite that we recreate the past. Of course, the learned author could never have foreseen the appearance of a modeme, but it does help to resolve some of the difficulties in the original formulation. To begin with, the monads are not windowless because now they have a partner. If there are appetitions they can only belong to the modemes, just as, if there are perceptions they can only belong to the monads. Thirdly, if there is a pre-established harmony that cannot be between body and soul but rather between monads and modemes. Fourthly, the relation between monads and modemes may well imply a common cause in the sense of a common origin, but on no account does this imply a 'final' cause or any gradually unfolding plan.

Let us consider these points in a little more detail. Since the monad would appear to be a more complete concept than the modeme the question might well be asked: Why do the monads appear before the modemes and not the modemes before the monads? Perhaps the answer might be found in the way we construe the relation between organic and inorganic nature. In his *Critique of Judgement* Kant argues that there are two types of causality, one that is open-ended and another that is closed. What we mean by an open-ended system is one in which there is some gradation or scale, that things which are effects presuppose others that are causes, and that these in turn entail other causes but at quite a different level. What we mean by a closed system, on the other hand, is one in which there is dependence both as we ascend and descend, that is, one thing may be the effect of another as we ascend, but also the cause of the same as we descend. But if we think of something as possible in that way then it can only be a work of human artifice (that is, *a priori* by virtue of the purpose supplied by a rational mind but *aposteriori* by virtue of the materials that are needed to produce it). A work of nature, however, is one in which the parts through their own causality produce one another in regard to both their quiddity and their being. Each part exists not merely for the sake of the others, but rather, each part is a vital organ that produces all the others. (That is, each part acts spontaneously and not just mechanically). However, such a formula and despite its seeming plausibility is basically flawed, since dynamism can be expressed not only in terms of what is useful but also in terms of what is not. And this completely negates the Kantian dogma. Rather should one say that in art is it the durability of the part that reflects the durability of the whole, and the destructibility of the whole which reflects the destructibility of all the parts, but that in nature can we connect both the obsolescence of any part with the durability of any whole, and the obsolescence of any whole with the durability of any part

But to return to the subject at hand, what Leibniz argues in respect to a certain provenance is that the perfect agreement of substances having no connection as such attests to the fact that they must also have a cause that is common to them both. However, having dispensed with the idea of a 'final cause', what is meant by a 'common cause' can only be a *specific development* (albeit of one and the same substance). Perhaps this point can be illustrated in the following way. To the extent we might say that something which is relatively recent is also much easier to explain, the implication is not that something much older is also more vague and obscure, rather, that our *knowledge* is more vague and obscure. That is, if we wish to know what is the cause of the Eiffel Tower or the cause of the pyramids then from a certain perspective this is entirely the same, since we know in both cases that there must have been equipment, materials, and manpower. But of course, the construction of the Eiffel Tower is much better understood than the construction of the Egyptian pyramids, and that is because the *evidence* is that much closer to hand. In the same way, so far as it concerns the *cause* of monads and modemes, it may be more proper to regard this as knowledge following on formation rather than formation following on design. However, if looked at from the viewpoint of divine agency (if indeed there be such a thing) then the only conclusion must be that not everything that has eventuated was planned from the beginning. Given the age of the universe, and a Creator who has set it into motion, it is not difficult to appreciate how a small mistake may have burgeoned into something quite unintended or unforeseen.

Chapter 14

**The Different Forms
of Government**

In accounting for the different forms of government, it is customary to divide them in such a manner, that if the power of making laws resides in the hands of one then this is what we call a monarchy; if it resides in the hands of some then this is what we call an aristocracy; and if it resides in the hands of many then this is what we call a democracy. Thus in recommending democracy as the form of government best suited to the nature of man Locke argues that . . .

> it being necessary to that which is one body to move
> one way; it is necessary the Body should move that way
> whither the greater force carries it, which is the consent
> of the majority. (TTG Second Treatise Ch. VIII No. 96).

However, there is a problem about this, since in terms of what we mean by unity, or the relation between whole and part, there is a difference where it concerns the relation between the ruler and the ruled than there is between similitude and dissimilitude as such. That is, where it concerns the question which parts are similar and which parts are not, it matters little how they might be separated or combined, given that this is merely a question of degree. Certainly, we do not perceive what is round to partake of what is angular, or what is soft to partake of what is rigid, but that is not to say we cannot combine these qualities, as, for instance, a cannon ball which is round and rigid, or a cushion which is angular and soft. But in the case of parts that are active and parts that are not it is a contentious issue how they are to be combined, and that is because there must be a threshold for what it means to be active in and of itself. If the different parts that comprise such a whole are equal in number this will not supply a result, or at least, not supply a result for how such a relationship might be viewed. Thus, in arguing that a body will always move in the direction that it is carried by a greater force, it is not clear whether Locke means that the many will always be moved in relation to what is *sectional*, or that the many will always be moved in relation to what is *whole*. After all, we do not need many parts to impart motion to a thing (otherwise we could not have a monarchy or an aristocracy), and if there are more active parts than there are inactive ones, it raises the question in what sense they are active at all. Or at least, in what sense they comprise a group that is dominant or in what sense they comprise a group that is docile.

In the *Republic* (Book VI) Plato argues that rulership should never be by the mob, since if we would not entrust our goods to those who are thieves, or our music to those who are deaf, then neither should we make custodians of those who are ignorant. The origin of a quality such as courage or justice does not reside in those things that may be gleaned through the senses, but in a suprasensible realm accessible only to the sagacious. What we mean by justice is not the justice of many, what we mean by honour is not the honour of many, what we mean by truth is not the truth of many, rather only that which can be separated from the thickets and the brushwood. The man who aspires to do great things should be someone who cultivates the pleasures of the mind and leaves the body to itself. He should be generous in spirit and shun the trappings of wealth, he should have a retentive memory and a willingness to learn, he should be courageous, temperate, and fair. However, if we were to place our trust in the majority then what we would have would be a mere cacophony of sounds, not elevated discourse but a hankering after trifles. The best of all governments then, is government by the few, those able to see beyond the clouds of obscurantism, of mixed emotions and fetid desires.

But if philosophical wisdom should be the basis for the state, there are certain other forms which are not quite in keeping with this ideal, that is, such polities as timocracy, oligarchy, democracy, and tyranny. What we mean by a timocracy is something that mixes honour and virtue, a ruling and a warrior class, that is, which practices gallantry at the same time as generating fear. How it differs from an aristocracy is that it does not admit philosophers into the corridors of power but keeps them at arm's length, which favours those who are capable of waging war through cunning and guile, not those who seek peace through diplomacy and tact. What it has in common with an oligarchy is that it is covetous of money; it has been trained not in poetry and the arts but in flattery and deceit. By an oligarchy, on the other hand, we mean a community which desires property and wealth above all else—it is the rich who hold the purse strings and the poor who kneel at their feet. A fee will be levied as the prerequisite for citizenship, and those who cannot afford this will be barred from every privilege of the state. What it has in common with a democracy is that there will always be a certain self-division or self-dissent, only this will take a different form in the one case than it will in the other. The oligarch will become a sponger and a miser; his generous nature will be threatened by a more venal set of desires. Such a person will be at war with himself but his better instincts will overcome his baser ones. The democrat on the other hand will experience a similar tension, but he will not accede to his better nature, rather to what is common and ill-disposed. He will abandon the virtues of prudence and modesty, preferring rather the vices of vanity and ambition. In fine, if oligarchy could be called the politics of stinginess, then democracy could be called the politics of envy. What is characteristic of democracy is that it is full of dissembling and cant; it not only treats equals as equal but the superior as equal as well. To be free in this sense means to be frivolous and unthinking, not bound by the law but by the joys of the moment, the whispers of the hour, the events of the day. And this in turn leads on to tyranny, since the same disease that swallowed up oligarchy will eventually swallow up democracy; only in this case where there is a reaction in the opposite direction, an excess of liberty giving rise to an excess of oppression.

These sentiments are echoed by Montesquieu who argues that democracy may be excessive in two ways—there may be an excess of inequality which issues in aristocracy, and there may be an excess of equality which issues in despotism. Equality in a state of nature is something men forgo when they enter into civil society, but it is reclaimed when they are accorded equality before the law. But if they are equal as citizens, they are not also equal as husbands, or councillors, or magistrates. And so, a division of duties must be respected as much as a division of offices, equality before the law not exempting the citizenry from that duty each has as an instrument of the state. Where, however, the people are incapable of bearing or sustaining that power which has been assigned them, they will not only envy a magistrate but of the whole of the magistracy, they will not only envy a lawyer but of the whole of the legal profession, they will not only envy an infantryman but of the whole of the military. Under these circumstances, the merit of high office will be supplanted by the envy of the hangers on, the integrity of the virtuous by the turpitude of the weak, the prudence of a captain by the recklessness of a crew. This will then spill over into a general condition of frivolity and sloth, the raiding of public coffers, the selling of suffrages, the most pernicious and thorough undermining of the state. But no matter how well they have fared this will only bring the citizenry that much closer to the brink, of succumbing to a charmer or the rantings of a despot.

In the case of Rousseau, he begins with the general observation that for any action, there must be two distinct elements, the will or the disposition, and the capacity or the wherewithal. By analogy, he then applies this to the polity and suggests there must be two distinct powers, one which corresponds to the *form* and the other which corresponds to the *matter*. As to the form this is in essence a popular will or the will of the majority. As to the matter this is in essence an administrative will, or a power which decides how the law should be applied without exception. But what we mean by a 'popular' or 'sovereign' will must be understood in two respects (a) so far as it reflects the whole of which the individual is merely a part, and (b) so far as it reflects the part for which no other exists as a whole. Thus, so far as it is a unity it is what we call the Sovereign, and so far as it is a multiplicity it is what we call the State. In respect to the meaning of the government or the executive, then this is an intermediary between these different forms, that is, between an implicit form which we call 'the general will' and an explicit form which we call 'the popular voice'

In order to explore this in a little more detail, we need to begin by acknowledging that what is general must always retain at least some degree of generality, and what is particular must always retain at least some degree of particularity. That is, to the degree we ask a judge to be impartial we do not demand that he be completely free from all private engagement; that he suppress his natural feelings or his opinions and his values. If there were some higher power for which a judge was merely the medium, then there is no reason why the 'interest' of such a one should take precedence over the 'interest' of he whose conduct was under scrutiny. Since the wrongdoer at least *knows* what he is after, and this is part of the 'general will', on what grounds might the latter (i.e. the general will) ever turn or be used against itself? Thus, if by a judge or a magistrate we mean someone who is free from bias, we do not mean also free from *interest*, or at least, what is in the interest of the plaintiff, or in the interest of fairness, or in the interest of the common good.

So far therefore as there is a difference between the power of the sovereign and the power of the executive, then this must be expressed in terms of a difference in their *functions* as well. Not only that, but since we recognize that the citizenry will have a role in the making of the law, so also must they in the execution of the law, only here by electing those persons they deem best suited to the task. The populace itself could be described as a kind of magistracy, both that from which any rulers will be drawn and that *on whose behalf* any judgements will be made. It is advisable therefore that the many be governed by the few, only, however, in terms of what the many regard as being in their 'interest', not what is effectively in the interests of but few.

Now let us address the general claim that democracy is something that tends towards anarchy, and that anarchy is something that tends towards tyranny. Strictly speaking, if we are going to say that anarchy is a corrupted form of democracy, then we should also say that tyranny is a corrupted form of monarchy. That way, we can avoid connecting the differentiae with any particular genus rather than the genus with any particular species. Neither should we allow ourselves to fall victim to any kind of determinism—there is just as much evidence linking tyranny with anarchy as there is linking anarchy with democracy.

Let us begin by addressing some of the factors at work in the case of the French Revolution. In1788 facing financial ruin in the aftermath of the American War of Independence, the French monarch Louis XVI ordered a meeting of the Estates General to consider how the matter might be handled. Up till then the Estates General had been a largely advisory body consisting of the clergy, the nobility, and the commoners. However, since the bourgeoisie (or middle class) had been steadily growing in influence and number, this 'Third Estate' was able to proclaim itself a National Assembly, and invited the other Estates to join in the work of national reform. Worried about its size and influence, Louis XVI then ordered a transfer of troops from the eastern frontier to the vicinity of Paris and Versailles. This in turn incited the general populace who sided with the rebels, and resulted in the storming of the Bastille, a symbolic gesture which ushered in the new regime. The confusion which ensued guaranteed the National Assembly that its newly won status would be preserved, and ultimately paved the way for widespread constitutional reform. In just a matter of a few years very many important reforms had taken place, but principally the abolition of feudalism, the removal of tithes and all clerical privileges. In 1793 the constitution was amended to allow for a new ruling body, the Directory, which oversaw the administration and execution of the laws. But the Directory was a failure principally for two reasons (a) it was a corrupt and ineffectual government, and (b) there was growing sympathy for a more military style of leadership. In 1799 the highly regarded general Napoleon Bonaparte was able, by means of a coup d'état, to elect himself First Consul of the Republic of France. This is a good example of the kind of revolution that can proceed from below (i.e. from a state of simmering discontent) or from above (i.e. from a simple usurpation or annexation of the throne), thus connecting anarchy with tyranny just as much as anarchy with democracy.

Or to consider another case, in the middle and latter part of the nineteenth century Italy had established itself as a constitutional monarchy, but there was also provision for a parliamentary form of government. The upper house, the senate, was a body of notables appointed by the king, but possessed of little power, while the lower house, the Chamber of Deputies, acted as a check on the cabinet, which in turn administered and carried out the laws. After the First World War, however, Italy was beset by a number of crises. In the first place, the country had been so weakened by the war effort that its industry was in tatters, its currency was inflated, and there were food shortages plus high unemployment in every town and village. In addition to this there were certain radical elements, which, buoyed by the success of the Bolshevik Revolution in Russia, urged the workers to seize and operate industrial plants, to subdue and overthrow their landlords. This in turn lead to the formation of a group of nationalists who hankered after past glories, who were as one not so much in respect to their programme, but rather in respect to their general disaffection. This then became the movement known as *fascism,* and it took as its leader the young and ambitious Benito Mussolini. By employing the tactic of countering violence with violence, the fascists were able to overwhelm their opponents, and oust them from local administrative positions. By 1922 these marauding bandits (known as Blackshirts) had gained such complete ascendancy that they forced the king to appoint their leader as prime minister. From this point on *Il Duce* was able to stifle the parliament and enact discriminatory laws which were completely at odds with the general wishes of the people. After the Second World War and the defeat of fascism, a new constitution was drawn up, which, like the original Albertine Statute allowed for a two-chamber parliament, but which, unlike its predecessor, gave them equal status and equal rights. In order for any proposal to become law it must receive the approval of both houses, with or without due amendments. Today, Italy is a vibrant democracy with a multitude of parties and a heritage it can be proud of. This is a good example of how tyranny may be connected with anarchy but not democracy with what is anarchic.

In comparing Plato and Rousseau, the key issue is whether by rulership we mean something that rests on the existence of certain *virtues*, or on the existence of certain *freedoms*. Since Rousseau places greater stress on the individual and the welfare of the individual, his solution to state domination is to create an intermediary body between the sovereign and the people, which in turn creates a distinction between the *ought* and the *is* of rulership. By the former we mean the role of government in stabilizing the relation between sovereign and people, by the latter, neutralizing the relation between sovereign and people. If by a corporate will we also mean a particular will then in this case the government will be at its strongest, and it will usurp the role of the people. But if by a corporate will we mean the will of the people then in this case the government will be at its weakest, and it will usurp the role of the sovereign. Thus, in order that the executive be limited and prevented from abuse what is requisite is that it be governed by the people, and be bound by the dictates of their will. Plato on the other hand places much greater stress on training and education, and so presumably would support an hereditary rather than elective form of government. That is, government not only by the few but also *for* the few. The true aristocrat is someone who cultivates an elevated lifestyle, who has seen through the fog of deception and cant, who holds sway not through braggadocio but through discipline and self-control.

However, whatever the truth of this, there are several objections that could be raised to such a 'born and bred' kind of elitism. In the first place, we are by no means convinced that virtue *is* something that can be taught, or something that can be implanted, even though it is certainly possible to instill a sense of morality. More likely it is a person's property or assets that will be handed down, not his wisdom or his virtue. A more serious objection is that what these rulers will aim for is only the preservation of a certain settled outlook or clearly established norms, and thus that where this is leading the masses may not be a state of enlightenment but rather to a state of subservience. (Consider the role of the church during the Middle Ages and its persecution of non-conformists. In this case the kind of 'aristocracy' that it represents was certainly not a boon to the state)

Where it concerns the question of freedom and in what sense this is conjunctive with equality, then what we mean by this is equal treatment for equals, not the belittling of those who have shown themselves to be exceptional in one respect or another. That is, whilst we recognize that all men are equal before the law that is not to say that some should not be regarded more highly, or at least, that rewards should not be given according to the contribution that each of them might make. Liberty therefore is not the same as envy and neither is it the same as licence; no man has the right to abuse himself or act contrary to his conscience, just as no man has the right to dispossess another or deprive him of his life. To love one's neighbour as oneself is not just a directive of reason but of common sense; just as the directive to respect oneself and to respect the law are equally efficacious as an end. If this were not the case, or there was not some natural duty to treat all men alike then there would be a descent into barbarism, and a person's hold on life might hinge on nothing more than the lenity or severity of his master. But again, to be well respected means to be treated equally, and that will always be so unless there are other factors that may be brought in to play.

As to the relation between freedom and the law, we need to distinguish between physical freedom and what is meant by freedom of the will. Physical freedom means the absence of restraint, or anything which may restrict a person in his actions or his deeds. That is, it is the capacity or means for the execution of that upon which one has determined or resolved. Freedom of the will, on the other hand, involves a choice between two opposites, as perhaps when a person judges that one thing is of greater value than another, or that one action is more pleasing than another. In the case of due compliance to the law then a person who does so is acting in accordance with his knowledge of the outcome, that he will not be punished, just as a person who violates the law is acting in accordance with his ignorance of the outcome, or at least, his uncertainty it will go unpunished. What it means in this case therefore, as it does in any other, is the *degree* to which a person may be deemed to be free, by virtue of being capable of acting both rationally and designedly. If a person judges that certain sanctions are unduly harsh then this may deter him from embarking on any course he has in mind; if he judges that certain sanctions are unduly weak then this may encourage him to embark upon his course. But that does not mean these judgements are anything *but* subjective, or that there is some objective standard that tells us what really is excessive or extreme. One person may be deterred from jaywalking simply because he fears he will be fined; another person may not be deterred from stealing even if there is a considerable likelihood he will be caught.. It all depends on how we view the relation between risk and reward.

There is also the question of a choice which is moral rather than legal, or in defiance of the law, and that is the case when a person is directed by his conscience or his faith. Thus an externally imposed penalty, although a dissuasion in many instances, can never divest a person of that right he has to express dissent, or to draw strength from such convictions as are not in keeping with those of the state. Of course there are those who would argue that since one man's right corresponds to another's duty, what it means to have a 'right' is not thereby what it means to be free in any unrestricted sense, that is, to simply follow one's passions or be captive to one's beliefs. However, in respect to the relation between law and liberty we need to be careful about the kind of assumptions that we make, or at least, whether it is question how something is to be promoted or whether it is a question how something is to be *shared*. A division of rights and duties only indicates how any burden *must* be shared, but not also, how any interests *might* be joined. That is, individuals may cooperate for the sake of a good which they hold to be common, but the state should never impose itself on the citizenry for the sake of what it believes to be comprehensively for their own good. Hence some latitude must be given to the expression of dissent, if there is a clear voice and this is expressed in a manner not intended to cause mayhem or alarm.

In the case of Machiavelli the approach that he adopts to the wielding of power is somewhat more cynical (or at least, that is so in the case of *The Prince*). He begins by addressing what we mean by the different forms of government, or at least the different varieties, since he dispenses with republics and considers only those that are ancient and those that are modern. Hereditary states are the easiest to maintain, since all one need do is toe the line and not depart from the accepted wisdom and the accepted customs. So far as it concerns newly created states then we need to distinguish between the mixed, or those that have been joined to the old, and the pure, or those that have been acquired by a variety of means, be that patronage, merit, or good fortune. The most important question however is not so much how men may acquire their kingdoms and principalities as how they may hold onto them. And in this respect the best advice is to show an indomitable spirit, not to curry favour or exhort men by persuasion, rather, to compel them by guile and by force.

Human nature for Machiavelli is fundamentally flawed, but what is detestable as a common trait is the shallowness and fickleness of humankind. The only difference between the Prince with his selfish motives and the people with their selfish motives is that the latter are credulous whereas the former is not; rather he is cunning and proficient in obtaining what he wants. The people are always fickle and they are always chasing after baubles, the Prince on the other hand is only changeful when it suits him—for the most part he builds his reputation on the strength of his army not the strength of his convictions. He inverts the way we would ordinarily regard virtue and vice—normally, we would account the former praiseworthy and the latter blameworthy, but for Machiavelli there is nothing to be gained by seeking the plaudits of the mob, ultimately it is only vice that is worth coveting, providing it does not impinge on one's authority or one's esteem. The people only believe that certain things are commendable because they are weak and effeminate, whereas the Prince realizes that there is nothing that stands strong apart from fortune, and that in order to overcome this he must be versatile and ruthless, not merciful and just. Of course, that is not to say the Prince should not avoid being hated by his subjects, but that is not the same as being hated by the nobles who are always jealous, rather, not tampering with their property or their wives.

The problem with this however is that there is no indication as to how power might be used to regulate our behaviour other than reflecting the way that men do *actually* behave, which in the case of Machiavelli is particularly insidious. We might consider this from the viewpoint of an institutionalized set of rules, both understood in the abstract and from the viewpoint of that conduct it requires. In the game of cricket for instance, we have the implements, a bat and a ball, two opposing sides, and an umpire at either end. The role of the umpire however is not in any way to meddle or engage with the players, it is, quite simply, to administer the rules as he sees fit. And essentially this is what we mean by the administration of the state, on the one side do we have the instruments of power and on the other the citizenry as a whole. The question never arises whether a man may be good in his private dealings but bad in his public duties, or good in his public duties but bad in his private life.

However, if Plato has a problem understanding what we mean by liberty rather than licence, then for Aristotle it is more about the orderly rather than indiscriminate wielding of power. In the Politics (Ch. III. iv) he argues that whilst a good man must also be a good citizen it is not necessarily the case that a good citizen must also be a good man. And yet on what grounds does this assertion rest? Since in any constitution there will always be a diversity of functions just as there is a diversity of powers, what we mean by the good or the best must always be subject to that end it is intended to supply. And so if there is a bifurcation in the means there must also be a bifurcation in the ends, a good carpenter not necessarily being a good husband and a good husband not necessarily being a good carpenter. But more especially when we consider certain pairings, the pairing of father and son, the pairing of master and servant, the pairing of buyer and seller, then it should be clear that what we mean by virtue or duty in one sense is not necessarily what we mean by virtue or duty in another. In the way then that we might characterize a good man as free the good man must also be a ruler, whereas the man who obeys, whilst a good citizen, is not also good in the way we have just outlined. But to be a ruler or a statesman in the best sense is not to have inherited or acquired such a station, rather to have *honed* it, as a cook does by serving an apprenticeship, or a doctor does by serving an internship, or a lawyer does by serving as a clerk.

As for the argument that a ruler is someone who learns his art by being ruled, this is no different from saying that a person learns to thieve by being robbed or learns to forge by being duped. Or to press the analogy with a game of cricket, it is a little like saying that a team is better because it is bowling, or better because it is batting, when the real question is whether a game is better by virtue of having at least *some* rules or better by virtue of not having any. Of course, it is true that Aristotle does at times flirt with the idea of the rule of law, but this is just a brief diversion; it is not long before we are back beating the old drum, singing the praises of those who are the strongest or fittest. In order that the gifted have dominion over their fellows, it is requisite that there be some attribute which sets them apart, be that entitlement by birth, entitlement by riches, or entitlement by skill. But there are some men of such impeccable virtue that their capacity for statecraft soars above the rest; they therefore should not be constrained by the law but rather serve as its embodiment, sole contributors in the making and the shaping of the state. Such a panegyric however does little to allay our suspicions, since he does not spell out who it is that is going to lead us to the Promised Land, be that Moses, Hitler, Gandhi or Genghis Khan.

And as Rawls quite rightly points out, what we mean by 'majority rule' must be tempered by certain broader considerations, for instance, how the ideal underlies the real so far as any original position is concerned, and how the better must underlie the best so far as any practical outcome is concerned. As we have already seen (Ch.12) there may be a tiered relation between (a) negative duties, (b) positive rights and (c) collective agreements. Thus, where it concerns an arrangement which is mutually advantageous those who choose to restrict their freedom have a right to expect similar acquiescence on the part of those who have benefited from just such an accord. There are two aspects to this however; there is both the principle from which it proceeds and the outcome on which it relies. If there is no assurance the other party will satisfy his part then there is no reason the agent will do so either. Hence this whole arrangement hinges on something that is agreed to by both, and as a matter of general principle, the belief that public utility should always override our purely private concerns.

What we mean by a pact or a promise is an act done with the public intention of incurring an obligation not only with respect to the promiser but also the promisee. The important point about this is that what we mean by a moral obligation is not something that derives from any public institution, nor, from any particular theory of punishment. Rather, what it relies on is a principle which is known in and of itself, that is, a principle which is virtuous or a principle which is just. This particular viewpoint therefore (that of an ethical agent) must be distinguished from that of any general societal practice or any legally binding set of rules. It goes without saying that no matter what the activity we are dealing with there will always be need of certain rules, be that the rules for social engagement, the rules for a game such as chess, or the rules for any seasoned group of actors. But that does not prove that all such behaviour must always be moral, only that there may be a certain shading in the way these rules are taken and applied. There may be a question of decency when a person is snubbed because he is a Muslim or a Jew, there may be a question of seemliness when a cricketer refuses to walk even though he knows he is out, there may be a question of fitness when an actor is drunk or flirtatious on the set. But that is not to say that in any of these instances it is our basic morality that has been spurned—it may just be a question of the prevailing culture or the prevailing sentiment, not what is just or equitable in itself.

In regard to the second, then we must recognize that majority rule or a majority decision is very often the only way we can arrive at an outcome which is likely to achieve what is best. The jury system is a good example of the kind of mechanism that serves the end of what is fair, or at least fairer than any other system we may choose to introduce. Even though the members of a jury may have no legal expertise, their views are considered valuable in weighing the evidence and reaching a conclusion deemed to be impartial if not always fully informed. If, however, we had only the magistracy or the appellant court, then although there might be a surfeit of experts that does not mean there would also be a surfeit of common sense. Judges and magistrates, therefore, are useful in the administration of civil law, but not so useful in criminal trials or when there are more serious issues that require a more deliberative or down to earth approach. Or let us consider this from the viewpoint of the highest order system for the making of rules, that is, the question of constitutional reform. In this case what we are dealing with is a group of experts who pool their resources and collate their findings in order to achieve what they believe to be for the best. Of course, that is not to say there will always be complete agreement where it concerns a particular point of law, but there is no doubt that an exchange of views will always be preferable to what is authoritative or peremptory in itself. And even an elitist such as Plato would have to admit that there may be just as much a correction and calibration through the airing of different opinions, than there is a narrowing of vision if decisions are made ad hoc, or merely for the sake of just a few.

Chapter 15

Of Civil Dissent

In the way the contract theory of government is expressed through different writers, its basis may be the most expedient arrangement of wills as in the case of Hobbes, or it may incorporate a sense of what is ethical and just, as in the case of Locke. Thus, in the case of a shopkeeper who pays the mafia to ensure his business remains solvent we might describe this as expedient but on no account fitting and just. On the other hand, the reason the law punishes theft and fraud is not because it is grossly inexpedient but rather because it is a breach of certain civil and proprietary rights. Where however it concerns the question of consent then what this means in terms of any initial condition may be no less favourable to the former than it is to the latter. And that is because it is much easier to accede to a system when we know who is the master and who is the servant—where agreement is binding and there is no prospect of dissent. No doubt this may seem a little odd, but in the context we are discussing it may make more sense if there is a clear assignment of roles rather than something vague or ill-defined.

Let us pursue this a little further through a discussion about the relation between will and force. In terms of what we have previously called proposing rather than inducing a belief, then this may involve a counting of consequences but then again it may not. That is, under certain circumstances a bad intent may be coupled with a true belief and under other circumstances a good intent may be coupled with a false belief. In the case of the latter, however, what it means to void a promise as the result of certain intervening events is not the same as what it means to void it *ab initio*, that is, when a person is not acting under duress. If a person fails to deliver on a promise because he is physically unable to, then what this means is that there are intervening circumstances, not because he has a change of heart. On the other hand, if a terrorist is holding a gun to your head and you are required to lie to the authorities, you cannot be accused of having a bad intent if it is your welfare or your family's welfare that is at stake. Thus, in terms of the relation between force and will, in certain situations it may not always be clear which of the two should be preferred

The point is, although we must formally consent before any obligation can arise, this does not mean that such is a strict condition or requirement, since 'formal consent' may only mean explicit consent in the presence or absence of any attendant force. So far as it concerns the absence of force however, then what we mean by the strict condition for doing one's duty consists in the possibility that there may a division or partial mismatching of interests. The reason a person is required not to meddle with his neighbour is because their interests may not always be the same, and we must respect the right of others to do as they wish just as they must ours under the same or similar circumstances. However, the question of competing interests or aims should not be confused with the question of consent or compliance as such, since it is not a clash of interests that is implicit in consent but rather consent that is implicit in any advancement of an interest. When a parent asks a child if he has done his homework, then there may well be a difference in their aims, the parent deeming it to be in the interests of the child, the child not deeming it to be in his own. But to respond to such a question is not to use the formula 'I am truthful when I say I have done my homework' as if it were equivalent to 'I am lying when I say I have done my homework' since it is the duty that antecedes the right not the right that antecedes the formal duty. The question of consent can only be valid if there is at least some parity between the parties concerned, but in the contract theory of government, it is an open question whether this does or does not involve some element of permissible force.

For Locke it is clear that it does not, since his starting point is that justice must always be impartial, and that this can only be achieved if men voluntarily renounce their right to be the judge in their own case. However, if there is a problem with the theory of consent, it seems to stem from the fact that even if the majority agrees to support the body politic it does not follow that a minority must do the same. Rousseau's answer as we have seen is that the individual should be bound in a double relationship, namely as a member of the sovereign towards the citizenry as a *part*, and as a member of the citizenry towards the sovereign as a *whole*. The individual in a state of nature does not renounce his rights but rather ties them over; he binds himself to a corporate will just as the corporate will must be bound to its members. This in turn leads on to the creation of a general or indivisible will which represents the true interest of all its members; not merely that which is summed or appended to produce such and such a 'majority' result.

We also need to be aware how this idea of a 'majority will' may be worked into a particular argument, although more in terms of what is an inalienable right rather than any consciously constructed good. In *TTG* (*Second Treatise* Ch. XI. 140) Locke argues that a system of taxation must be supported by the 'will of the people', understood as a majority of wills, and that its absence would be a clear breach of the law of property, which no person could be expected to forego. The view that he adopts is that funds will always be necessary for the protection of the people, to pay for infrastructure and for an adequate system of defence. What he fails to make clear is the method that might be adopted for the sharing of such an impost, or how, through the redistribution of income it might not alleviate certain indispensable needs. For if, as could be argued, the public good should include not just protection from foreign powers but some minimal standard of living, then what Locke would really appear to be arguing for is entrenched privilege and wealth. That is, it is not the majority who would object to being taxed, only those who had acquired their wealth through title and birth, or were covetous in the extreme.

Another problem with treating property as an inalienable right is that it is not clear under what circumstances, or on what grounds, it might ever be overturned. For in whatever sense there might be a power to usurp 'the will of the people', the question remains: what would be the rationale or reason for doing so? Since in many countries what is meant by *capital* or the *business sector* is something more or less taken for granted, why is it that a government would choose to remove it if it was the very thing that was propping it up? Are we, at one extreme, contemplating a massive redistribution of wealth that favours some specific elite or are we, at the other extreme, contemplating a massive redistribution that favours the rising working class (something which Locke could never have envisioned)? It is not clear therefore whether it is a particular principle that is at odds with an entrenched minority (i.e justice vs cronyism), or whether it is a particular principle that is at odds with a majority of wills (i.e. private enterprise vs socialism or collectivism) And of course what this overlooks is that there may be occasions when a government has perfectly good reason to divest a person of his assets, and that is when it is the result of illegal or ill-gotten gain.

Now this has important implications for the meaning of dissent, since if there is no 'common good' (understood as some *predominant* interest group) then neither is there any univocal end towards which all men might be made to strive. Fundamentally, and apart from those occasions when it is the majority that actually *does* speak, there is no reason why a minority or minority group should conform to the majority view, given that the prevailing sentiment may be nothing more than what the largest minority thinks. If we have confidence in our democratic institutions, then the question of dissent or disobedience concerns only the question of minority rights or a representation to the majority of what some section believes to be for the good of all. The question of minority rights, however, should not be confounded with the question of a class of experts or technocrats, whether in Marx's sense as some provisional power (the vanguard of the people) or in Plato's sense as some ruling elite (the philosopher kings). There is a vast difference between revolution which is achieved through action and revolution which is achieved through thought, just as there is between scientific innovation and any forces which may be harnessed to nullify their effects. Many of the rights which we hold to be sacrosanct, the right to vote, the right to work, the right to equal treatment, were not achieved by technocrats but rather by ordinary men with grit, determination and the courage of their convictions (Emeline Pankhurst, Martin Luther King). On the other hand, where it concerns scientific innovators such as Galileo and Newton then what they achieved was the result of intellectual vigour, not on any account the result of protest or hard-won reform. In this case what we tend to find are authorities hell-bent on suppressing such enquiry or anything not in keeping with their own deeply held beliefs. (In the time of Galileo this was the institution of the Church; in more recent times it tends to take a slightly different form, as for instance, the proponents of Intelligent Design.)

We also need to be clear about the difference between the spirit of any amendment or bill of rights and a particular morality which self-serving individuals may seek to impose on the majority in the form of some universal desideratum. So far as it concerns the first, then in terms of those values enshrined in the constitution our judgement may well be that the current laws are not in keeping with its spirit or intent. As we have earlier seen, to be treated equally means to be given equal consideration unless there are some relevant distinctions where it concerns the application of a rule or the denial of some more fundamental right. In the case of certain racial minorities, say perhaps Hispanics or blacks who are living in a predominantly white community, if no grounds can be found for regarding them as less worthy than their fellows, then neither should they be denied access to things such as education, employment, and health insurance. Where therefore there is evidence of discrimination or neglect, one might at least expect they would receive a sympathetic hearing from the courts. In the case of a practice such as homosexuality on the other hand the stance we take might be somewhat different, since if gays are allowed to flaunt their sexuality, it is not nearly so clear how the rights of such a group are being neglected or abused.

But if we are going to appeal to some common conception of justice as that which is implicit in the *will* of the majority, then there must be some clearly recognizable body that does in fact admit to this description. That is, what we mean by the *majority* must be understood in some specific or codified sense—it is not merely an aggregate of interests or some shifting interests that are never the same. There are two ways that we might construe the meaning of 'majority rule' (a) where it concerns the greater of two goods (and the aim is to achieve a complete alignment of all viewpoints) or (b) where it concerns the lesser of two evils (and the aim is to achieve a simple majority of all viewpoints) Thus, where it concerns the jury system, what we hope for is a solid majority if not complete unanimity; in the case of elections, what we hope for is some meaningful consensus or the sum of half plus one. To succeed in gaining a majority of votes however does not necessarily mean to have tapped into the majority 'interest', rather perhaps only ministered to some minority or sectional claim. Or to express this in a formula that Rousseau might well approve of, we need to deduct the number of interests that have not been realized from the number that have been in order to arrive at a 'real interest' or what is keeping with the least number of dissatisfied voters. For instance, if a candidate knows that there is a large section within his constituency that is in favour of euthanasia and a large section that is opposed to it, then his instincts will tell him he must walk a fine line between appeasing certain interests and ignoring certain others. (That is, it may not be in his 'interest' to support it or oppose it).

What can be said of the majority, however, can also be said of any minority, only in this case where it is the *force* of any majority that is matched by the *will* of any minority. What we mean by civil disobedience, however, is not exactly either of these, or at least, not something that supports either a majority or a minority agenda. There is certainly a presumption in favour of the latter, but this stems from the failure to recognize that minority protests will only be relevant when we have faith in our democratic institutions, not when they are in a state of flux or in need of wholesale reform. Any action opposed to a purely local or municipal law does not necessarily constitute outright defiance, rather, only when such a law stands shoulder to shoulder with the highest laws of the land. Hence, federal rather than state law is the real touchstone, and that concerns breaches in the areas of taxation, conscription, and various types of discrimination. There are two ways we might approach this. If the law in question is a basically sound one, e.g. upholding racial or sexual equality, then anything opposed to it may simply be illicit and without warrant or design. On the other hand, since the means by which we arrive at a just constitution can never be perfect, it may sometimes be necessary to comply with unjust laws provided there is not too great a deviation from that higher end they are meant to sub serve.

Apropos the question of a broader agenda for civil disobedience, perhaps we might approach this from an historical perspective. During the struggle for Indian independence there were a number of events that shaped its course and its final outcome. These events were the direct result of one very pugnacious and defiant man, Mohandas 'Mahatma' Gandhi. Having already witnessed racial violence during his time in South Africa, on his return to India, Gandhi was incensed by the fact his fellow countrymen were forced to pay a tax on salt, something so indispensable to their everyday needs. On 11 March 1930 he and his followers marched from their ashram in Sabarmati to the coast of Dandi with the intention of extracting salt from sea water in defiance of the general ordinances of the day. On 6 April, he raised a handful of salt as a symbolic gesture and a snub to the British. He also directed a raid on two salt pans near Bombay which lead to violent and bloody confrontations. Another key event occurred in 1932 when the British attempted to introduce separate representation into the Indian parliament, consisting of various groups such as Sikhs, Muslims, Hindus and the Untouchables. Gandhi was opposed to the idea of a separate electorate for the Untouchables, since he believed that this would perpetuate their minority status and keep them under the dominion of the ruling elites. Given that there could be no retreat from this position Gandhi started a fast on the 20th September, which finally ended on 26th September when a compromise was struck. There would no longer be segregation of the different groups but a kind of proportional representation which allocated seats not on a sectional but strictly numerical basis. To summarize these events, in the first instance such action was in no way incompatible with the majority *will* but rather in support of it, in the second instance, such action was in no way incompatible with a principle of fairness, replacing class distinctions with equality of status.

Given certain formal conditions civil disobedience could be defined as a political act which is contrary to the law, done with the express purpose of bringing about a change in the law through means that are peaceable rather than unruly. We need thus to distinguish it from other forms of protest or dissent; those in the first instance that could be called violent, and those in the second instance that could be called private. So far as it concerns the first the question that needs to be asked is this: What does it mean to be violent? Does it mean to be violent towards ourselves, to be violent towards our neighbours, to be disrespectful and covetous of their possessions? If we take this to include all of the above, then many acts we might otherwise deem moderate would have to be considered vehement in the extreme. (Would we say that Gandhi was wrong for fasting near to death?) To be more generous to our definition, we would probably prefer a division somewhere between injury to others, and injury to their property or ourselves. This also chimes in with the meaning of a criminal act, since we are well-disposed to consider a person both vicious and violent if his actions are injurious and he does not take responsibility for anything that he does. On the other hand, it may not obviate all the difficulties therein entailed, since to say that something is the cause of harm does not mean that it may not also in some sense be termed non-violent. A legal strike could be said to be something that sits uncomfortably between the extremes of non-violent protest as a means, and bloody confrontation as an end. In the case of textile workers protesting low wages this may not be so obvious, but in the case of the transport union initiating a work to rule order this may have dire consequences for those neither directly nor even remotely involved. Or in the case of the Coal Miner's Strike that enveloped Britain during the 1980s, there were widespread clashes between workers and police, most notably in the skirmish dubbed 'the Battle of Orgreave'.

For the most part however, we have just as clear a conception of the difference between the violent and the non-violent as we do between the forceful and the violent. Assuming force to be a means of ensuring stability in our relations with one another, we might describe violence as the illegitimate use of force, although in these terms not exclusively from the viewpoint of either the government or the citizenry. The government may have to employ reasonable force to quell a riot or an insurrection, but it may also be guilty if it initiates policies only after sowing the seeds of panic and general insecurity. Hence, legitimate force implies that the government is sympathetic to the values, beliefs, and ideology of its members; that it seeks a just end to every dispute, and that it does not suppress dissent when there are relevant and pressing issues at stake.

To address the question of the difference between the public and the private, it should be clear that civil disobedience is a conscientious act done in the public arena and for the sake of the public good. It sits therefore between legal protest in the sense of disputes about the application of law, and conscientious refusal in the sense of non-compliance on moral or religious grounds. The reason we do not hold it to be conjunctive with legal protest is that there is a difference between those judgements reached in particular cases and the nature of a law that is simply iniquitous in itself. The reason we do not hold it to be conjunctive with simple refusal is that there is a difference between justice in terms of purely moral or religious sanctions and justice in the sense of what is binding on us all (Of course we do not deny that religious customs may also be worked into any legal or criminal code.)

Let us consider this in a little more detail. Where it concerns the question of certain flagrant injustices then our protests will always be public, but where it concerns the question of certain faulty procedures then our protests will always be private. Thus, if a person has an issue with the administration of the law then there is little he can do except badger the authorities in the hope that things may change. He may also appeal to the general public for support, but this he should do through argument and persuasion not through invective and rabble-rousing. Or we might view this in respect to the jurisdiction of a law, federal laws having wider application than state laws and state laws having wider application than local laws. Thus, if a person judges that a local law is in violation of a state law, or a state law is in violation of a federal law, then this is not to deny that there is any validity *in* the law, but rather *which* law has the most currency in the case that is presently at hand. As we have earlier argued, protests that are directed towards local authorities are not in themselves civilly disobedient, they only become so when local ordinances are ratified by the highest laws of the land. Conversely, a state official might quite openly depart from a rule that is generally efficacious on the ground that in any given instance this may not be in keeping with its spirit or intent. Just as in the case of legal protest, in no way can this be said to constitute the breach of any fit law.

So far, however, as it concerns the relation between civil disobedience and simple refusal, then there is both a point of agreement and a point of divergence. Conscientious objection may take a form that is both open and artless or closed and concealed. Army conscripts who burn their draft cards in defiance of the authorities are acting openly, and in clear contravention of the law. On the other hand, those who harboured Jews during the Nazi regime were certainly not doing so openly, presumably because they were so contemptuous of the law it mattered little whether their activities were or might ever see the light of day. Another issue is the relevance of a legal sanction, and how far a person should be accepting and not evasive in any standpoint he might take. There may be doubts about a person's sincerity if he not only defies the law but also refuses any punishment in its wake. Of course, in the case of a secret engagement, one might hope not only that there were no consequences for the agent but also that it was completely successful in its aim. For the most part however, if a person is honest and upright he will not resile from those decisions he has made, preferring a good conscience to the whims of a ruler, death by the sword to any kind of recantation (e.g. Sir Thomas More during the reign of Henry VIII)

The real reason however that we distinguish between conscientious refusal and civil disobedience is because of how it touches on the question of a person's motivation, and what it means to act from private regard or a sense of private duty, and from public regard, or a sense of what is publicly useful. In the case of the first, although we would not say that a person's actions should always be in keeping with his own good neither would we say it must always be in keeping with the demands of others. A person who refuses to accept a blood transfusion on religious grounds may not be acting in defiance of any clearly promulgated law but there is no doubt if this became a common practice it would endanger many lives. Or consider the case of a person who refuses to take up arms at the outset of war. Even granted that there is a difference between territorial disputes and the basic right to self-defence, a person cannot be made to participate in such activity if he sees this as a simple violation of his will.[1] Quiet clearly, it is far too simplistic to ask a conscientious objector what would happen if everyone acted as he has, and that is because (a) we recognize the right of refusal when such refusal is not an evil in itself, and (b) we recognize there may be a valid distinction between the pursuit of certain reasonable as opposed to illegitimate ends. Even in the case of public utility or the public good, not only are we not obliged to obey an unjust law at all times neither are we always obliged to obey a just one. Or at least in the case of the latter, a law that contravenes what we deem to be morally requisite. Although in principle one should always tell the truth it may at times be proper to tell a lie, and that is when there are more serious consequences that need to be taken into account.

In the foregoing, we have argued that civil disobedience is an act contrary to the law, done with the express purpose of removing that law because it is perceived to be unjust. It also implies that one is duty-bound to accept those sanctions and penalties that are attendant upon such action. This then resolves the issue whether one is simply a flagrant objector opposed to every form of governmental control or a selective objector, in which case one may be acting entirely in accordance with one's rights. However, we may also need to consider this against a wider backdrop, and that is whether political power is being wielded moderately or excessively. No matter what the type of government we are dealing with it will always be reliant upon force to some degree, but there is a great deal of difference between one that favours fairness and one that favours despotism or cronyism. In the present context, we would like to think the government we are dealing with is one that remains true to its ideals, that it balances the rights of an employer with the rights of an employee, the rights of a prosecutor with the rights of a defendant, the rights of a magnate with the rights of a worker. On the other hand, in the case of a tyrant then what this requires may be something a great deal more extreme. As we have already said, conscientious objection may not only be open it may also be clandestine; and there may be no alternative if what we are dealing with is a particularly repressive regime. So far as it concerns the nature of terrorism, then this is even more directly opposed to achieving reform through peaceful or conciliatory means. On the whole it tends to replace quiescence with disquiet, confidence with uncertainty, and fit punishment with degradation and despair. It may be used both by governments to divide the citizenry and in a more globalized economy against governments to confuse them and undermine their support. Fundamentally however it is a weapon of the weak and not the strong— it is only useful at a point where its perpetrators are unable to envisage a more sober and rational set of means.

[1] Hobbes, Leviathan Ch XXI p.16

Chapter 16

Law and Liberty

The word *free* may be applied to any object that is unbound or unrestricted in its movements, be that, what is dependent on another but not absolutely so, or what is unrestricted in and of itself. But more properly the *liberty* that a thing has concerns its ability to act both rationally and resolutely, not irrationally, or without purpose and design. Thus, the actions of a beaver may be orderly but on no account would we call them rational, the actions of a hoarder may be rational but on no account would we call them purposeful; in neither case therefore is there evidence of what it means to be truly free. As concerns the relation between freedom and necessity, then what is free cannot be what is necessitated, and what is necessitated cannot be what is free. Thus, when it is said that every desire or inclination must proceed from some cause, and this from another cause, and so on until we arrive at what is uncaused, then it is not true liberty we are dealing with but rather only licence. A stone has no more the liberty to be fired from a sling than it does from a gun. In much the same way, when we say a person has the capacity to be lawless or unruly, we do not mean the necessity to be so disposed, only the licence to behave in a way that is not in his own or his neighbour's true interest

In treating further of the distinction between liberty and licence, let us consider the former as being in some sense a directive issued by one person for the instruction of another. In this case, what we mean quite explicitly is the issuing of a command, something that presupposes an author, an object, and an aim. Whether the injunction in question be entirely reasonable or just one person is coerced to the degree that another person is not. However, we may also need to distinguish between legitimate and arbitrary power, since there is a difference if power is exercised in conjunction with moral imperatives or power is exercised in conjunction with the will of the agent. Certainly, we do not say it is improper for a parent to admonish a child, and that is because it is fair and reasonable that an elder should instruct a child (moral imperative). But in respect to the wielding of political power then in the way we view this due consideration must be given to the question of a person's moral right to act as he sees fit, or do what he simply believes will prove effective as an end. The use of power could be said to be legitimate if (a) those that make the laws are also subject to the laws, and (b) the law confines itself to the aim of ensuring public peace. Thus, in terms of what it means to be free, if this is true liberty and not merely caprice, then it must be connected to a person's basic entitlement, that is, what he has a basic claim or *right* to do.

Where it concerns the meaning of a right then we need to address this from two viewpoints: (a) when it is logically connected with a duty, and (b) when it supports the idea of what is equal or just. In the first instance and as we have earlier seen, rights and duties are merely two sides of the same coin, since a person cannot expect others to respect his interests if he is not equally respectful of theirs. However, we need to be clear about the implications that follow from the *abuse* of a right and the implications that follow from the *observance* of a right. In the typical situation that we are dealing with, there can only be the abuse of a right when a person is unmindful of those boundaries within which he may reasonably act. On the other hand, to be respectful of a right may also mean to be accepting of rights outside that sphere to which they would normally apply. (As, for instance, when a right is accompanied by some physical or mental disability). This also raises questions about the relation between liberty and the state. To proclaim and enforce the law may be in keeping with the existence of certain rights, but what we mean by this is not that the state is the creator of rights, rather only their protector and guardian. Quite clearly, the state cannot be the maker of rights if these are the result of our moral progress, since this is a collective awakening and something that may be amenable to persuasion but not to duress. The right to life and liberty is surely more important than the right to work, the right to work is surely more important than the right to strike, the right to strike is surely more important than the right to form a sporting team etc. And all of which pertains to our moral consciousness, since it is not a matter of whether something can be enforced as to whether it *ought* to be enforced, that is, whether it carries sufficient weight in terms of what we ideally deem to be proper and just.

Of course, in the way we might describe the use of power as being arbitrary it is not necessarily the case that it is also abusive, since the abuse of power does not follow from the simple exercise of power, assuming this to be something pernicious in and of itself. From a certain perspective (and in terms of what is meant by the rule of law) we might well say this, but to be abusive only means to go beyond that right we are *allowed*, not ignore some simple rule that prescribes what we *ought* or *ought* not to do. If we are considering the validity of a system of law, then we need to attend to the question how it might actually apply, not whether there are some ideal values and from which it must never depart. No doubt a sovereign is not under an obligation to obey his advisors in any autocratic state, but that is not to say he cannot exercise his judgement wisely, that he may not be peaceable rather than belligerent, responsible rather than unruly. And so, in terms of our previous discussion about the nature of belief, in the way we connect this with a sanction or a threat we might also be more sanguine about the kind of leadership necessary to achieve a fair result. A duly acknowledged sovereign who issues a command is, it could be said, *proposing* a belief, and this is no less so than in the case of any legislative body, or any body of officials appointed by the people. On the other hand, in the case of a brigand or a robber who demands money from a bank clerk, then although it is equally true he may be issuing a command we would not in the same way say it carried any weight or was worthy of due compliance. An act of intimidation or thuggery may well involve the raising of a belief, but on no account would we regard this as either truthful or deceitful, since if there is no *consent* to the enjoining of such an end then neither can there be a comparison or the matching of any particular means.

The real crux of the matter, however, is not what we mean by a recognizable authority but rather what we mean by an efficacious sanction. After all, there may be no difference when we say that a sovereign is someone who *proposes* the belief his subjects will be punished if they disobey him and a policeman who *proposes* the belief that any citizen will be fined if caught littering on the street. But it may be a different matter if the sovereign is someone who proposes a false belief or a policeman someone who accepts a bribe rather than doing what his job demands of him. In *The Prince* (Ch. XVIII) Machiavelli argues that 'there are two ways of striving for mastery, one in accordance with the laws, the other by force . . .' and further on ' . . . a prudent Prince neither can nor ought to keep his word when to keep it is hurtful to him and the causes which led him to pledge it are removed'. Strangely enough we find Spinoza arguing in much the same vein when he states: 'The pledging of faith to any man, where one has but verbally promised to do this or that . . . remains so long valid as the will of him that gave his word remains unchanged. If he then comes to the conclusion . . . that more harm than profit will come of his promise . . . then by natural right he will break the same. (*A Political Treatise*. Of Natural Right Sec.12).

This is a good example of the problem that ensues when we do not clearly distinguish between the propriety of any action and the effectiveness of any sanction. What these writers are saying is that in the absence of any proper restraint, be that internal or external, a leader may rightfully do what he simply deems to be in his 'best' interest. And yet we would surely recoil from such an assertion, since in this case there is not only the indifferent use but the *abuse* of the will, that is, an inability or unwillingness to act at all in accordance with one's conscience or one's sense of right and wrong. Even if a person has nothing to fear from the breach of a promise, we would surely not say that he has the right to renege on his commitment or waver in his resolve. In more practical terms however, and no matter what the form of government there will always be a considerable difference between a policeman who is caught stealing, and a politician who is caught disowning any pledge.

We also need to consider the implication of regarding a sanction as simply the *prediction* that such and such an action will incur such and such results. Thus, a person could be said to be under an obligation to obey his superior so long as there was a high probability that disobedience would result in harm befalling him. An obvious objection to this is that it is not the certainty or uncertainty of achieving a particular result that is at stake, rather the legitimacy or authority of that person who is issuing the command. Thus, in the case of a bank robber threatening a teller's life, there may be nothing to suggest he would not make good such a threat. But since what we are dealing with is the wholly unjustified use of force, on no account could a person be said to be under the strict duty to do as he is told. Of course, that is not to say that it may not be prudent to do so, but self-preservation as an end is not the same as duty or virtue as an end. Another objection is that in the way we might regard a set of rules, to regard them as what is external may be very different from taking them as what is internal. As something external, this may mean nothing more than the application of certain signals or cues; as something internal on the other hand, awareness of what it means to be connected as a whole. Thus, a rat may be trained to do something by means of a positive stimulus, or dissuaded from doing something by means of a negative stimulus. However, a rat does not possess the insight that what it is doing is following a *coherent* body of rules, and so, it cannot appreciate what it means to belong to something called the 'kingdom of rats'.

This leads on to the suggestion that what we mean by law is perhaps not any specific directive but rather those rules or norms from which any such directives are derived. Quite clearly, what we mean by a legal code is not something invariably connected with a set of negative sanctions or a set of moral directives; otherwise, men could act no otherwise than in seeming contravention of the law. Thus, to act in accordance with the law must, to some degree, incorporate the idea of a manual or set of instructions for how the game should be played. This we have earlier seen in the case of a contest such as cricket. Likewise, in the game of bridge, if a person revokes or plays a card out of turn then he may be punished by the deduction of points or a number of tricks. But the act of revoking is not necessitated by the fact of playing bridge, only the decision that a person makes in the way he plays his cards. Similarly, although the law requires that a person who drives a motor vehicle must hold the appropriate permit, the reason for this is not that otherwise he will always drive poorly, rather, because it requires a degree of proficiency to begin with. And if driving is empowering for a person, then this could be said no less but only more so for something such as the institution we call marriage. Although there is no legal requirement to marry, what the law does is formalize an arrangement through which the necessary and appropriate ends can be met. In fact in these terms, a person is almost freer to behave in a way that he might otherwise do, since although the law may penalize a person for driving poorly it does not penalize him for being adulterous (or at least not in most Western countries, even if it provides the ground for a legal divorce). Nor does it require that a person give evidence in a court of law when this could be prejudicial to a spouse.

The point about all this is that there is a difference in respect to the legitimacy of any claim when this proceeds from some original act, and the legitimacy of any act, when this proceeds from what is empowering and not disabling in itself. A person who receives a loan or makes a promise is under an obligation to return that loan or fulfil that promise. But that is not quite the same as what we mean by liberty in a less restricted use of that word. As we have already said, the right that a person has to walk his dog means that any other must respect that right, but more broadly, what one person chooses to do or what he can do may not always be amenable to or within the purview of any other. If a person is a good pianist or a good golfer, then this is the sort of thing he may choose as his career, but the law does not punish a person simply because he cannot play a musical instrument or putt a golf ball. Where it concerns a bequest or a will, the power that a person has extends much further than his capacity to put pen to paper, since there is both a set of rules for any witnesses and a change of status for any beneficiaries.

Looked at in a broader sense there may not only be the question how a person benefits from the good will of others but also how he might withdraw from their disaffection as well. Although liability at one extreme *may* involve the consequences of acting rightly, or at least incurring any favour, liability at the other extreme *must* involve the consequences of acting wrongly, and hence incurring any wrath. To this extent, it is necessary to distinguish between a duty and a liability. The fact that a person has a duty to respect the rights of others also means he is liable to any punishment should he fail to do so. On the other hand, if a person has borrowed his neighbour's wheelbarrow then although he may be responsible for its return this is contingent upon a demand that he do so. In the absence of any such demand then although he may be *disposed* to return it he is not obliged to. The same is true if a person has been notified of the whereabouts of a stolen item, and yet makes no effort to claim it from its current holder.

In the case of withdrawing from a bad will, then what we mean is being immune from such a will, as for instance, the freedom that a politician has under parliamentary privilege, or the freedom that a diplomat has when serving on foreign soil. However, if liability is not a duty then immunity is not a right, since it does not prevent others from making certain claims, however futile or churlish these may be. There are many other instances when the power conferred on one person does not correspond to the duty imposed on any other. The power of a judge indemnifies him against any civil action in case there is a mistrial, if he ventures outside his jurisdiction, if he makes inaccurate or defamatory remarks. In the same way, a person who is suffering from lung cancer may take action against a tobacco company and win the case in court, but that does not mean it will prevent the tobacco industry from engaging in false advertising or continuing to sell their products into the future.

As we have already seen (Ch.10) duties may be classified in accordance with the sanctions we call legal, moral, and social but only in the first instance where this corresponds to a demonstrable right. However, duties themselves may be further subdivided, since we may also distinguish between a duty that is abstract and a duty that is real. No doubt, the fervour that one has for one's Creator, the respect that one has towards one's teachers, the friendliness that one has towards one's neighbour—these are all legitimate expressions of what is good and worthy in itself. On the other hand, in the case of our legal duties or our self-regarding duties then this may not be so obvious or clear-cut, since questions may arise on both counts as to how they in fact should be viewed. In the case of a 'self-regarding' duty this could be construed as nothing more than naked self-interest, and very far from what is truly efficacious in itself (e.g. the kind of obligations that we impose on ourselves). In the same way, where it concerns our legal duties then these should not be construed as obedience to a purely arbitrary will, rather, to the equal allocation of our freedom or our rights. Quite clearly, what is necessary here is the recognition of certain rights that are *protected* by the law, not the conferring and dissolving of rights by a mere fiat or any action suited merely to the moment.

Hence if we are going to distinguish between an abstract and a real duty, then of course, we also need to distinguish between an abstract and a real right. Abstract right implies the existence of different forms of coercion such that there may be nullity in their total effect. This also has implications for the way we regard the penal code in its relation to the judiciary as a whole. For instance, if a particular court makes a ruling on a matter for which it has no proper jurisdiction then it may be overturned on appeal to a higher court. The implication may therefore be that the judge has been 'sanctioned' even if there is no discernible interest in any ruling he has sought to introduce. From our own perspective, what we mean by the negation of a negation can only apply in the case of a duty, not a right; that is, when it is the negation of something that prevents us from acting dutifully (i.e. the negation of desire) or, when it is the negation of duty itself (i.e. an act of malevolence). What we mean by a right, properly speaking, is something that concerns a particular *interest* not a particular *will*, otherwise there would be no basis for any alignment just as there is for any division of interests. If you observe a school of fish swimming around a pond then you might describe this as a 'harmony of wills' but on no account a 'harmony of interests', since we would never impose a system on fish, as we would on people, to control any competing desires they might have. Thus, a system of rights and duties is a means of ensuring that in any community there will be at least some consensus and not a constant bickering or feuding over ends.

Alternatively, we might consider this in terms of a right that is substantive and a right that is prospective. What we mean by the former is some characteristic or quality that is binding at all times, that is, something that is pre-political rather than based on custom and usage. Thus, it is commonly said that all men have the right to 'life, liberty, and property' (Locke) or that 'all human beings are born free and equal in dignity and rights' (Declaration of Human Rights adopted by the United Nations 1948). One of the problems that we have with this mantra is that it is not altogether clear how or under what circumstances it might actually be applied. If we take the view that every person has at least a minimal worth, then no doubt there are certain practices that should always be outlawed. We do not condone torture, we do not condone drug trafficking, we do not condone slavery. It is an altogether different matter, however, if what we are saying is there should be a universal standard for self-improvement or self-realization, since then it is nothing more than conjecture what all men should strive for in this kingdom of ends. Not only that, but in seeking to remove the obstacles that prevent men from achieving 'equal' rights the danger is that there may also be a lack of regard for those customs and traditions that make every nation unique. The call to different communities to amend their practices or live up to their ideals could be also construed as a clash of cultures, or the attempt by some to impose their values on those less 'enlightened' or 'sophisticated' in their ways.

As far as it concerns a right that is prospective, then there are two ways we might approach this (a) in terms of custom and usage, that is, what constitutes the basis for a primitive system of law, and (b) in terms of some future ideal by means of which any current condition may be compared. To consider the first of these, so far as we have defined a 'right of nature' in relation to a 'state of nature', then this means the right to defend oneself in case of attack. But, in and of itself, it has no moral import; it is not so much prescriptive as it is the simple urge to stay alive. Leaving aside this hypothesis of a pre-political state, law arises in the first instance when there is a claim that acquires a particular colouration, when it is praiseworthy and not just prudent to adopt such and such a set of habits or routines. When a person experiences shame or remorse at the perpetration of a wrong, then this arises from the expectation of how unfavourably his peers and loved ones might react. Thus, it is not so much the existence of a duty as a moral claim that results from the identification of the one and the many. In respect to the second of these points, this concerns a particular social movement, or the emergence of a certain consciousness that is ultimately ratified or endorsed through the state. There are many such movements that could be cited—the Suffragette movement in the eighteenth century, the Trade Union Movement in the nineteenth century, the animal rights and anti-nuclear movements in the twentieth century. These are all good examples of a progressive ideal, not recognized in any hitherto established body of laws.

Now let us consider the relation between the individual and the community when there is some basic assumption about an individual or collective will. So far as rights and duties could be said to be correlated then what this means is that they must be external in their origin. So far as it is an external right that gives rise to an internal duty, then from our own perspective what this means is that a person may have the desire to obey the law out of respect for the law and no otherwise. So far as it is an internal right that gives rise to an external duty then from our own perspective what this means is that a particular consciousness may be transformed into some collective or universal good. It is important in this instance, therefore, not to confound the sense in which legality may be underpinned by a moral imperative, with legality as the objectified expression of a person's desire to be free or to act with impunity. A person would not so much be 'forced to be free' as 'free to be forced' if his intention were firstly to enslave himself and then seek ratification through and in conjunction with the state—which is exactly what would happen if the state were deemed capable of fusing both individual and collective being. For surely, the very existence of slavery as a social force proves that it is possible to have a legal duty without a legal right, just as it is, to have a legal right without a legal duty (in the case of despotism). Therefore, to abolish such a practice requires the emergence of a social conscience from behind the veil of ignorance, not the restoration of the self through the most circuitous and arbitrary of means.

We might also consider this internal aspect of law from the viewpoint of the internal consistency of a body of rules or norms. Thus, according to Rawls, every legislator should adopt guidelines for the creation of laws and these include: (a) ensuring that the laws are publicly known and promulgated, (b) ensuring that they are administered fairly and impartially (c) ensuring that they are general in both their content and their aim (d) ensuring that they do not exceed the powers of those in whom they are vested etc. On the other hand, we might also approach the external aspect of the law from the viewpoint of adherence to any directive or compliance to any command. In the classical command theory, law derives from a superior who has the power or right to inflict pain on those who will not yield to his urgings or his requests. Thus, the notion of a general law in these terms does not preclude the prospect it may advance the interests of the ruler without advancing the interests of his subjects. So far then, as there is a dividing point for what it means to be dutiful in the sense of being just, we may discern this in the way the law relates to our past deeds, but in no way as being abusive, and the way it pertains to our future deeds, but in no way as being quite vacuous. In the worst-case scenario, retroactive legislation may be a useful tool in the hands of a tyrannical or brutal regime. This is especially so when respect for the sanctity of human life is lacking and criminal proceedings are brought against those who have neither the capacity nor the means to mount a defence. The reason we demand that rules be applicable in advance is because they must be seen as *guiding* and not *censuring* human behaviour, hence, on no account for deviation from what could never have been known in the first place. In the best-case scenario, retroactive legislation may assume a very different guise if what we are dealing with is the repeal of a law that is universally deemed iniquitous or unjust. So far as it concerns a prospective right, then a change in public sentiment or a change in conscience may demand that there be a change in the law itself, and even if that means doing so *ex post facto*.

Chapter 17

On Slavery

As we saw in our discussion on liberty and law, what it means to act freely is to act both rationally and designedly, but it should be clear this is not always to act for the sake of, rather not to act in defiance of, a clearly established set of rules. Thus, a person is acting both rationally and designedly when he buys and sells, when he enters into an agreement for the assignment of goods, when he prospers in any enterprise without injury to his fellow men. What is permissible does not necessarily exclude an element of complacency any more than it does an element of fellow-feeling. A person can be both an industrialist and a philanthropist, a legislator and a charity worker. On the other hand, as for those things that expressly forbidden by the law they invariably concern arrangements that are harmful, but most especially any injury one person may seek to visit upon another. There are two ways we may regard such activity, in the first place, from the viewpoint of certain basic or inalienable rights that can never be ceded, and in the second place, from the viewpoint of a means that is conditional or delimited by such and such end.

In the case of the first, there are certain basic rights that must be regarded as indissoluble, no matter how much force is used to prise them from their roots. We might conceive of this in the following way.

Quite clearly, a person cannot be denied the basic prerequisites of life, he cannot be denied the right to food or sustenance, to work the land, or produce the things that sustain him and those who depend on him. Neither can he be commanded to harm himself, or be denied the right to defend himself if subject to attack. As concerns those who threaten his property or his livelihood, then it is a matter for the law how far he may go in restraining such offenders, but there must always be at least some right to safeguard his procurements or what he has striven for in the course of his life. Likewise, no man can be made to accuse himself or bear false witness against his neighbour, to demean himself or seek repentance through a less than dignified means. In all these things, therefore, we would say that a man was free and within his rights to resist the injunctions or directives of others, even in the instance they are deemed to be his superiors.

In the case of the second, what we mean is that if the end is discretionary then the means must be discretionary, but that if the end is not discretionary, then neither will there be any question about a means that are or are not fit. That is, the reason it is wrong or morally abhorrent to treat a person as a means does not hinge on the question whether it is proper to treat him in isolation from any end, rather whether it is proper to deprive a person of as much freedom as is had by the rest of his fellow men. Thus, it all depends on the circumstances whether there is or is not any question about a means. A lawyer is the means to the recovery of a person's assets, an orthodontist is the means to the recovery of a person's teeth—we do not say that it is wrong for either a lawyer or an orthodontist to be *used* in such a manner, and that is because there is clear agreement before any such relationship is entered into. An end such as the recovery of a person's teeth is very different from the end such as the forfeiture of a person's goods—in the latter instance, the means must be adjudged as subordinate to the end, since this is the denial or disruption of a person's basic rights. There is a difference between an act such as murder or theft when this is the *forcible* seizure of a means, and an act such as benevolence or philanthropy when this is the *voluntary* relinquishment of a means.

Now let us embark on a discussion about the relation between public and private power. Public power as we have earlier said is power exercised by those in their capacity as officials or representatives of the state, from either privilege or duty. Private power it could be said is power exercised by those who assume responsibility for their fellows, or when two persons engage with one another as in the case of a contract. However, we might also adopt a slightly different approach to this by suggesting that public power is the meting out of any penalty in respect to directives of the state, and that private power is the meting out of any penalty in respect to some association or group. In the sense in which a sanction is operative but not also revocable then ultimately this is what we mean by any sanction imposed by the state, since if public order is the end then most assuredly there can only be private regulation as its means. However, as we have already seen in the case of a person's right to marry or to make a will, the law may confer certain privileges without imposing certain duties. Even here, however, although there may be nothing by way of a coercive order there may yet be something by way of a negated effect, or the refusal to accord certain rights if they are nascent and not yet sprung from the womb. Thus, in respect to a divorce hearing, the voiding of a contract undertaken for immoral purposes, or the prohibiting of minors from drinking and voting—these could all be construed as sanctions that nullify some existing condition, or in the case of the second, prevent in the present what is only applicatory in the future.

To address once more the relation between public and private power, there are certain spheres of activity in which state intervention may be neither appropriate nor effective, and that is the right that a person has to join an assembly, to take part in any duly formed guild, association or group. In the case of a Trade Union or a sporting club, then the most severe sanction may be expulsion or the revoking of a person's right to retain full membership, but that is not the kind of recourse that could be described as injurious in the extreme. Unless the rules of such an association are in direct conflict with those prescribed by the state, there is no reason why the aims and objectives of the former *should* be subordinate to the aims and objectives of the latter. In acting in his private capacity, an individual need only be mindful of what falls within some narrowly circumscribed sphere of interest, whereas in acting in his public capacity, he needs also to be mindful of what is for the good of all.

However, there might also be a circumstance in which the freedom to act is so straitened or constrained that no such harmony exists between the two—when public power is so pervasive it touches the very core of what it means to be autonomous or self-sufficient. Thus, slavery might be described as the involuntary servitude or perpetual service of a human being in return for the basic necessities of life, and without those benefits that might normally apply. Or to express this a little differently, although we might describe a murder- suicide as the forcible seizure of both a means and an end, in the case of slavery we might describe this as the forcible seizure of both a body and a *will*. In saying that we are not suggesting it may not be more or less extreme, simply, that no matter what form it assumes it has no legitimacy in and of itself. Whether it be the unconditional surrender of an enemy or the drudgery that is demanded of a serf, where there is nothing given there can be nothing gotten, and he who sells himself obeys neither his instincts nor his reason.

The practice of slavery has a long and bloody history dating back to Greek and Roman times, but more so in the case of the latter, where it was a distinct feature of both city and rural life. In medieval Europe it was gradually replaced by the institution known as serfdom, later abolished in home countries, in colonies, and eventually as an international trade. So far as it concerns disobedience and rebellion on the part of the slaves themselves, let us consider two significant historical events, firstly the Haitian uprising (1791-1804) and secondly the American Civil War (1861-65).

By the mid seventeenth century the French desire to expand its outposts had reached the Caribbean Sea, and together with the Spanish it controlled the island of Saint Dominique. With an increasing demand for products such as rum, molasses, and coffee, the West Indies became a centre of trade in the New World. And this in turn fuelled the demand for more and more slaves, a practice which involved traffic between Africa, the Americas, and Europe. But despite the peace and stability that ensued well into the next century, there was growing friction between the ruling whites and those slaves who had become freedmen, or in the case of half-castes what were known as mulattoes. With the Revolution on mainland France and the outing of Louis XVI in 1789, the voice of discontent became ever more raucous, and this spilled over in 1791 when there was a violent uprising in the Northern Province. British intervention only intensified the problem and made the rebels more determined, whilst at the same time placing a strain on the relation between blacks and mulattoes, and increasing the colour divide rather than dissolving it. Desperate to quell the outbreak the British then recruited the largely black population to fight on their behalf, but it was a wasted effort since the war was already lost, mainly on account of disease and malnutrition. By 1801 a Constitution had been established which prohibited discrimination on the basis of colour or race, and affirmed the equality of all men under the one indivisible law. Attempts by Napoleon Bonaparte to reinstate the system were totally crushed when blacks and mulattoes finally joined forces, and on 1 January 1804 Saint Dominique was officially proclaimed an independent state.

When the *Mayflower* arrived on the shores of the North American continent in 1620, there was already a flourishing slave trade, since it was so prevalent in Europe no one would think twice about transporting Negroes to this newly discovered land. Moreover, as Montesquieu would write in *The Spirit of Laws* . . .

It is hardly to be believed that God, who is a wise Being, should place a soul, especially a good soul, in such a black ugly body. (Book I Ch.XV)

Thus, while the white servant had his origins in common with the white master, the origins of the Negro slave were lost in the arid deserts and humid rainforests of the African hinterland. In the beginning, the use of slaves was restricted to the cultivation of such things as sugar and tobacco, which many believed would fall into disuse with an increase in industry and other forms of husbandry. What sealed their fate was the invention of the cotton gin, a device that made it possible to extract seed from lint and thereby dramatically improve the production of cotton needed for the European mills. However, to call this an economic boon would be to grossly misrepresent the true situation, since the greater production of cotton also meant an oversupply on the world market, just as, the need for slaves also meant there was a greater price that had to be paid for them. Effectively, what this did was make the Southern planters more dependent on their Northern neighbours, since it was the North that benefited from the sale of equipment whilst the produce itself was being mortgaged to the hilt. Therefore, if slavery was not viable from an economic point of view, then on what grounds could it be justified or according to what logic could it be sustained? The simple answer is that slavery so permeated the white consciousness that it had become the overriding index of social prestige and success. At the apex of this social pyramid, there were several hundred planters each with several hundred slaves. Below these were the aristocratic families with up to a hundred slaves, then the gentry with at least ten slaves, and last but not least, the yeomen with at least one or more slaves. Thus, social improvement tended to mean acquiring more and more slaves, and emulating the behaviour of those who lived a life of luxury on sprawling and sequestered plantations.

The question over slavery reached its head in 1860 when Abraham Lincoln was elected president of the newly founded Union. After his speech in 1858, when he declared that 'no government can endure being half free and half slave' there was a great deal of panic in the South, which lead to the succession of several states starting with Southern Carolina, and then others such as Mississippi, Alabama, Georgia, and Texas. Border states such as Missouri and Kentucky remained true to the Union. The war itself began with a dispute over Fort Sumter, a Union stronghold just outside Charleston harbour but which for territorial reasons was laid claim to by the South. As the war progressed it became increasingly clear there was a role for the blacks, not just to fill the empty ranks, but also to demonstrate that they could rise above the station they had been allotted by their brutal overseers. Without waiting for the President to act, several Union commanders had already organized an unofficial regiment of black troops, composed of former slaves from states such as Georgia and Southern Carolina. By the end of the war, about one in every ten Union soldiers was an African American, and they fought with distinction at Petersburg, Missouri, Virginia, and most especially at Fort Wagner, even though almost half died under heavy Confederate fire. The South tried to argue that the use of slaves was a barbaric departure from the rules of warfare, but it was they who were lacking in scruples, since no doubt if any had been returned their fate would have been no different than before. The valour of these men is a good illustration of how a sense of duty can *negate* a sense of entitlement, or at least, the cowardice of those who preferred prejudice to equity and were shamefaced in their denial of certain basic human rights.

Of course, there is a considerable difference between the meaning of a slave rebellion in the former case and what we mean by it in the latter case, since in the latter case the action taken is not so much by the slaves as on behalf of the slaves. As we have already argued, there are broadly two ways we may conceive of the state—one that founds it on the will (Hegel) and the other that founds it on an interest (Hobbes). To consider the first of these, in conceiving the relation between rights and duties we may do this in terms of: (a) there being some semblance of form but not content; (b) there being some semblance of both form and content; or (c) there being sameness in both form and content. In the case of (a) a slave is someone who has no rights and hence no duties, although there may be some similitude in respect to the latter. In the case of (b), when a person achieves a degree of respect then his rights may acquire a certain purport, or at least they may be matched with certain duties. In the case of (c) what we mean by duty in the absence of certain interests becomes duty as the actualization of certain interests. In the same way, what we mean by a right as something directed *against* the state becomes what we mean by something to be *incorporated* within the state.

Where it concerns the second, then we need to attend to our original distinction between the forcible seizure of a means and the voluntary relinquishment of a means. In terms of the relation between the individual and the state, what was construed as the forcible seizure of a means becomes the forcible seizure of an end, and what was construed as the voluntary relinquishment of a means becomes the voluntary relinquishment of an end. In other words, so far as it concerns a voluntary relinquishment then the implication is that the state permits its citizens to act apart from but not outside the law, or at least that the law should not be seen to infiltrate every aspect of their lives. So far as it concerns a forcible seizure the implication is that the state may exercise supreme authority over its citizens, but only when there are reasonable grounds for any course it may undertake. Thus, in the case of something such as the death penalty, this does not extinguish the bond between rights and duties (as if the individual could conceivably appropriate this as his right) but rather strengthens it, by recognizing that the *might* of some may not be in accordance with what is a *right* for all. Hence, the taking of a person's life under certain circumstances could well be justified by arguing that the framework for lawful action is also the framework that prevents its infraction.

In terms of the distinction we have already drawn between a free and involuntary end, this also raises the rather vexed question: Is the victim the means to the wrongdoer or is the wrongdoer the means to the state? In other words, it raises a further question about the relation between right and power, that is, not just how far the state has the means but the cogency for behaving in the way that it does. Supporters of capital punishment would argue that right derives from power, or at least, that the power to destroy what is good must be checked by the power to destroy what is evil. Opponents of capital punishment would argue that although the state has certain powers that should never be overridden, it does not follow it also has the right to destroy life, only to preserve it. As we have already argued, a right is not something created by the state but rather *protected* by the state; it already exists in the life of the community and in those associations that make it up. And if associations have rights that are in no way bound up with the state then this applies equally to any individual with claims against it. We do not say of an infant or a lunatic that since it is under no obligation then neither does it have any rights; rather, we distinguish between an innocent incapacity and the evil in being mistreated, or the capacity to seek protection and the evil in being ignored. In much the same way, if there is some relation between the forcible seizure of a means and the forcible seizure of an end, then this will be different for a master than it will be for a slave. For the master, the forcible seizure of a means is conditional upon the forcible seizure of an end, since to enslave a person does not at the same time accord one the right to deprive him of his life. (That is, we have to distinguish between the taking of a life and the subjugation of a *will*.) For the slave on the other hand the forcible seizure of an end is conditional upon the forcible seizure of a means, since if a person does not have the right to harm himself then neither does he to enslave himself; or assign to any other such a right as is not properly his from the moment of birth. (By that of course we mean the right to give but not to take life).

However, this is not the only way we might conceive of state power in the sense of the forcible seizure of an end; we also need to consider the broader context, or what is entailed in the relation between different nation-states. In times of conflict, there is a general convention that whatever is captured becomes the property of the victors. Thus, what we mean is the legal convention whereby the invaded territories, and everything in them, become subject to the will of the aggressor. In effect, however, what this means may not always be so clear, since if the victors are disposed to be merciful, then a person may choose imprisonment rather than allow himself to be put to the sword. And hence the right to kill must be distinguished from the right to enslave, since even in captivity a person must retain some rights, or at least the right to nourishment for any service he performs. Neither does it follow that those who are born of a slave must be bound into slavery, rather, only for such time as there are means to keep them within their bonds. The right to enslave is something that progresses from the agent to the object not the object to the agent, and hence not to the advantage of the former but to the advantage of the latter; otherwise there would be no end to war or drudgery as a basic form of life.

Returning to our discussion about the state, one of the problems with conceiving of it as a natural phenomenon, is that it tends to confound freedom as unimpeded action with freedom when what we really mean is self-fulfillment or the overcoming of base desires. In an earlier chapter (Ch.12) we compared the development of the state to the growth in a plant or a tree. In this connection slavery might be likened to the way the whole is dependent upon the part, or at least, the way any part may be parasitic upon the whole. Yet does that mean it could ever be justified in these terms, that is, taking it to be an aberrant growth but not one that was prejudicial to the well-being of the whole? This is no less the case if we take slavery to be an implicit condition for the existence of certain basic and indispensable rights. We would surely not say that slavery was a necessary 'moment' which connects the absence of rights and duties with the identity of rights and duties- as if we were just as much a prey to our passions at one level as we are the masters of our own destiny at quite another. Fundamentally we can only overcome force through freedom- not force through force- and we need to be clear about precisely what this means. The Abolitionist Bill introduced into British Parliament in 1833 was not the result of certain ineluctable forces but rather the perseverance of a band of committed men such as William Wilberforce and Thomas Clarkson.

Neither would we accept that there is any valid distinction between the legality and the propriety of slavery based on a distinction between the morally superior and the morally equal. There are those who would argue that not only can the physical and moral be compared in respect to their relative strength, they can also be contrasted in respect to their relative worth. In the case of the latter, a 'just' or 'natural' form of slavery occurs when the master is morally superior and the slave is physically superior, much in the way that the farmer is superior to the ox. An 'unjust' or perverse form of slavery occurs when the master is physically superior and the slave is morally superior, as when a barbarous people such as the Macedonians conquer a civilized people such as the Greeks. Where, however, physical prowess is supported by moral superiority, then what this proves is that even in times of war what is legal may also be what is just. Thus, if the Greeks were to conquer the Macedonians not just because they happened to be wiser but also stronger, it would not be surprising if they were also less harsh in the manner they treated their captives.

The only problem here is that if there is some doubt about unlimited force as a means, then this applies no less to the question of unlimited servitude as an end. Whilst it is true that there are some who would argue that force is 'just' (in keeping with the law) and others that it is 'unjust' (in contravention of the law), this is no less so in the case of enslavement, for on the one hand we have the argument that all men should be treated equally, and on the other, that some men *may* be treated unequally. In the *Politics* Aristotle argues . . .

> . . . it is according to nature that even the art of war . . . should in a sense be a way of acquiring property; and that it must be used against wild beasts and against such men as are by nature intended to be ruled over but refuse; for that is the kind of warfare that is by nature just. (Politics Book I viii 1256b20-25)

But this is to make a means into an end and an end in to a means— it no more proves that there is 'justice' in the taming of obduracy than that there is 'justice' in the taming of wild beasts.

So far as it concerns the alleged 'naturalness' of being ruled in some fixed or permanent way, this may be true in some instances, as in the relation between child and parent or patient and nurse, but that is only for as long as a patient remains a patient or a child remains a child. There is no evidence of any formal or strict distinction between truly 'rational' and what could be termed more 'passionate' natures. To act foolishly, to act intemperately, may to some degree be to act without reason, but that does not mean to act without a will, or be incapable of directing one's will towards some end that is proper and just. There is no such thing as a man who is entirely lacking in reason or entirely lacking in passion, only the extremes of ruthlessness on the one hand and tenderheartedness on the other. To be cruel to a snake may not be to be cruel to any prey but it may be to any offspring. To be cruel to a golf stick may not be to be cruel to any opponent but it may be to any improvement. To admonish a child may not be cruel to any future ambitions but it may be to any incipient sloth. It all depends on whether we are acting out of fear, frustration or love. The fact that we are fussy about our pets, about our clothes, about our cars, proves that there is no arbitrary point at which we become indifferent towards these things, or regard them as any the less worthy of our care and respect. Therefore, to describe a slave as merely a body without a soul or a chassis without an engine, is a little like defining a river as any stretch of water no longer than the Thames and no wider than the Nile.

Or if it is argued that there is such a thing as an *interest* that is common to both a master and a slave, then we need to address this in terms of other couplings that imply a certain rule, as for instance, between parent and child or teacher and pupil. The slave, it might be argued, is a kind of 'living tool', a piece of property that serves the ends of a master but is capable of using other tools as well. Hence, the role of a slave is that of an agent not that of a producer—the tasks of the field are done by horses and ploughs, the tasks of the household are done by servants and their overseers. It remains a moot point however, how far a slave might have respect for its master just as a master has affection for its slave, to what extent there may be true loyalty and not merely trepidation at the prospect of any blunder or slip. Quite clearly, if there is no basis for comparing the virility of the stronger with the infirmity of the weaker then neither is there for comparing the welfare of the vassal with the welfare of the liege—the one is simply strength by stealth, the other, impotence or a lack of due regard for self. Neither should sympathy or consideration for a 'living tool' be used to justify ill treatment or indifference towards a 'dumb tool'—as if the latter were merely a plaything in the hands of either a master or a slave. A slave, it might be argued, is someone who lacks reason but is capable of striving for it, and so, someone who may benefit from the wisdom or instruction of his betters. An animal, on the other hand, is entirely at the mercy of its instincts and its fears; it cannot foresee or plan for any contingencies just as they might arise. Hence in some sense it must also be regarded as a 'useful' tool, only in this instance for the role that it plays in production, not for the sake of any more gentlemanly pursuits. But again, there is no settled rule as to how any such relationship may be viewed—fundamentally, there is a vast difference if this proceeds from the instinct to be caring or the instinct to be cruel. Just as a human who is free may sometimes be enslaved by his fears or his beliefs, so an animal in captivity may sometimes find relief through the timeliness and not the tardiness of its death.

Chapter 18

On Representative Government

As we saw earlier, one of the problems with majority rule is that it is not altogether clear who is to rule and who is to be ruled, that although it might be suggestive of a certain self-rule all this really does is give a license to the mob, that is, not rule by reason but rule by passion. A particular artifice for overcoming this could be called 'distributive justice in reverse', that is, that by starting with a ratio such as 10:1, then 1000 men could be reduced to 100 or 100 men could be reduced to 10, thereby in some sense converting a majority into a minority. Oddly enough, what we mean by a *representative* government is a relatively new phenomenon. Traditionally this may have had something to do with the way that power sharing was construed, since from a certain perspective majority rule was not only contrasted but also compared with rule by the few, as also was rule by the virtuous with rule by the wicked. In the Athenian model equal weight had to be given to things such as property, birth, and numerical strength, which tended to obscure the prospect of anything else, since it would be pointless if there was only a representation of the rich or a representation of the poor. Rousseau was trenchantly opposed to the idea, since although the popular will could express itself as either a unity or a multiplicity in no way could a minority be made to stand in for the majority, or at least, not where the legislative was concerned. Pioneers of modern democracy such as Locke and Montesquieu were certainly well aware of it, but it was not until John Stuart Mill that it was given a fuller and more detailed explication.

Although we have already treated of the relation between democracy and anarchy, let us restate some of the objections that could raised to majority rule, beginning with the direct and continuous participation of all citizens in the affairs of the state. In the Athenian model, a relevant distinction was drawn between the equal distribution of power on the one hand and the unequal distribution of talent on the other, that is, that since some men were equal in some respects but unequal in others, what they were due depended largely on what contribution they could or were willing to make. Effectively, what this meant is that the basis for political power stemmed from attributes that were either inclusive (i.e. freedom) or attributes that were exclusive (i.e. birth, status, wealth). In these terms, it is not difficult to see why democracy became synonymous with a system in which offices were determined by lot, and equality consisted in 'ruling and being ruled in turn'.

This was also relevant in a certain historical sense, since the ratio between what was given and what was owing concerned the contribution of different *groups* within society, leaving aside the differences between the individuals who made up these groups. Democracy was thought to supply one thing, freedom, aristocracy another, virtue, and oligarchy another, wealth. It thus focused on the question which class deserved the highest honours, since justice for the individual concerned only what was equal and not commensurate in its kind. Such a view persisted throughout the Middle Ages, as did distinctions based on wealth, privilege and status. From a modern perspective however, the real issue is not whether there is an equal or unequal distribution of power as where the line should be drawn between private liberty and the *demands* of the state. In a more frenetic and complex world individuals are not so willing to involve themselves in public affairs if they have no bearing on their own welfare (otherwise than to complain), and so, their participation in the political process will be minimal compared to other and more pressing concerns. In particular this is certainly the case with 'choice by lot', since it tends to be confined to things such as military conscription and jury service—in other words, be somewhat disinclined to undertake. Not only that, but with the advent of mass communication everyone has the opportunity to scrutinize the workings of parliament, to engage in public debate, to voice their opinions through the media, the Internet and the press.

Another objection is that what we mean by democracy should not so much be government by the people as government *for* the people, that is, that government should be something of *benefit* to all its members, not just the right it affords them to be the masters in their own affairs. This is linked to the idea that what is composite or multiform must also be cacophonous, whereas what is uniform or frictionless must also be harmonious. Quite clearly, majority rule cannot obviate the fact that in any division the greater part will always be favoured even if this is not true of the undivided whole (Consider a country such as Ireland where a religious majority in Ulster is not what constitutes a majority overall.) In another respect, it also concerns the question whether any sampling of a community reflects what is true of that community as a whole. If the members of parliament are less than any constituency, and any constituency is less than any electorate, then it is a moot point whether any majority within the parliament does in fact reflect what the majority supports. Nor, on the other hand, does it do anything to overcome the existence of entrenched majorities, since in these terms a person may be badly treated simply because he is Jewish, black, or poor. Hence, there is a clear conflict between individual rights and collective agreements, or individual agreements and collective rights. In order thus to make order out of chaos or justice out of inequity we must admit a standard of good which is different from the good of individuals, a 'common good' which overrides all such disparate and uncoordinated ends. In the famous formula of Rousseau, a common good is not something to be gleaned from an assemblage or amalgam of wills but only something that can be abstracted from a range of interests—that is, something that assumes both a point of agreement and a point of divergence.

A further question is whether a majority decision is necessarily the best decision given such criteria as might fairly be applied. In the case of the jury system, it would certainly be better if we could obtain a solid majority rather than a flat majority, and that is because we are more concerned with the strictures of justice than obtaining a barely tolerable result. However, so far as it concerns the difference between the greater of two goods or the lesser of two evils, then this may rest on nothing more than our particular point of view. Whether it concerns the choice of brevity over prolixity, thriftiness over extravagance, or gluttony over abstinence; all that is requisite may be a simple preference given the situation in which we happen to find ourselves.

But what if the idea of a 'greater good' and a 'lesser evil' could be combined or there was a coupling of their respective means, would we then be just as satisfied in obtaining a simple majority? For instance, let us consider the result of a plebiscite over some pressing issue in which 45 per cent of the population chose option A, 40 per cent chose option B, and 15 per cent chose option C. If as it so happened all those who chose C preferred B to A, then that would raise the support for B to 55 per cent, giving it an absolute majority (leaving aside the question how the other preferences might also be distributed). In these terms, an absolute majority would be the 'greater of two goods' in the sense of what was better than a bare majority, and a second preference would be the 'lesser of two evils' in the sense of what was better than the option most disliked.

To pursue our enquiries, let us consider what we mean by the delegation of power against the backdrop of: (a) a choice by lot; (b) a choice by election, and; (c) a choice by merit. What we mean by a choice by lot is any kind of arbitrary distribution of tasks, either choosing in a purely indiscriminate way or rotating the roles of individuals so that each receives an equal share. So far as it concerns a choice by election then what we mean is any kind of assignment taken as an expression of will, although of course, to a smaller number of persons than those who are actually doing the assigning. In respect to a choice by merit, what we mean is the acquisition of any position or station through skill and not luck, through ability and not birth, through a demonstration of one's readiness and aptitude for the task that lies at hand. As for the meaning of delegation, we need to be clear about the difference between delegation and affiliation. An affiliate is someone who associates as a subordinate or underling, as might also be said of an affiliate church or an affiliate business. A delegate on the other hand is someone who acts on behalf of another, and where the implication is that he is an ambassador for that person, as the conveyor of a petition or a request. We can think of this more concretely perhaps as the delegate for a body of ratepayers, the delegate for a body of sportsmen, or the delegate for a body of workers. What we are implying therefore is that there will be both representation *to* someone and representation *through* someone, but not necessarily, what is representative in and of itself.

The question this then raises is why someone such as Rousseau although trenchantly opposed to deputies is nonetheless quite favourable to aristocracies. The answer lies in the way he conceives of the different instruments of power, and how these may be divided in one way and yet combined in quite another. Since the government is an intermediary between the sovereign and the state, it draws partly on the influence of the former and partly on the influence of the latter. Effectively, what this means is that in its corporate guise it may also engage with the sovereign, but that in its composite guise it may also engage with the state. In the first instance, what we mean by the prince is also what we mean by the ruler (tyranny), in the second instance what we mean by the prince is also what we mean by the people (anarchy). However, given the basic difference between the sovereign as a body that makes the laws and the people as a body that obeys them, the functionaries who administer the laws must always be selected from the latter, and be beholden to it as its instrument but not its end. A magistrate therefore can never act on his own behalf or against the wishes of the community, nor can the interests of the criminal ever be aligned with the interests of the state. Quite clearly what Rousseau is proposing is that the people should elect their magistrates rather than have them appointed, and hence that this could be more on account of their connections rather than their aptitude or skill.

From our own perspective, there are two major objections to this: firstly, it supposes the administration of law to serve no further end than the will of the people; and secondly, it supposes the government to be a corporate and not just a composite whole. In respect to the first of these, although we would agree a magistrate or an official is not someone who should be swayed by bias, it does not mean a certain weight should not be given to his experience or his skill. A magistrate is not someone who acts simply in the place of the state, or in the place of the people, he is someone able to exercise discretion and proffer advice when it is proper he should do so. In respect to the second, if the government can be conceived of as having a corporate will just as the sovereign does a general will, then this raises the prospect the individual may be stripped of his identity, since he cannot serve both the interests of the government and the interests of the sovereign. It probably seems odd that Rousseau would not countenance a coupling of choice by election and choice by merit—that if we are going to elect a person, why should we not also be cognizant of any expertise he might be able to bring to the role? Especially where it concerns the legal establishment, we would probably prefer to leave to an expert what is within the domain of an expert, and not embroil ourselves in matters we do not really understand.

In respect to an earlier discussion about equality of treatment (Ch.6) we approached this from the viewpoint of what it means to be endowed with certain indispensable rights. Now let us approach this in terms of what it means to be equally gifted on the one hand or equally industrious on the other. Where it concerns the former, then what we mean are such things as strength and intelligence; where it concerns the latter then what we mean are such things as merit and desert. In particular, merit and desert have a bearing on distributive justice, that is, when a person acquires status as the result of any labours he may have wrought. Aristotle handles this by suggesting that power should be distributed according to the capacity that different groups have to advance their competing claims. But then the question remains: What constitutes merit and desert as distinct from what is naturally or inherently unequal, and what constitutes use or convenience as distinct from what is naturally or inherently equal? In respect to the second part of this, then the answer must surely be those *relationships* that are unequal, or where one person owes fealty or allegiance to another. Parents and offspring are not equal, masters and servants are not equal, teachers and pupils are not equal. The role of elders is to discipline and to instruct, the role of juveniles is to listen and to learn. In respect to the first part of this question, the answer must surely be in terms of any sectional interest that is equally applicable, in a democracy the value of being free, in an oligarchy the value of being rich, in an aristocracy the value of being virtuous. (Aristotle in his classification of governments does not here attend to the more restrictive sense of 'desert' as we would ordinarily understand it, that is, what is acquired and not innate)

Tracing the ideas of Aristotle and Rousseau back to their roots, then it is clear that what we are dealing with is an *organic* or *apriori* conception of society. For just as a muscle develops to become more supple so does the state develop to become more cohesive, only not by incorporating what is expedient but rather by incorporating what is wise. We might, however, take a somewhat different approach to this by suggesting that civil society is the result of a mere artifice, or that it may be possible to reverse the 'natural' order of things by fusing disparate means to produce harmonious ends. And in terms of what we mean by 'representative government', this is exactly what we are doing, introducing such a device when the need or necessity for it outstrips its faults. Particular wills are the expression of a general will but in a very different sense from what is arbitrary or indifferent, that is, in the sense in which a single will is normalized by incorporating the idea of a multiplicity of wills. In the particular form of government that we call 'representative', the wills of a number of individuals are compressed into the will of a single individual, but not by being made conformable to it, rather in the way this will is taken to be the expression of their *broadly* consentient views.

Let us pursue this in terms of what we mean by representation quite specifically in the context of a particular *system* of government. In the account that Hobbes gives of a monarchical government, he argues that in order for men to be freed from the vagaries of nature, it is necessary that they appoint one person to act on their behalf, and that for his sake, they must relinquish all their rights. In the account that we have given, if we take not one representative, but rather some body of representatives (e.g. Parliament or Congress etc.) then there is a curious parallel between what is singular, as what is incorporated within a multiplicity of wills, and a multiplicity of wills, as what is incorporated within a singular will. On the other hand, so far as there is a seeming point of agreement in one respect there is a more obvious point of divergence in another. Since Hobbes argues that the sovereign is in no way beholden to his subjects, this not only runs counter to any kind of compromise but any kind of limitation on his unrestricted power as well. Montesquieu in his wisdom thus divides government into three species, the republican, the monarchic, and the autocratic, where the implication is that a constitution is something that connects a democracy with an aristocracy but divides a monarchy from an autocracy.

Of course, in the way that we say something is representative we are not necessarily saying that it is also *representational*, rather, we are using it in a broader and more figurative sense. For instance, in the way that Rawls speaks of a representative man, what he means is someone who represents a particular office or social rung. Or, in the way that Leibniz speaks of the relation between whole and part, what he means is that it is the latter which symbolizes or exemplifies the former from a particular point of view. In neither case, however, does this capture the true sense of what we mean by 'representative government', but then again neither does it altogether eschew the sense this might convey. There are those who would argue that a representative is someone who should embody a particular set of characteristics, that is, the aims and purposes of whoever or whatever they represent. At an associational level, we might consider this in terms of the relation between a broadcasting company and any delegate seeking sponsorships or advertising, between the Chamber of Commerce and any spokesperson articulating the views of the business sector, between the Church and any ordained minister servicing the needs of his parishioners.

The question remains however: Is representation at the level of an association also what we mean by representation in the case of the state? There are those who would argue that fairness in a political system can never be achieved unless all people are *equally* represented, and that this is impossible if certain sectors or minorities are pushed to one side. What we mean by 'government by the people' should ideally therefore be a representative cross-section of the population as a whole. Another claim is that if there is any link between a representative and that sector or group he represents then this should not only be mental but also emotional, that there is a difference between the capacity to empathize with another through imagination, and first-hand knowledge of just exactly what he is going through. Thus 'to represent' in Leibnizian terms should not be to identify with another quite generally but in some more determinate way. However, to stipulate in what way two interests are the same, may not be to indicate on what grounds they are also *laudable,* or at least, guarantee good government rather than corruption on the part of all those concerned. We would surely not say that a gangster was a fit person to represent a precinct simply because it was run by the mafia, any more than we would, that a Jew or a Protestant was the only person capable of representing a largely Jewish or Protestant community. The effect of this may not be to overcome a sense of alienation through a certain 'fellow feeling', rather, galvanize these forces and give them undue weight in comparison to others more worthy of our support.

There is also a considerable difference between acting in the public interest and acting in the interest of some specific coterie or group. There are those who would argue that there is no such thing as the 'public interest', and that this is simply a subterfuge for narrow and self-interested aims, but we must be careful to distinguish between representation when this pertains to equality of treatment, and representation when this pertains to majority rule. No doubt, there are many cases where various groups within society have been ostracized or outlawed, but that is not to say the role of government is to bring them into the fold, or act as an arbitrator in every dispute that may arise. The government is a powerful entity with vast resources and an iron resolve, and this usually ensures any consensus will be skewed towards its ends. Yet even if we do not accede to the notion of a disinterested pursuit of public good, we must admit that governments can and certainly do act in the general interest, especially where it concerns matters such as defence, environmental degradation, and acting on the effects of climate change.

If therefore we cannot accede to this idea that there must be a 'common characteristic' for both the rulers and the ruled, what, would we say, is the proper function of any duly elected person or duly elected elite? Let us take a brief sojourn back to the Greeks. Towards the end of the *Meno,* Plato embarks on a discussion about the relation between virtue and knowledge. He firstly observes that knowledge and virtue are the sorts of things that tend towards our good or enhance our sense of what we mean by the good. Yet the question remains: How do we know if it is the same or a different kind of good we are dealing with? For instance, let us consider some of the things we might regard as being useful, such things as beauty, strength, and wealth. To be useful in these terms does not mean to be unconditionally good, since beauty may be used to demean the ugly, strength may be used to destroy the frail, and wealth may be used to dispossess the poor. What we take to be good must thus include some *relevant* use, not simply what it means to be useful in itself. In the same way, moral qualities such as courage, justice, and nobility must be exercised with due moderation, otherwise they will degenerate into forms either too lax or too severe. This is also true of what it means to instruct or instill a particular skill, since to teach someone the art of citizenship is very different from what it means to teach someone the art of stealing. Yet, even if we do not admit that what is taught must also be what is good, or at least be *always* what is good, that does not mean there is not a kind of wisdom which informs us in one sense, and a kind of folly that blinds us in quite another. Virtue, thus, may well be a kind of wisdom but it is also a cautionary kind of thing, like revising our plans or decisions when our 'better judgement' tells us that we should. In much the same way, what we mean by the political art is neither something that is inborn nor something that is taught; rather it is a certain aptitude that we practice and rehearse as the course of our lives unfold. Some things that we acquire are also things we are taught, but the skill of a politician is not like the skill of a mason or the skill of a potter; there is no graduate school for politicians, no entitlement as there is for the amassment of wealth. A politician is someone who possesses common sense and nous, a certain perceptiveness and skill, but that is not something he is owing his equals, rather it is something that sets him apart.

However, in an age of constant media exposure, we may also need to consider this against the backdrop of certain pressures that are brought to bear, both from within and from without. In respect to the former, so far as a person is a member of some political party then he is also bound by its rules, as he is by the kind of ideology that underlies any policy or agenda reform. In saying that, it should not be assumed that the elected party has received unqualified support for every policy it may seek to bring about (the so-called 'mandate' theory), rather, that their policies have been deemed preferable to any others that have been proposed. In respect to the question of a certain outward pressure, we need to address this from the viewpoint of what it is taxing and not merely convenient for any politician to undertake. In some respects, it may be useful for one person to 'stand in for' or 'represent' the will of the many, but just as a doctor does not minister to the healthy, neither should a politician be someone who panders to certain interests if they have already been met. A vote winner should not overstep the mark by trying to be 'all things to all men', but neither should he ignore the appeals of his opponents and heed only those of his supporters and friends. What we mean by being 'disinterested' is giving voice to a range of grievances and concerns that are nascent, or that without support, might otherwise never see the light of day.

In respect to the claim that a representative is someone who should do no more and no less than address the concerns of his constituents (just as a lawyer might the interests of a client) this is open to the objection that it is not clear in what any 'consentient' interest might be said to consist. That is, it is not entirely clear how we might arrive at any true consensus of interests or how the wisdom of a politician might be weighed against the wisdom of the mob. Of course, it is true that politicians should always be sensitive to a shift in the public mood, but there is a considerable difference between acting shrewdly or decisively, and responding to the wishes of those who are neither better motivated nor better informed about the issues that are at stake. In most federalist systems there is clear recognition that representatives must work not in isolation but rather as a group; that they are tied not only to the needs of their constituency but to the nation as a whole. Thus, what it means to 'stand in' for something could be taken in both a partial or local sense, and a global or more pervasive sense. As to those who would argue (e.g. Thomas Paine) that a rotational system is necessary when there is any ascension to power, this is a little like saying that we should hand the treasury to a spendthrift or entrust our children to those with base and immoral desires. To grant an equal right does not mean that there are no rights for the able, to choose by lot does not mean to act by default, to check unbridled power does not mean there are not some who are more adept at using it. The point is, no matter what our style or form of government we cannot do without good leaders and good institutions, and we cannot create this condition unless we are willing to cede power to those who are best able to deploy it and for the enrichment of all.

Chapter 19

The Spirit of Democracy

To begin with, let us consider the difference between public and private interest as this might exhibit itself in the case of: (a) a monarchy; (b) an aristocracy; and (c) a democracy. In the case of a monarchy, what we mean by the making and revoking of law resides in a single person, and so, there cannot be any conflict between his interest and the interest of any other. In this case, the person who has the power to command also has the right to command, and so, he cannot be conscious of any interest that is opposed or not in keeping with his own. However, this may not be the case if there any pre-established rules—it depends on how effectively the sovereign's power might be stymied or curtailed. In the case of an aristocracy, it is still a single body we are dealing with, but this must also be tempered by considerations of a just distribution of power. That is, inequality and the consequent strife may ensue if there is not a rein on self-love, or if equal status is not accorded each of the parts that make it up. Even if it is the people and not the nobility who are under the yoke, the ruling body must exercise a degree of self—control, otherwise order would descend into chaos and sobriety would descend into drunkenness. Inequalities are most prevalent when there is an inequality of wealth, as for instance, when wealth is hereditary, or when simmering rivalries become an open wound and different families attempt to outdo one another. In the case of a democracy, legal enactments are no longer tied to self-aggrandizement but self-respect, or at least a greater respect for the law and that end it is meant to subjoin. In these terms, there is a much clearer awareness of what is for the common good and not merely for the sake of private gain.

However, to consider this in a little more detail what exactly do we mean by the 'common good' or the 'public interest'? The notion of a public as distinct from a private interest would seem to echo the difference between a real and an apparent interest, or at least what a person *deems* to be in his best interest and what is 'truly' in his best interest. However, although we may begin with the idea of a true or genuine interest, what this means in its public acceptation is very much a matter for debate. In the case of Rousseau, the common good is not simply an amalgam of interests, but rather some essential part or what is distinctive in itself. It is not the sum of the interests but the sum of the differences that needs to be reckoned with in the final account. On the other hand, in the case of Mill, the argument is more along the lines that the interest of the individual should be subordinate to the interest of the group, and that what really matters is the quantity, not how it is distributed or divided. But if the former is somewhat questionable in terms of what it postulates as an end, then the latter is no less so, since it seems to reify the interests of groups and treat them as if they were wholes.

In *Considerations on Representative Government*, (Part VI) Mill makes the general observation that in monarchies and aristocracies, individual interests may be opposed to more benevolent concerns, that unreasonable systems of taxation may be imposed, that the ruling elite may exercise its authority despotically, that it may covet and claim undue privileges. He then goes on to suggest that this may be no less so in the case of democracies, that the ruling power may be in the hands of purely sectional interests, and that this undermines an impartial regard for the good of all. Even if there is lip service to principles such as equal opportunity or love of one's country, narrower and more deep-seated interests will always prevail. Thus, what could be said of any ruling or tyrannical elite could be said no less of any ruling or tyrannical class.

The trouble with this is that although it may well be possible to identify certain divisions within society it is not nearly so clear why this implies any divisiveness as well. Mill cites the gulf between Catholics and Protestants, Negroes and whites, the skilled and the unskilled. But the question remains: What constitutes a particular class as distinct from a particular interest, and how can they be connected in the way that Mill would have us believe? Why is it that Protestants and Catholics cannot live side by side, that negroes and whites cannot live side by side, that workers and employers cannot live side by side? Moreover, even if they don't live peaceably side by side, what has this to do with any form of government? The treatment of blacks during the 1950s and 1960s in the southern states of America could well be described as a 'tyranny of the majority' but might this not equally be said of the treatment of Jews during the Nazi era, even if a great deal more extreme? Yet according to Mill's logic, it seems this could only be said of the former, since the Nazi regime was not a democratic government. We are not so much concerned with the 'silent minority' or the complacent majority as we are with discrimination and oppression as a tool of the majority. It may be true that in Islamic countries it is the Christians who are mistreated, and in Christian countries the Muslims who are mistreated, but that may be on account of certain cultural differences, not any kind of authority or rule. As to the claim that a rising class of workers may be able to limit competition in the marketplace, or impose taxes on the rich, or bring about a levelling of wages, then again, it is not altogether clear how this might be attained. Perhaps the same could be said of the Athenian model of democracy, but the fact is, wherever there is a laissez faire economy this will always be in favour of the rich.

It may be one thing to suggest that a person will be more sensible of his immediate interests than he will be of those more remote; but it is an altogether different matter if you are going to say that class interests which just happen to be in the majority will always outstrip class interests which just happen to be in the minority. It is merely an assumption that the majority interest represents a different interest than what is in the interests of all, since the fabric we weave may involve a disaffected majority just as much as it does a disaffected minority. In the case that we cited in an earlier chapter, Gandhi's reason for preferring a system of proportional representation was because of the confict that existed between various groups; and that is different from the logic that says every minority should be treated as an end in itself. This also touches on something we have already discussed, whether the best system of government should be not only representative but *representational* as well. Based on this premise we then have the idea of a proportional system of voting, that minorities have just as much a right to the expression of their views as do those with greater numbers on their side. Various schemes have been touted for ensuring that minorities are given an equal say, as perhaps, that there should be at least three candidates for every seat, or that a person be given three votes split in any way that he might choose. There is even the quite fantastic idea that the number of voters should be divided by the number of seats, and that a person may vote for someone within his own constituency or the nation as a whole. (The implication here is that preferences will be necessary to achieve a certain threshold)

To pursue our enquiries, let us again address the question whether a majority interest can be tyrannical in the way that a minority interest can be self-serving. For instance, if within the general community there were a majority of Catholics, and among the Freemasons, a majority of bankers, does that mean that it is the Catholics who rule the religious community and the bankers who rule the Freemasons? In the same way, even if society were divided into plebeians and noblemen, does it follow that the wealthy must always be dismissive of the poor, or that the many must always be mistrustful of the privileged? Furthermore, how does this help us address the real meaning of majority rule? Let us undertake the following thought experiment beginning with the different ratios: (a) 1:10; (b) 3:10; (c) 7:10; and (d) 9:10. Quite clearly, the first of these will be a mirror image of the last, since if we begin with the median point then two will be the difference between three and seven, and four will be the difference between one and nine. Thus, in purely hypothetical terms let us call these the governments that constitute (a) a monocracy, (b) an aristocracy, (c) a democracy and (d) an omniocracy. What this also implies is that if a minority (3:10) is reflective of a majority (7:10), then an omniocracy (9:10) must also be reflective of a monocracy (1:10).

Now let us address this in terms of: (a) a comparison of active and inactive parts; and (b) a comparison of positive and negative outcomes in relation to whatever proposal might be put to the vote. In the way that different thinkers have treated of the forms of government (e.g. Hobbes, Rousseau) it is common practice to define monarchy as rule by a single person, aristocracy as rule by an elite and democracy as rule by the many. This suggests that what we are dealing with is a condition in which there is one active and many inactive parts, some active and some inactive parts, or many active and few inactive parts. In the case of the latter, however, we might adopt a slightly different approach by suggesting there are complementary pairings as well as conflicting ends. In other words, if we have nine parts and two are paired (i.e. one positive and one negative) then we have a substantial majority, and if we have eleven parts and ten are paired (i.e. five positive and five negative) then we have bare majority. Let us call this the principle of diminishing returns.

However, if our assumption is that we can arrive at the idea of democracy through different and yet not incompatible means, then this is not what we have succeeded in doing at all. To begin with, although it is true that an omniocracy may well be compared to a democracy so far as it concerns the strength of any opinion, there is no guarantee that what we arrive at will always satisfy at least a minimal set of requirements. That is, it does not guarantee a result in the case of an even number of voters, since the voting may also be deadlocked. (This is underscored by the fact that for an even number of voters the remainder must always be +2.) Looked at in the other way: Suppose we have a body that comprises four active parts ABCD and six inactive parts EFGHIJ, or six active parts and four inactive ones. In the first case, what we have could be termed an aristocracy; in the second case, what we have could be termed a democracy. The question is: Does this also constitute the basis for minority and majority rule? In other words, by an aristocracy do we mean a system in which there are more inactive rather than active parts, just as in a democracy there are more active rather than inactive ones?

It appears upon a closer analysis that it does not, or at least, that we also need to distinguish between the parts as they are in themselves and the parts as they are in relation to any whole. Perhaps we can illustrate this point in the following way. In the case of a body of persons as has just been cited, let us suppose we were to halve the number of parts, so that we have AB as one composite and EFG as another. Now the body of persons AB as a ruling minority would not change in respect to the size of the whole, since two persons could just as well rule a body of three as it could six (although perhaps less effectively). However, in respect to a certain majority what would you say about this, that there was or was not any change in the meaning of majority rule? In a certain sense no, since both constitute a bare majority, although more strictly in the case of the second when we have +1 as our remainder. Let us now suppose we were to double the number of parts by incorporating the body KLMNOPQRST, adding KLMN to ABCD and OPQRST to EFGHIJ. In respect to a certain majority, what would you now say about this, that there was or was not any change in the meaning of majority rule? Since in the first instance we have described EFGHIJ as the active members, so in the second instance let us describe EFGHIJOPQRST as the active members. The question is; Is this a *necessary* condition for majority rule? It seems that it is not, since the bare majority here is eleven not twelve, and so, which member should we exclude if we have more than we require? The three parts EFG that were indispensable when we halved our original number, have now become superfluous once we double our original number (or at least one of them has). The majority in the sense of a floating conglomerate must thus be viewed quite differently from a minority in the sense of a fixed or determinate ratio (in this case 2:3).

Now let us review what we have previously said about the relation between whole and part. In the case of a country such as Ireland what we mean by the majority in one respect is not what we mean by the majority in another. Thus, if we take the six counties of Northern Ireland, then it is the Protestants who will be in the ascendancy, but if we take the entire country, then it is the Catholics who will be in the ascendancy. In this instance, what we mean by an alienated minority will vary depending on how we construe the relation between all or only some of the parts. However, in the case of a representative body such as Congress or Parliament, there is a difference if we say the whole is *composed* of all its parts and that the parts are *representative* of the whole, that is, that they mirror it in this respect or that. As we saw in a previous chapter, it could be argued that the majority of a majority (i.e. the majority of representatives drawn from a majority of districts) is not really a majority at all, and that there is no guarantee their views will 'reflect' the views of the constituency as a whole. On the other hand, what this *assumes* is that a common interest can really only be a single interest, and that it is a single or block interest which links the representative to those who have vested him with power. In thinking of a representative body this way, we are doing so as Leibniz might, that is, by regarding a part as in some sense symbolic of the whole. But in what sense does Parliament really typify society as a whole? Apart from everything else, this vastly underestimates the intelligence of the 'average' voter, or suggests that what he identifies with may be something of an understandable but nonetheless quite superficial kind. That is, that a Catholic will vote for a candidate simply because he is Catholic, a Jew will vote for a candidate simply because he is Jewish, a wharfie will vote for a candidate simply because he is a Trade Unionist etc. A person of average intelligence is not someone who simply supports a colour divide or a religious faith; rather, he is someone who judges each issue on its merits and draws the relevant conclusions accordingly.

Let us address in more detail the meaning of a 'common' as opposed to purely singular interest. In terms of a difference in policy or viewpoint, then what it is that divides two candidates must also be what it is that divides any constituency of voters. For instance, let us say that one candidate is in favour of euthanasia and another candidate is opposed to euthanasia. How then might this be relevant as an issue and how might it contribute to any debate? For every policy that a candidate puts forward, and for every position that a candidate adopts, let us say that there are three possibilities: (a) that it will elicit a strong response; (b) that it will elicit a weak but nonetheless discernible response; and (c) that it will elicit no response. And that in keeping with this there will be two broad categories: (a) those who are in favour or opposed; and (b) those who are indifferent or undecided. If further we deduct the number of irresolute voters from the number of committed voters, then this will leave us with a body that is either strongly in favour or opposed, or mildly in favour or opposed. When, therefore, we sum these strong and weak alliances as they pertain to different policies or platforms, this will constitute a critical threshold for the way we may arrive at any outcome.

This also raises questions about the ability of citizens to 'see the bigger picture', not to be tied to their immediate welfare but to be mindful of the greater good. Let us approach this from the viewpoint of what we mean by a rational as opposed to appetitive desire. There are two ways a person's fortune may be connected with his moral state, and that is: (a) when it supports the idea of what is *just*; or (b) when it supports the idea of what is *good*. In the case of the former, what we mean by virtue consists in being impervious to fortune; in the case of the latter, what we mean by virtue consists in making a proper use of the same. From our own perspective, the real crux of the matter is how we connect utility and freedom, since there is a difference if we say that a person should be happy in the face of good fortune and that he should be tenacious in the face of adversity. However, in a more relevant setting, let us consider this in terms of the different approach that may be taken to the question of good citizenship. In his work on representative government, Mill makes the general observation that

> . . . on average, a person who cares for other people,
> for his country, or for mankind, is a happier man than

one who does not; but of what use is it to preach this doctrine to a man who cares for nothing but his own ease, or his own pocket?

> (*Considerations on Representative Government*
> Part VI Infirmities and Dangers)

On the other hand, compare this rather casual regard for exalted principles with the observation of Montesquieu

> . . . in moderate governments, the love of one's country, shame, and the fear of blame are restraining motives, capable of preventing a multitude of crimes. Here the greatest punishment of a bad action is conviction.'

> (*The Spirit of Laws* Vol.1 Book VI
> Of The Severity of Punishments).

And which of these would we prefer? Quite clearly the latter, since this affords a better glimpse of what it means to be a *responsible* member of the State.

Or let us address this in terms of the distinction between positive and negative freedom, as outlined by Berlin in his classic essay 'Two Concepts of Liberty'[1] The kind of virtue we might connect with negative freedom is one that pertains to the idea of a 'self-regarding' duty. In other words, the aim of virtue is to achieve a well-founded rather than faulty sense of what it means to act for one's own good. However, the important point is that a person is *equally free* whether he pursues his good as a rational end or he pursues his good as an appetitive end. A right therefore is simply the power that one has to do or to forbear, and a duty, not what a person denies of himself, but what he hopes to achieve in the timely way that he acts. The kind of virtue, on the other hand, we connect with positive freedom is that of acting in accordance with reason and taking responsibility for any decisions that we make. So far as a person is prone to passion then he is also enslaved by his hopes and his fears—the aim of virtue therefore should be to direct him towards his 'better self', not allow him to fall prey to purely capricious and fleeting desires.

This treatment has led some writers to suppose that what we mean by positive and negative freedom are diametrically opposed, even though Berlin himself admits that this stems from the kind of arguments that only Plato or Hegel might adduce. Let us address this from the viewpoint of both liberalism and idealism. The way that a liberal argues might be as follows: (a) Since pleasure and pain can be compared quantitatively but not the latter qualitatively, there can be no qualitatively worse pleasures or qualitatively better pains that are in any way comparable, rather, only a diverging point for what is painful or pleasurable in itself. That is, although some pleasures may be nobler than others that does not mean there is a higher and a lower 'self', rather all pleasures should be sought no matter how trivial or mundane they may seem. (b) From the fact that some men have exceptional or superior talents, it does not follow they must also have privileges, or at least that is, a greater right to the allocation of societal good. In other words, one person's happiness can only complement the happiness of others; in no sense does it constitute an exclusive or restricted domain.

The way that an idealist (such as Rousseau) argues might be as follows: (a) In their natural or primordial condition men will always be subject to less pleasure than pain and hence to more injury than complaisance. Hence, the only way a person can safeguard his rights is to enter into a contract that serves the common good. (b) However, to the degree that there is alienation of any particular will then this must be twofold—in the first place, on the part of the agent, and in the second place on the part of the community, willing its own good and willing its own end. (c) Freedom therefore means acting in accordance with reason but not appetite or desire. And since there can be no true freedom unless there is regulation as well, what is requisite is an instrument or agency for the making of universal rules. This agency, which embodies the notion of a guaranteed right, is what we call the state.

In comparing these views our first reaction might be that they are as far apart as 'the starry sky and the deep blue sea', but perhaps this is somewhat deceptive. Berlin himself clearly supports the liberal mantra, he points to the 'monstrous impersonation' whereby the rational self although not real, is nonetheless 'revealed' at some momentous instant, more or less like Paul's conversion on the road to Damascus. However, similar doubts could be raised about liberalism, or at least one of its mainstays, utilitarianism, in line with what we have previously said. Although utilitarianism would appear to support the sovereignty of the individual and the claim that what we mean by a 'common interest' is only an aggregate of interests, what this also does in a roundabout way is abstract from individual being and posit a 'common identity' which is peculiar to no one. Since it does not support any meaningful distinction between quality and quantity, it is open to the objection that there can only be an 'average utility' and the kind of trade-offs that do nothing to prevent any basic inequalities, or the hardships felt by those less 'worthy' than the rest. Another question raised by this is what we mean by human nature, or at least, the sort of instincts and motives that govern every man. For some writers (e.g. Hobbes) the way they conceive of a state of nature makes it clear that what they mean by the individual is something inherently self-seeking. For other writers (e.g. Rousseau) the way they conceive of a state of nature makes it clear that what they mean by the individual is something much more complex in its makeup. It is not inconceivable therefore, that at the root of both idealism and liberalism is there not some lofty conception of man, but rather that great shibboleth called 'enlightened self-interest'.

As we have earlier seen, the notion of a public as distinct from a private good would appear to hinge on the difference between what is really in a person's interest and what is *seemingly* in a person's interest, assuming of course, that all auxiliary claims can be marched into line. This, however, is not only evident in the case of an idealist such as

Rousseau but also for someone such as Spinoza. In his broad political theory Spinoza argues that a person's right is also the capacity he has to do and to forbear, that it consists in just this power, and that what a man does he does according to the laws of his innermost being. And that does not simply mean to follow the laws of reason, since life teaches us it is no more within our compass to have a sound mind than it is to have a sound body, and so, there is just as much a 'right' to be directed by our passions as there is to be directed by our reason. In their everyday intercourse, there is a difference if one man is bound to another in respect to his body or bound to another in respect to his spirit. In the first case, this concerns the damage or violence that one person may visit upon another, in the second, it concerns the recompense that one person demands of another by virtue of any favours he might have performed. However, concerning the duty to be loyal this lasts only so long as there is the fear of reprisal, that is, so long as the level of danger remains the same. What men fear in a state of nature is just the result of fear itself, darkness and insecurity in the face of any looming opposition; what men fear in civil society is an even greater threat, the loss of peace and stability wrought by the agency of the state. To this end, all power should be vested in the multitude or those who have been chosen as the guardian of their rights. It also follows that the only way we can define evil is what threatens the common good, and in defiance of any duly promulgated laws. In a state of nature, on the other hand, there can be no such thing as wrongdoing, since men can do no otherwise than obey their instincts, and if these are faulty this can only be an injustice to themselves.

Now let us summarize this from the viewpoint of liberty on the one hand and empowerment on the other. Liberty and necessity are as one, just as right and power are as one, since the fundamental or overriding rule is that a person should persevere in his being and follow his instincts no matter where they may take him. Empowerment on the other hand alters the relation between reason and desire, by allowing the former to direct the latter rather than the latter to act of itself. The important thing about this, however, is that it is impossible to do wrong in a state of nature, and that just as we can match public and private good in one respect so we can match public and private ill in another. Or at least, that if there is a basis for distinguishing between public and private good, so also must there be between public wrong or wrong to another, and private wrong or wrong to oneself. It remains an open question, however, whether virtue should or should not include some element of proper restraint. In the present case it appears that for the sake of our own self-sufficiency, it may sometimes be necessary to perform acts we would not otherwise consider provident or wise.

And that is why there is a considerable difference in the kind of approach that Spinoza adopts, and the sort of course that we would recommend. In its discretionary power a government may choose to allow gambling if the indications are it is a problem for the few but not a problem for the many. In the case of drug taking, on the other hand, where there is a much clearer link between private and public harm, it may well be necessary to introduce a range of measures that are much more restrictive in their kind. Where it concerns idealism there may also be a point of divergence, since to say that government should check the tendency to act irrationally is not to commit oneself to the further claim that it should direct its members to the end of acting wisely. Or, that man is free so far as he obeys his own laws but that he can only attain perfection through and in conjunction with the state. One of the problems with the notion of a 'general will' or a 'categorical imperative' is that it seems to prescribe a particular morality that is universally binding, not by adhering to the spirit but simply the letter of the law. It is the mark of a truly tolerant society, however, that it permits associations such as the Jehovah's Witnesses, the Freemasons, the Amish, that is, associations that foster different ideals with the consent of all their members, no matter what suspicions may be lurking in the wider community.

Let us pursue this and along the following lines. It has been routinely argued by those of a liberal persuasion that the only grounds for punishment is the harm that one person inflicts on another, and that his own good is not a sufficient warrant for the prevention of any choices he might make. It could be said, for instance, that the state should never intervene to prevent a person from becoming drunk, since to do so could generate more harm than it was intended to combat. However, in this case it is not so much a question of weighing up the consequences, as it is the sort of means that may or could be duly applied. It might be possible to establish a range of measures to prevent all manner of ills, but the reason the state does not do so is that it is limited in those resources that are available. If a drunkard is brandishing a knife or making a public nuisance of himself then the police may well be called on, but it is not the same as if he is simply relaxing, half-seas over, in the sanctity of his kitchen or his living room. We also need to be clear about the difference between physical and moral harm when this is or is not accompanied by a natural or a legal *sanction*. Under certain circumstances, the state may be silent where it concerns the kind of activity that places a person in moral danger, but not where the danger issues in physical or pecuniary harm, as for instance, when gambling debts precipitate an act of embezzlement or pornography precipitates an act of abuse. Here, the state must intervene to protect its members, and quite specifically where there has been a violation of their rights, be they *in rem* or *in personem*. But that is not to say the state may not also have a more immediate concern for its members as in the case of drug taking, since if it can prevent the supply of drugs, does it not also have a moral obligation as well?

Thus, when the government passes legislation to support something such as equal opportunity for the disabled, or the expulsion of militant trade unions, we would not say that this detracts from the freedom of all its citizens, but rather enhances it instead. We would also say the same of any campaign that seeks to dissuade a person from anything that may be harmful to his health. (e.g. anti-vaccination). Some would call this paternalism; we would prefer to call it a kind of restrained benevolence. One of the problems with the catchword *utility* is that it may tell us what is more or less good and what is more or less bad, but not necessarily, what is qualitatively *better*. Where it concerns the question of a 'common good', we would hold this to be not just the question of a compounding but an *aligning* of interests as well. Certainly, it is better if we can produce more good than less, but that does not mean we should not pursue what is *essentially* good, or at least consider not just our physical but our moral development as well. Since we can discern no difference between public and private ill, it is perfectly reasonable that punishment will be inefficacious or unprofitable when it exceeds the magnitude of the crime. In this respect we are thinking of evil as a common store that may be added to or subtracted from; we are not thinking of any difference between the harm to the wrongdoer and the harm to the victim. Neither are we thinking of any difference between the harm to the victim and the harm to the self. That however is not the case where it concerns the relation between public and private good. Since we recognize a difference between public and private good, it raises certain questions as to whether or not a consensus of interests also implies a misalignment of interests, and whether a person should be compelled to perform certain deeds if only to set a good example for his fellows. Hence, if it is not proper to prevent a person from supporting those in need, neither should it be deemed appropriate to act in a manner prejudicial to one's own enrichment or good.

[1] I. Berlin *Four Essays on Liberty* Oxford University Press Oxford 1969.

Chapter 20

On the Separation of Powers

As we have already seen in writers as diverse as Plato and Hobbes, a common assumption about the nature of government is that it may be subject to change; that tyranny, for instance, is a vitiated form of monarchy, oligarchy a vitiated form of aristocracy, and anarchy a vitiated form of democracy. In order to prevent this, there were those amongst the ancients who suggested that the distribution of power should be treated in a way that was inclusive rather than exclusive—and this is exactly what we mean by a mixed constitution.

Drawing on his extensive knowledge of the Roman Empire, Polybius in the *Histories* (Ch. VI) demonstrates how a bond can be achieved between those elements in society, that, acting separately, would not be nearly so fit for their own protection or defence. Broadly speaking there was a ruling class consisting of the consuls, a privileged class consisting of the senate, and a common class consisting of the people. The consuls had the task of supervising the magistrates, of bringing ambassadors before the senate, and of seeing to the execution of such decrees as were issued by it. It also had the role of convening the people, of placing business before them, and of enacting their decisions. The role of the senate was first and foremost to maintain the treasury, to regulate income and expenditure, to provide for the construction and repair of public buildings. It was also charged with responsibility for handling a range of disputes both internal and external, crimes against the state, squabbling amongst its allies, the declaration of war etc.. As to the people, it was their role to ensure that good offices received their proper rewards and ill offices their proper penalties. It was they ultimately who had the power over life and death, and without their full participation the accused could always seek reprieve through exile or expatriation to another place.

The nature of the relationship between these parts could be described as one of mutual dependence not mutual antagonism, since although each was wary of the other's interest, they were also respectful of it as well. The consuls were in need of the senate so far as it concerned any provisions that might be forthcoming—they were also answerable to it at the end of each year. Likewise, they were equally in awe of the people, since agreements and treaties could not be concluded without the consent of the latter. The senate was in need of the people, since it could not administer penalties against state enemies unless there were ratification by the general assembly. Even in the case of laws that directly affected the senators themselves, these only took effect upon acceptance or rejection by the populace. On the other hand, since so many workers and agents were involved in the construction and repair of public buildings, it was clearly in the interests of the citizenry to respect the wishes of the senate. They were also beholden to it as they were to the consuls in another respect—most of the judges in important trials were drawn from the senate, and so in times of war they had little choice but to remain faithful to their superiors.

Aristotle takes a somewhat different approach to this, since he firstly identifies three different kinds of powers (which he calls the deliberative, the administrative, and the judicial) and then applies a certain set of procedures in analyzing the role of each. Essentially what this does is answer the question (a) who are the real contributors in the sense of which section of society do they represent, and (b) how are they chosen; by appointment, by election, or by lot. The important point about all this, however, is that it only very roughly accords with a general distinction between law-making, law-administration, and law-adjudication, since it is one thing to consider the *instruments* of government and quite another its general ends. Neither Aristotle nor Polybius had any real idea of a balanced constitution, that is, the need to ensure that not too much power was concentrated in the hands of a few. In the case of Polybius there must be some doubt about the way he handles the question of judicial procedures, since on the one hand, he seems to allow that the people may have the power over life and death, and on the other, that they are subject to those judges appointed by the senate. In the case of Aristotle there is a somewhat curious treatment of the executive, since an official is someone not only able to issue orders but to engage in decision-making and take action on his own behalf.

However, to say that the ancients had no real appreciation of a balanced constitution does not mean they had no idea how power might be shared, only, that they did not view this in terms of a set of mutual checks and balances. Certainly, Aristotle was well aware of the need for a robust middle class to offset the conflict between rich and poor, as also the importance of the deliberative faculty, but he did not connect this with the functions we would call the legislative, the executive, and the judiciary. The notion of a set of checks and balances was something that evolved slowly over time, and during the Renaissance, it typically took the form of an arrangement between social forces that ensured none overrode the effectiveness of any other. For Francesco Guicciardini (1483-1540) this was more a question of which should be the predominant power, since he saw the nobility as a necessary means for curbing both the influence of the people and the influence of the state.

Let us consider these ideas in a little more detail. The Great Council, which in principle comprised the body of the people, had the right to vote and elect individuals to high office but not the right to deliberate or influence the national agenda. Because of the inevitable disorder that results from open discussion, it would not be proper for the people to be directly engaged in law making, but merely to judge wisely of those proposals that were put before them. Not only that, but sovereignty in these terms should not be regarded as the expression of a bare majority but rather of a solid majority, just as a jury verdict is not acceptable if it is merely half plus one. The kind of scheme that prevents the many from seeking public office will also ensure that it is not any collective good that is advanced, but only the good of individuals, understood as the wisdom of a few in contrast to the ignorance of the many. Hence, the ruling class may co-opt those classes that are beneath it, but it must not cede or hand power to those it regards as less deserving than itself. The senate, which comprises the body of nobles (or priors), has the task of deliberating in most matters that concern the welfare of the state, but it does so not as a conduit for factional interests, rather, as different individuals seeking best outcomes for the country as a whole. Since policy and legislation require a higher degree of expertise than the simple choice of a candidate, the senate provides a forum for sustained debate, and, because of its size and makeup, discretion in the matter of due deliberation.

However, the real secret to good government is the fact that action can be taken quickly, that resolutions are effective, that remedies are immediate, which is only possible if there is a single personality, the Gonfalonier, who is head of state. Elected by the people but not accountable to them, the Gonfalonier enjoys this post for the duration of his life, thus ensuring that he can prosecute important legal trials without the fear of plots and innuendo. However, since there is a danger such a personage may act above the law and not merely in accordance with it, means must exist for the priors to bring charges against him, provided it is not done more than once for the duration of their office. All in all, the important point is that such a system is not favourable to a set of checks and balances, but rather, unlimited power in the case of the senate, due deference in the case of the people, and wariness in the case of the Crown. The senate checks the influence of the people by co-opting intermediate classes but only in support of itself, and it checks the influence of the Crown by requiring a two-thirds majority in the case of any charges laid against it. The fundamental aim however is to combine the benefits of a meritocracy with the benefits of an aristocracy, to draw wisdom from the senate and provide fairness for the citizenry.

The notion of a mixed constitution was also something that lent itself easily to the British, especially under the rule of the Plantagenets who strengthened the institutions of government and laid the foundation for the House of Commons. In 1642 Charles I confirmed this general scheme by declaring that the Kingdom was a balance between three Estates, the Crown, the House of Lords, and the House of Commons. However, one of the things that writers at this time realized was that in order to have a balanced constitution, it was necessary that that be between the *functions* of government and not merely the parts that made up its basic fabric. To this end, there was a stipulation that one power could not act without the cooperation of the others, and thus, that there had to be a right of veto just as there was of general assent. Whereas for Guicciardini, there is a distinct gulf between the senate and the people, in nineteenth century England the House of Commons was becoming a truly representative body, and that meant attending to the broader interests of the populace. In the kind of tripartite system we are discussing, the executive was deemed a branch of the legislative, neither completely separate from it nor completely aligned with it. The House of Commons and the House of Lords were a check upon each another by virtue of the right to reject anything put before them, and the Crown was a check upon them both, acting as the final arbiter for any injunction put before it. This power was in turn checked by the privilege of Parliament to enquire into the activities of the Crown, but not through impeachment, only through the removal of its assistants or advisors. The role of the nobility was especially important, since it set a good example and acted as a bulwark against any disaffection from within.

What however became known as the separation of powers could better be described as the separation of functions, the shift away from a matching of powers to a better appreciation of what they were in and of themselves. A good example of this is Locke's *Two Treatises of Government* written in response to the views of Sir Robert Filmer, presaging many of the reforms of the eighteenth and nineteenth centuries. Scholars have long debated whether this was intended as a defence of the Glorious Revolution of 1688, although on the weight of evidence, this may not have been the case at all. Whereas Hobbes was the ultimate political theorist Locke was the ultimate political adviser, and if there is one principle that stands out above all else, it is that virtue could only be discerned in the *trust* that men place in one another. From this there followed: (a) the need to prioritize the different functions of government, and (b) the need to ensure that those who made the law were not above the law, that is, to strengthen what we would nowadays call the rule of law. The legislative is regarded as the supreme body, since this is the body not only chosen by the people but also subject to their will. It is divided from the executive in principle, if not in practice, since whoever crafts the laws should not be exempt from their observance, and that can only be so if the task of making the laws is distinguished from the task of administering them. This is also made plain through the idea of their having a corporate existence—that while the legislative may be temporarily inactive there must always be an overriding force to ensure that it effectively remains intact. Of course, that does not preclude the prospect that the executive may reside in a single person, but Locke is careful to distinguish between a public person as the embodiment of the Commonwealth and a private person who acts contrary to the spirit and the letter of the law. The *Second Treatise* concludes with a rather unconvincing attempt to justify insurrection and rebellion on such dubious grounds as the removal of property, or destabilizing the parliament through despotic means.

From an historical perspective the question is: How effective were Locke's ideas and how successful was he in achieving the outcome he might have hoped for? The answer to this lies in recognizing how separation must always be distinguished from any rupturing of the same; that in order to prevent the abuse of power it is necessary to prevent its unravelling as well. Whilst the executive and the legislative might ideally be said to comprise two separate selves, in reality it was the Crown that held the balance of power. This was true for a number of reasons, but amongst other things, because the House of Commons at the time was not a truly representative body, rather, only a vehicle for the nobles and the landed gentry. Moreover, because of an ongoing struggle between the Parliamentarians and the Crown, what the Glorious Revolution achieved was not really the removal of tyranny but the replacement of one evil by another. In the presence of an effective sovereignty, there had at least been some semblance of stability, but once that was gone, how could the system be re-energized or be brought back in any effectual form?

The solution concerned the ability of Parliament to reorganize and reorient itself in keeping with a more stable set of rules. In the eighteenth century, what was called the cabinet comprised a small committee of ministers that helped strengthen the ties between the three powers already outlined. It did this in a number of ways, but essentially by raising the profile of the House of Commons. Having said that, it should not be assumed that the role of the Crown was in any sense diminished, since there is no doubt that the Sovereign exercised a pervasive influence over the cabinet, that he could fill it with his advisers, or that he could just as well ignore it when it suited him to do so. All this began to change however during the American War of Independence when there was a more galvanized and robust opposition, and the transition to what we today would call the party-political system. In order to shore up its defences the Parliament realized that cabinet would have to be stabilized, and it did this by capping its number and confining it to those who held responsible office. This was further strengthened by the election of a prime minister who brought the different administrative bodies into line, and effectively became the head of state.

For Locke, one of the major issues in his theory of government was the question of divided sovereignty, that is, which power was best suited to exercise supreme authority. He is at pains to stress the importance of the legislative as distinct from the executive, and that this ultimately resides in the will of people- only with whose consent it remains valid and binding. Since all delegated power must be limited by the end for which it is given, the legislature may at any time be dissolved and placed in the hands of those the people deem best able to realize their ends. To trust in God therefore was also in a sense to trust in a government that was made by the people. This, however, was quite different in the case of Montesquieu, who takes a more considered approach to the question of powers and a more analytic approach to the question of functions. Montesquieu was a great Enlightenment thinker whose name is most closely associated with the expression 'separation of powers', but in a sense this is somewhat misleading, since what we are presented with is an interwoven fabric and not a systematic body of ideas.

To begin with, let us consider how Montesquieu approaches the question of instrumentality, and more specifically, how this gave rise to certain elements that are evident in our present-day judiciary. In the *TTG* Locke identifies a power that is separate from both the legislative and the executive, which he calls the federative. Because of his commitment to natural law and the fraternal relations between men, he argues there must be a power directed outwards, in the case of treaties, alliances, hostile engagements etc., in other words, everything that comes within the gamut of what we would nowadays call foreign affairs. In a somewhat different vein, Montesquieu argues that the role of the executive concerns not just matters that pertain to civil law but also those that are dependent on the universal law of all nations. This, therefore, is not really a distinct power but something that should always remain under the aegis of the executive. The advantage in adopting such an approach is that it paves the way for an independent body to oversee global divisions, rather than allowing natural law to dictate the course that every nation *should* pursue. It is important that we do not confound the ideas of dependence and independence, since just as one independent state cannot be made dependent upon another, neither can national law be made dependent upon any imaginary alter ego. As we shall see later on, it can be quite a tricky matter to balance the requirements of municipal law with the demands of international law, taking justice in a more abstract and thoroughgoing way.

The dividing point for Locke and Montesquieu concerns the question of how individual liberty should be preserved, since Locke most closely connects this with the legislative, whilst Montesquieu most closely connects this with the judiciary. If the legislative is the supreme authority but also beholden to the people, then there will be a progressive effect in both the way the law is administered and the way the law is adjudicated. (This is similar to the views of Tom Paine, although he argues that the government is to the constitution what the judicature is to the legislature.) On the other hand, if the aim of government is to ensure that no man is in fear or awe of any other, then the judgement in individual cases must be distinguished from both the creation and application of the laws. Whilst Locke appreciates that a person who both makes and administers the laws may be tempted to disobey them, he does not recognize (as perhaps Rawls does) that this also applies to the legal system, and that the rights of individuals may be just as thoroughly abused when they are brought before the courts. Hence, Montesquieu is very careful to represent the judiciary as a kind of invisible force, and judges more likely to be reserved than outspoken in any views they might support. What therefore we mean by an independent judiciary should encompass a variety of things: (a) a passive rather than active role in relation to the executive; (b) a clear distinction between the individual and any office that he holds; (c) a jury system supervised by judges versed in the law; (d) a bar for arraigning officials suspected of fraudulent or misleading conduct etc.

Where it concerns the question of a balanced constitution, Montesquieu adopts the view that this must incorporate a system of checks and balances, whilst at the same time not denying there may be a blending or mixing of powers. In the first place, he wishes to revive a monarchical system of government by suggesting that the executive should be placed in the hands of a single person, without in a traditional sense also being able to influence the making of legislation.

The executive should not be viewed as an arm of the legislative, merely a means of keeping it in check, or at least of balancing the different elements that make it up, that being the people on the one hand and the nobility on the other. The role of the executive is also highlighted by the fact it may be necessary to check the power of the legislative so that it does not become despotic, and to respect the dignity of the person who has been entrusted with the execution of the laws. It should be noted however that although Montesquieu takes a very different approach to this than Locke, this is by no means without wisdom or warrant, since the system as a totality is so loaded with impediments that it prevents any part from encroaching upon any other. Not only that, but in a sense the executive is the buckle that joins both the powers and the functions of government, if we take this to mean the nobility and common folk on the one hand and the legislative and judiciary on the other. Since the judiciary is itself an independent power, and the legislative at least able to scrutinize the conduct of officials, there is no way the executive could act unilaterally or in any sense exert an influence all on its own. Ultimately, Montesquieu's aim is to ensure that the needs of individuals are met so far as this concerns their status or class and that the rights of individuals are met so far as there is equal liberty for all.

Turning now to Rousseau, although we would not consider his model to be a particularly practical one it does bear some resemblance to that outlined by Guicciardini. Both, in some sense, support the idea of an elective government, only in the case of Guicciardini an elective monarchy, in the case of Rousseau an elective aristocracy. Both also believe in a balancing of forces, in the case of Guicciardini, through the agency of the legislative, in the case of Rousseau, through the agency of the executive. Since for Rousseau there is no such thing as a legislature that is truly representative, then such a role can only be supplied by the executive. An elective aristocracy therefore means the election of magistrates and officials who have been drawn from the body of the people. For Guicciardini popular assemblies are a means of checking tyrannical aims and providing a basis for the legitimate use of public power. Hence, there is no reason why the people should not choose the head of state, only not *from* them, but through a system of merit based on virtue rather than ambition. An elective monarchy therefore means the election of a sovereign not from the body of the people but through preselection by the senate. In seeking to achieve a balance between the different powers within government, Guicciardini does this through a particular social class that he then redefines in terms of the existing political order. The senate is the bastion of all noble ideals; it represents a body of committed persons best qualified to carry out the affairs of state. Not only does it regulate the activities of the sovereign and the people, it drives a wedge between the art of persuasion and something that is altogether more extreme.

For Rousseau, there are various relations that need to be accounted for, and they are: (a) the relation between sovereign and state; (b) the relation between sovereign and prince; (c) the relation between state and prince. So far as it concerns (a) then the sovereign being one can only be something singular, and the share that each citizen has will also be reflected in their number, the smaller the number the greater the share, the greater the number the smaller the share. So far as it concerns (b) and (c), then the executive or prince represents a desirable means along a sliding scale that regulates the relation between sovereign and state. Since all 'will' proceeds from the apex and all 'force' proceeds from the base, the general aim will be to align these different influences by creating a kind of 'golden' mean. In the case of Guicciardini 'will' and 'force' are entirely the same—if the Senate has the 'will' then it also has the means to check the sovereign.

The relation between force and will also raises the question of what we mean by an invariant will. In a previous discussion about the relation between a common and a singular interest (Ch.19) we have made the point that this need not reflect the difference between what is 'moral' and what is 'selfish', rather, what galvanizes our passions or what makes us more phlegmatic. And that is because in any representative system there will always be something we take to be common, if not in reality then at least in its prospect. If the electorate is deadlocked on a particular issue and one candidate is in favour of it whereas another is opposed, then this will not be effective in how any determination may be reached, since there will be equal numbers on both sides of the fence. On the other hand, if a majority is in favour of it and both candidates are opposed, then again, this will not galvanize the voters but rather split them in separate ways. In this instance, what we mean by an invariant will is something we associate with a set of neutralizing or unproductive forces. But now let us consider how it might also apply in the case of a set of hostile or countervailing forces. Or at least, those forces at work in the case of the French Revolution.

For centuries French society was divided along rigid class lines, best known as the First, Second, and Third Estates. The First Estate comprised the Catholic clergy, those deemed responsible for the registration of births, deaths, and marriages, as well as managing hospitals and schools. Their holdings were about 10 per cent of the land. The Second Estate comprised the aristocracy, those whose influence was felt most strongly in the Church, in the army, and in the royal court. By the eighteenth century, they were also assuming a more entrepreneurial role, taking an interest in finance, insurance and shipping, as well as being unstinting supporters of the arts. The Third Estate comprised all those who by law qualified for neither the Church nor the nobility. Essentially this meant a small proportion that could be described as the upwardly mobile, and a much larger proportion that was tied or rooted to the land. So far as it concerned the former this was a rather diverse group, from the 'upper' bourgeoisie, the merchants, bankers and lawyers, to the 'lower' bourgeoisie, the artisans and shopkeepers. By far the largest collective, however, were the peasants, manual workers tilling and working the land. *In toto*, the Third Estate was estimated to own up to 60 per cent of the land.

The nobles, together with the upper bourgeoisie, paid relatively few taxes, and there was no central authority to verify what they had actually paid. However, this was altogether different at the bottom of the social order. Every peasant had to pay one tenth of his produce or earnings to the church (a tithe). As a landowner, every peasant was required to pay land tax, known as the *taille*. Every peasant was required to pay a tax based on the size of his household, as well as the use of the noble's mill, his oven, or his winepress. Every peasant was required to pay the salt tax, contracted out to government agents more intent on lining their own pockets. Other imposts included billeting for the army and the *corvee*, a compulsory work order on roads that were rarely used. When we consider the implications of all this, what was particularly pernicious was the imposition of the *taille*. We might estimate that 25 to 30 per cent of the land was owned by the nobles and 30 to 40 per cent by the peasantry. Given that only about one percent of the population comprised noblemen and ninety percent peasants (albeit, not all landholders), it seems extraordinary that on a *per capita* basis no land tax was imposed on the former. This was also exacerbated by the fact that tenant farmers were required to pay higher rents in lieu of such a tax, whereas a nobleman could cultivate the land he owned without any fees whatsoever. What we have at one extreme is a life of untold privileges and at the other a life of endless drudgery.

But if the French Revolution was not a peasant-inspired revolt then neither was it strictly a bourgeois-inspired revolt. Whilst it is true that the effects of the revolution were certainly favourable to the middle class, that is not to say the bourgeoisie were solely responsible for resolving the deadlock; rather, they might have helped precipitate it in the first place. That is, since it was the merchant class that aspired to the nobility and manufacturers who bought their entitlements, it was their action which ensured more wealth was placed in fewer and fewer hands, not the redistribution of wealth to those less fortunate than themselves. Given the inconsistencies in the way the taxes were levied, a life of privilege was ultimately destroyed by the fact that every section of society, no matter its size, was made to contribute to the needs and expenditure of the state. Or to express the pith of this in the words of Sir Winston Churchill, with added licence; 'Never in the field of human conflict was so little owed by so many to so few'.

Now let us consider how we might connect an invariant will with a set of complementary forces. One of the strengths of the British parliamentary system is its ability to marry a balanced constitution with a set of checks and balances, taking the former to mean a monarchical figurehead and two legislative houses. In this case a hereditary monarch could be described as the 'glue' holding all these constituents together. On the other hand, it is an altogether different matter if we begin with a set of checks and balances, and then attempt to ascertain from different *functions* how these should also be combined. If the legislature is a check on the executive, the executive is a check on the legislature, and the legislature is a check on itself, then what you have is a formula for inaction, not action.

In the case where we have merely the *functions* of government (and leaving aside a Presidential style), then in order to achieve a balanced constitution it may also be necessary to introduce a set of conjugate powers. Perhaps we might conceive of this in the following way. Let us dispense with the idea that both legislative houses are a check on one other, but that the upper house may amend or reject any legislation put before it. In the case of anything it amends, this may be returned to the lower house for its consideration or it may simply be returned in its original form. Ultimately however when legislation passes through the upper house it acquires a certain status, that is, it will either be accepted or rejected. So far as it concerns the executive, let us say what we have is a body or assembly appointed and not elected, completely separate from the legislature. A power sharing arrangement with the legislature would then concern the way this might be divided. Let us say there were twenty-one members. The most natural way we could divide this would be by creating a simple majority, the bare majority of one. In these terms such a body would be dominant, and anything put before it would be passed once this deciding vote was achieved. On the other hand, if we were to say that any decision was valid only when there was total or nil support, then its effectiveness would be greatly reduced. There might be a few occasions when only one or two supported any motion, just as there would when twenty or twenty-one did so. Let us then say that a 'fair' result was achieved when a certain percentage did so, either one third or two thirds. We might then adopt the rule that when less than one third voted for a motion it was automatically rejected, and that when more than two thirds voted for a motion it was automatically passed. The upshot of this is that the status of legislation *might* change if there was a vote by less than one third or more than two-thirds, but otherwise, it would remain as it was first of all. Thus, the legislature could be sure to retain the balance of power when there was a vote between seven and fourteen members. This would also enable us to achieve a degree of efficiency in two ways, in the first place in respect to where the general parameters should be set, and secondly in respect to where the particular parameters should be set. For instance, if you wanted the executive to have less influence in relation to the legislative, then you might change the parameters from one third and two thirds to one quarter and three quarters. On the other hand, if you wanted the executive to have more efficiency then you could change the upper mark from two thirds to three fifths, or if less efficiency, the lower mark from one third to two fifths.

Chapter 21

International Law

To begin with, let us consider three traditional ways that we may conceive of international law: (a) that it has no form and no content; (b) that it has form but no content; and (c) that it has both form and content. In the first case, we might regard the state as the source of law for its subjects but on no account beholden to anything from without, that is, as an instrument of the will but on no account for what is ordered. Just as men are naturally hostile to one other in a state of nature, so in the world at large are nations naturally suspicious of one another's aims. Thus, a commonwealth is self -sufficient to the degree it is able to ward off any outside threats, but also vulnerable if it does not have the means to provide for its own defence. In the case of the latter it may therefore be necessary to enter into a pact, but only so long as this fear or this danger remains present. The motive that any commonwealth has is thus effectively no different from that of any individual, to act in its best interest, and only to cede power when there is something better or pleasing to be had. Let us call this the theory of anarchism (or positivism in a more developed sense).

In the case of the second, we might regard the state not just as the source of law for its subjects but also for itself, that is, not only as a vehicle for self-aggrandizement but for regulation and self-control.

Dependence and independence are thus entirely in keeping with each other's aim; dependence means only how we view things in terms of a formal set of rules, self-sufficiency means only how we view things in terms of what is of interest to ourselves. Hence, we might consider this in the way we would a simple promise or a compact. The reason men pledge obedience to one another is for the sake of their mutual support, but what is implicit in this idea is very different from what is implicit in the idea of personal well-being. And accordingly, nations should be treated like responsible citizens, and if a nation does not fulfil its basic commitments, we should not assume it has acted in bad faith; rather, that it has simply been prevented from carrying out what it had otherwise always intended to pursue. Let us call this the theory of voluntarism.

In the case of the third, we might regard the state as the repository of certain basic norms, that there is a hierarchy of norms, and that what is more specific derives its import from what is more abstract or comprehensive in its kind. Thus, a person may have a specific duty to meet his contractual commitments, but that does not hinge on any correlative right, rather from a more general rule that stipulates how he is to act. And this in turn proceeds from some basic or primary postulate on which everything else depends. However, in saying this we are not suggesting that the object of the judicial system should be to maximize efficiency in the way that Hume suggests. Since it is not the case that particular judgements will be faulty or unseemly, what is requisite is that they attract at least a minimum amount of support. It is possible for one legal system to replace another but that is not because of any question about its efficiency, rather because there may be a loss in support on one front and a gain in support on some other. Let us call this the theory of legalism.

Now let us consider these different viewpoints in respect to the meaning of a *sanction*. In terms of the anarchic view, since each nation exhibits an independent will then the only relevant sanctions are those it imposes on itself, meaning by that, the force that is requisite in the case of attack or self-help. Since there is no such thing as a world legislature or any one body positively adhered to by all nations, neither is there any power to make or enforce laws, and so, nothing that could be said to be binding at all. International law is simply a misnomer for the kind of moralities promoted by different nations, but since there is no truly supranational interest then neither can there be any sanction for keeping it intact. In terms of the voluntarist view, if nations can be regarded as self-regulating and not simply self-interested, then there is no need for any sanctions imposed from without, rather only those that are generated from within. Together with the consent that must be given for any treaty, there is also the obligation that any nation has to ensure all its conditions will be met. Moreover, just as there is a sense in which moral rights may become legal rights when they are backed up by the machinery of the state, so is it the existence of a public conscience that determines how the members of one state will be aligned to that of any other. There is an implicit understanding therefore, that there should be a customary set of rules for how states behave not just in the present but also in the future.

In terms of the legalistic view, it is not so much the question of whether or not there are any truly binding sanctions (since these must always be admitted), but rather, from whence do they arise and how should they proceed. There is a difference if we regard a sanction as some act that breathes life into the law or strengthens it and something that proceeds from the law itself, that is, that ties in with the operation of certain other rules. A trade unionist may be expelled from the organization to which he belongs, but we would not call that a legal sanction even though it is broadly coercive in its kind. In the same way, when a person commits an act of fraud, we do not assume that he will automatically be punished any more than we do that he will automatically be caught, only, that it imposes an obligation on magistrates and other officials to act within their duly constituted bounds. A legal norm therefore may bear some relation to the issuing of a command but it is not this on which it relies, rather only some higher norm, or some higher statute, or the very constitution when the need for this occurs.

Of course, there are those who would argue that what we mean by war is itself a kind of sanction, but this really depends on one's viewpoint, since there is a difference between war as a justifiable cause, and war as a simple act of aggression. Not only that, but there has to be a question of how effective this may be, since nations do not wage war when there is the prospect of mutual gain, only if they are rapacious and are seeking a dividend all their own. It is much easier to impose a sanction when there is the necessary machinery for doing so, but that is not the case where it concerns the activities of rogue nations or renegade states. A rogue state is much more likely to be disruptive of the general order than a rogue individual, since in the latter case we have the necessary disincentives whereas in the former we do not. Moreover, to threaten a state which has a nuclear capacity may not only be futile but invite a more radical response than was ever one's aim. We also need to distinguish between the offender and the injured party when there is a question of reparation on the one hand and retaliation on the other. In the case of reparation, this could be described as the obligation that arises when there has been a breach of some agreement and an admission that this in fact has taken place. At this stage it is not properly a sanction, since the offending party may simply see reason and pay up, or refuse to admit that he was ever in the wrong. In the case of reprisal, we might call this the forcible interference in a state's sphere of interest either quite specifically or rather more broadly defined. Although normally illegal, such interference may be permitted when there is a clear infraction of the international code. This, however, is not what we mean by retorsion, an identical or similar act on the part of the aggrieved; rather, it is an act of enforcement sanctioned by the wider community for the express purpose of protecting those rights that have effectively been denied.

As we have already argued, what we mean by war is a unilateral and not a bilateral act, not a particular status but a particular action. For all practical purposes, war exists if there is a unilateral act of aggression preceded by a declaration of war; if not then it is little more than an act of brigandry. Whether the offended party has the intention or the wherewithal to respond is altogether beside the point—we do not say that a state of war does not exist because one legal entity has been swallowed up or can offer only token resistance to the agent. We need to be careful about the difference between a war of aggression and a war of defence, since we must distinguish between an illegal war in defiance of certain universal conventions, and any counteraction intended to stymie such a threat. From a certain perspective, an act of aggression may well be regarded as a unilateral act, but that may be no less so for something that is multilateral or collective; as when the members of a pact (e.g. the Kellogg-Briand Pact) are obliged to wage war against those who have illegally turned against their own. In the same way, resistance by force to legitimate reprisals is not only something altogether frowned on; it may attract a further raft of penalties in its wake.

However, in order to purge nations of the desire to make war we also need to purge them of the desire they have to foster their own peculiar interests, and this is altogether unrealistic, since the best we can hope for is some general consensus or some neutral middle ground. Even the existence of a court to try war criminals does not prove that international law can be effective as a tool, only that it supports the logic of all wars, that the vanquished must submit to those who are their masters A nation with certain aspirations, no less than a criminal, will not be deterred by the threat of prosecution when this is not what it had in mind to begin with. In reality, there is a fine line between those influences at work in the exercise of our reason and those influences at work in the exercise of our will. An army regular may be called on to make many difficult decisions in the heat of battle, which may involve following either the dictates of his conscience or the dictates of his superiors. If the latter, then this may result in punishment by his enemies if they are triumphant; if the former, then this may result in punishment by his countrymen if they deem it necessary. Either way there is an uneasy tension between the kind of sanctions(internal) that propel him in one direction and the kind of sanctions(external) that propel him in another.

Having dealt with the relation between dependence and independence let us now deal with the relation between independence and interdependence. What we mean by a state is a body of people occupying a particular territory and with a government exercising effective control. What we mean by the independence or sovereignty of the state is that it is not subject to any legal order or legislature superior to or outside its own. Recognizable bodies such as China, the Soviet Union, and Australia are good examples that fall into this category, but that would not be so if they were territorial units subject to the authority of others. The United States, for instance, comprises fifty states that are subject to a federal legislature, India was once under British rule, Algeria was once a French outpost, the state of Georgia was once a member of the Soviet Union—these are all good examples of territories that are or once were under the aegis of some superior power. The independence of any political body should not, however, be viewed in any fixed or invariant way, since to exercise autonomy is not entirely incompatible with any directives arising from without. In the case of something such as the EEC, member states are subject to certain manifest restrictions, and these include tariffs, the movement of workers, and the establishment of commercial ventures on foreign soil. In theory, the sovereign status of a country such as Britain might cause it to ignore such impositions, but in practice every effort is made to bring domestic law into line with the treaty's requirements.

So far as it concerns the relation between independence and interdependence, then there is a difference if it is the former that predominates or the latter that predominates. If the latter, then what we mean by independence is a little like the open market, each party showing no interest in the other and reciprocity fostered through unfettered activity of a largely selfish kind. We can see this at work in the adoption of a common currency such as the Euro, or sporting events such as the Olympic Games. However, since states have a clear interest in preventing certain outcomes e.g. pollution or climate change, then so also are they in need of legal instruments for the laying down of general rules. Interdependence in these terms will mean something more than mutual dependence; it means a willingness to comply with moral constraints provided there is due compliance on the part of others. There may also be certain provisos, as for instance, that no one be worse off by entering into such an agreement, and that there be an equal allotment of all the benefits and burdens that are therein implied.

If it is the former that predominates, then what we mean by independence is simply the right to act capriciously, to wage war without the least compunction, to inflict hardship on a weaker neighbour no matter how wrongful one's cause may be. In like manner, what we mean by interdependence will not be something more but rather less than mutual dependence, that is, the forging of any contract so long as it suits those whose interests are largely at stake. Since sovereignty will always override the obligation of either party, to renege on one's commitments is not to do the other harm, rather to return to some original condition before there was any such agreement at all. The creation of the Warsaw Pact may perhaps illustrate the kind of forces at work here. Despite the fact this treaty was intended solely for the security of its signatories, it did not prevent one member (the Soviet Union) from invading another (Hungary) and quashing any resistance to its autocratic rule.

To define a state, however, according to broadly relevant criteria may not always be to win the point, since the rise and fall of states is a common phenomenon, and so, due consideration may be an important element in the overall mix, especially where it concerns such borderline cases as San Marino or the Vatican City. But then we also need to distinguish between recognition in this purely evidentiary sense, and recognition as a *condition* for the making or creation of a state. This broadly follows the distinction between the theories we have called voluntarism and legalism. There are those who would argue that what we mean by 'the state' must comprise some qualities that are objectively verifiable, otherwise certain territories could be disqualified simply on account of their being inimical to their neighbours. On the other hand, even if we do not consider the international order to be a coherent body of rules, that does not preclude the prospect there may be a coterie of nations that are 'calling the shots', or at least, that those parts less vital must in some sense be dependent on those parts that are more so. Hence, there is a sense quite clearly in which recognition means the different ways states are situated vis-à-vis one another, and to what extent they are willing to deal with one another on roughly equivalent terms.

There is also the question whether recognition hinges on who is effectively *in* control or who is exercising *legitimate* control, and these different senses must be clearly distinguished. For instance, for many years following WW2 there was considerable resistance to the GDR as constituting a legitimate government, largely because its creation was deemed a breach of agreements already in place. But of course, that is not to say the East German authorities were not *effectively* in control, or that there was any likelihood of insurrection from within. Similarly, no matter how strongly one might disapprove of the way that General Franco came to power, there is no doubt he exercised complete and effective control for the duration of his rule. Therefore, a case could be made for saying that stable government, no matter how oppressive, must always be balanced against the pernicious effects of internal dissent or persistent criticism emanating from outside. On the other hand, because we recognize a state as being continuous does not mean we have to recognize a government as being continuous, or as anything but provisional in its kind (consider the Vichy government during the Nazi occupation). In these terms we are probably thinking of the legitimate authority as the one that has been overturned, and the unlawful government as the one that has taken its place.

So far as it concerns the question of what is *de facto* and what is *de jure*, then the real question is whether a government can be said to be exercising effective control, not whether it is ideologically or even culturally sound. To consider in the first place what we mean by *de facto* as distinct from *de jure* authority, this hinges on the question whether it is or is not tied to such and such a set of procedural rules. Hence a teacher, a Scout Master, and a clergyman, all exercise authority within a certain framework of rules, and these are the kind of rules that enable them to provide guidance and instruction of some quite specific kind. To *have* authority, however, is not the same as what it means to *be* an authority, just as the right to be an instructor is not the same as what it means to inspire confidence in and of itself. We might say of a clergyman or a priest that his authority derives from a bishop, of a teacher that his authority derives from a principal, of a shop assistant that his authority derives from a manager, but a philatelist or a geologist is not someone who has been granted a certain authority, rather someone who just *is* an authority, in the one case on stamps, in the other case on rocks. When we apply this to the strictures of international law then we need to be clear about the difference between the stability of any government and any doctrine or ideology it might profess. To take a case in point, although the Communist Party was able to exercise effective control in Russia shortly after the October Revolution of 1917, it was not until 1924 that the British government gave it its full and unreserved support. However, the fact that a Western democracy may be ill disposed towards a Communist state does not address the more pressing issue of what it means to be fully in charge. Stalin and Churchill, Kennedy and Khrushchev, may well have been great personal rivals, but we would not on that account describe the governments that they led as *de facto* rather than *de jure*—that is, it is not so much the perception of that which is consentient as the reality of that which is stable.

Looked at in another way, the distinction between *de facto* and *de jure* could be said to rest on the *intention* that one state has in its dealings with any other, that is, to grant it temporary acceptance or to recognize it more completely. The difficulty with this however is that since it is within the power of any state to withdraw its approval, the kind of recognition that this entails can never be anything but conditional, or at least conditional upon the decision not to do an about face. Another argument is that *de facto* recognition only exists when there is the prospect of unilateral withdrawal, whereas what we mean by *de jure* concerns some binding commitment as well. But again, there is a problem if we cannot distinguish between the spirit of any agreement that has been voluntarily entered into, and something that may be forcibly imposed from without. It may well be true that any state that enters into a contract is bound by the terms of that contract, but that only begs the question how such an agreement has been arrived at in the first place. Members of the EEC may certainly be bound by the Treaty of Rome, but that is not to say there is any 'supranational interest' that is altogether exclusive of their own. The claim that what is unilateral in its origin may become reciprocal in its effects, stems from the presumption that in order to become a member of the larger community any new state must prove its worth to those who have already won their stripes. In other words, a state can only become legal if it can see that it has in fact been recognized and to such and such a significant degree.

But again, this comes back to the question whether a legal norm or a legal postulate is something that *must* issue in political consequences, or whether it is political decisions that *may* or *may not* generate certain legal effects. If we were to argue that a state or government does not exist until it is recognized by the wider community then this will always issue in certain legal effects, or least, be treated in terms of an act that is legally binding. On the other hand, if we were to argue that political decisions must always remain free, then *ipso facto*, there can be no legal effects that are not subject to a change in the national will. Of course, it is true that certain consequences must follow if what we mean by that is empowerment, but that is not necessarily the case if there is conflict with a state's internal laws. Among the powers accorded to a newly recognized state are: (a) the right to sue in the courts of the states that recognize it; (b) the right to the seizure of property belonging to any previous government (c) the claim to immunity for its diplomatic representatives. On the other hand, even if the representatives of another state are immune from legal prosecution, that is not to say it is the judiciary that decides whether any entity should be treated as a state. This then raises the question whether a judgement arrived at in terms of municipal law must always be in keeping with the broader precepts of international law.

In international law, there is agreement in principle that the actions of a state remain the same no matter what the changes in its government, and so, what occurred in the past cannot be nullified or overturned by any decisions in the present. On the other hand, and strictly in terms of municipal law, then quite clearly those decisions of the judiciary will always be in keeping with its host, and so, what occurs in its present *or* what occurred in its past. This is especially so in countries where there is a separation of powers, since the judiciary may simply be following the executive, and if the executive has acted in a certain way, then the judiciary may have little choice but to accept this as valid and binding. In these terms, governments are not continuous, and if the actions of one government are regarded as lawful then the actions of another may not be. This point was well illustrated in a case between Great Britain and Costa Rica in 1923, when the British Government sought damages for the breach of certain concessions that had been granted British companies in 1917. These claims were upheld, since the ruling of the Chief Justice concerned only the question of effective control, not how far such a government was regarded as constitutional or rightfully installed. But hypothetically if such a case had been brought before a British court, then its ruling would have been determined by the actual status of Costa Rica at the time of these concessions, echoing the executive's decision to disavow the incumbent and hence rejecting its own set of claims. In fine, so far as it concerns the prevalence of municipal over international law, then political decisions may well have legal consequences, but on the whole, it should not be assumed that every political decision must be based on some analogous or prior legal norm.

But that said, this does not mean we are giving unqualified assent to the theory of voluntarism, only that there may be doubts about legal sanctions outside any purely voluntary arrangement where coexistent powers are concerned. Furthermore, we need to distinguish between the kinds of sanctions that could be called *apriori* (i.e. legal sanctions) and the kind of sanctions that could be called *aposteriori* (i.e. social and moral sanctions). In the case of a state that has joined the community of nations, it is clear it may be subject to *apriori* sanctions with or without its consent, and that international law is binding on all its members not because of any grudging acceptance but as a condition of entry first of all. Hence no matter how cordially some members may be asked to meet their commitments, that does not mean that a gap may not arise between the implementation of certain sanctions and those requirements on which they are based. In the case of a country such as Iraq (which joined the United Nations in 1945) then it is clear that the olive branch extended to it did not inspire an altogether fit response. After long-running disputes with Kurdistan and Iran, the decision to invade Kuwait in 1990 sparked a full-scale invasion which toppled its dictator and led to economic ruin. On the flip side it also created a power vacuum and a degree of strife that has since not been fully resolved. Or to take another example. When the British government in 1949 demanded compensation from Israel for the loss of British planes over Egyptian soil, this could not have been based on any legal requirements, since at that time Israel had not yet been recognized as a state. (Or there are some who would say Israel *had* been, only *de facto* not *de jure*.) The kind of compensation involved here could thus be described as a *posteriori* rather than *apriori*, that is, as a reaction to what was broadly seen as immoral or antisocial in its kind. Or consider the kind of sanctions imposed on South Africa during the 1970s and 80s—these were not in response to any legal infraction but rather to a form of social injustice, that is, to the system known as apartheid. Thus, in order to join the international fraternity what is requisite is that any aspirant not only abide by its legal but by its moral requirements as well.

Index